The Way It Was

Recollections on the Life and Times of an Opinionated Granny

Olga B. Kurtz

PublishAmerica
Baltimore

Softcover 9781462665785
PUBLISHED BY PUBLISHAMERICA, LLLP
www.publishamerica.com
Baltimore

Printed in the United States of America

To Moniza,
  Thank you for
helping us to understand.
Our best wishes for you
and your family.
                Olga Kutz
                   and
                Friends
                9 - 30 - 16

In memory of my mother

Julia Molohoskey Bechkowiak

Veechnaya Pamiyat
(eternal memory)

INTRODUCTION

The Way It Was originally came about when I was telling some stories about the family to Mary Anne and Vicky, my sisters, who hadn't heard those particular ones. They suggested I write them down for the younger generation. That's what I started doing with pleasure.

Most of the information about our family history on these pages came from stories my mother, Julia Molohoskey Bechkowiak told me. As much as I loved her stories, my deep regret is that I didn't ask enough questions of her or the other main characters when they were alive. Most of what I've written here is as I remember Mom telling me, or what I've been able to piece together with the help of my sisters, brother, other family members, and neighbors. (Please note: My memory now is not an indication of what I remember from the past. Honest!) I may have taken a few liberties with setting or motives, but where facts and dates are concerned, if I had any doubts I omitted the information rather than misrepresenting.

That pretty much explains how I started with the family history, but that's only a very few pages of the total number for this book. The rest of the book is about my life and experiences. That part developed gradually, but I will justify four very good reasons why the book expanded as much as it did. (I would frown on those who might call them rationalizations rather than reasons.)

1.   As I completed three other books during these many years, I brought to my fellow authors and members of the Akron Manuscript Club, whatever writing I had been doing during the time between our monthly meetings. When I brought the first chapters of what became *The Way It Was* , the group was attentive and also asked leading questions like: "What were the first months in America like?" and "What was it like to start school?" It seemed the group was interested in more. That's all the encouragement I needed.

2.   From memory I made a list of subjects I wanted to cover. Once I started, it didn't take many pages of writing to see that even

though I remembered general impressions and feelings of various events, what needed considerable investigation were dates, details, and facts. Vague impressions weren't enough. I needed specifics to support what I felt and why. In the process of pinning down facts, some part-information that lurked in my own mind got explained. As one example (see National Nightmare chapter), I remembered that Richard Nixon appointed Gerald Ford as Vice-President to take Spiro Agnew's place. The solution for that particular contingency wasn't in the original Constitution. I had no idea where Nixon got the authority to do this until I checked the information for that chapter, which naturally added to the length.

3.   The writing also expanded because of my age. There's been a lot of history in my life. I kept adding to my original list, events that for one reason or another, I thought should be included. Quite a few were added.

4.   Of course, I need not remind any of my family that I am, after all, The Matriarch. As such, I feel a heavy responsibility to lead and nurture you all in the path of *right thinking.*

5.   Most of **The Way It Was** was written in the years following the more current Great Recession that started in 2008. The facts of what started the Great Depression of 1929 and this Great Recession were very similar. In both situations, free market capitalism ran amok. Consider what conditions would be like for ordinary people during this Recession without the cushion of Social Security for the disabled or elderly, or without unemployment insurance or Food Stamps for those who lost jobs because of the economic forces or market manipulation.

Dear children of all ages, more important than anything, my wish would be that you might find these pages interesting enough to read them, and in doing so, you also get a feel for **The Way It Was**.

Luv tu all om yu,
The Matriarch

ACKNOWLEDGEMENTS

Writing about personal experiences is much different from telling about them. Talk is fleeting, but writing remains to be available to scrutiny. When I started writing this story, it didn't take long to realize that some of my memories were murky or patchy. When that happened, I contacted anyone I knew who might be helpful to achieve more accuracy.

Most often to verify family information, I called on my sisters, Mary Anne Smith and Victoria Kelsey, and brother, Russell Bechkowiak. There is however a fifteen year span in our ages, so there were some discrepancies in our recollections. In those instances I pulled seniority and am willing to take responsibility for my decisions. I also consulted cousin Steve Bralek on family matters.

Vicky is currently also doing more extensive genealogical research on our family. In the process, she has collected family pictures from many sources. Since she is very capable with the computer, the pictures in this book are included because she knew what needed to be done.

The Kulka family was our neighbor for many years. Tom Kulka and his sister, Helen Kulka Lindner, were good sources to confirm information about our old neighborhood.

Milora Beachy (now Van Antwerp) and I got to be friends through alphabetical seating in high school. After we graduated, we went our separate ways, but reconnected recently so that I was able to consult with her about Garfield High details.

Grace and Jack Spears and Frank and I knew each other from the Independents table at Akron U and remained friends through the years. I had a hard time pinning down tuition costs for our Akron U years and asked both Milora and Grace. When I finally did get official information, both of them had remembered costs quite accurately.

I am fortunate to be a member of the Akron Manuscript Club. It is the oldest writer's group in Ohio, organized in 1929. The members have reviewed almost every chapter of *The Way It Was* as well as most other recent writing I've done. Not only have they improved my work with corrections and suggestions, but they were encouraging as well.

My sincere thanks to all of you for your patience and your help.
Olga B. Kurtz

○   ○   ○

Other works by Olga B. Kurtz:
Crazy Spider and *Prisoner Prince*

○   ○   ○

CONTENTS

CHAPTER 1
SEREDNICA

Serednica was a village in Poland so small that during its existence, it never earned a spot on any map. Today it does not exist at all. It was completely destroyed after World War II. The village does however, survive in the memories of those who left it. My family was among them. I was a child almost four years old when we came to America. *The Way It Was* is about my life in this country. On occasion through the years, I would wonder what my life would have been like had the family stayed in Poland. From what I know of our village, I'm grateful the family had the courage to take the risks.

Serednica was very little different from any other village in Poland or Ukraine or Hungary for that matter. There were of course differences in language and clothing and even in building styles from place to place, but the villages themselves before World War I were very much alike.

There was always at least one church (or more), and perhaps a synagogue. There was always a postmaster or some other insignificant government representative, and at least one tavern (or more). There was usually a small school, and a place to buy staples like tea or coffee or tobacco or salt that the village could not provide for itself.

Travel by foot or horse or cart, was slow, so there was very little interaction between villages. Differences were emphasized. No name was given to the language spoken in Serednica. Rather, everyone understood *"po nashimo"* meaning *"in our way."* Should a rare visitor say *bandurki* instead of *kartofli* for potatoes, he would be branded as an outsider. He was not speaking *po nashimo*.

Wherever they happened to be, what all the farming villages had in common was poverty. This poverty was not superficial or temporary. It was mind-numbing, a lifetime of drudgery. If it was a good year for crops, then the coming winter was not so threatening. New boots or fabric for a skirt or shirt or pipe tobacco might be possible, and life did not seem so bleak. When the harvest was poor and the winter severe, there was hunger, illness, and suffering. Children lived very much like their parents and grandparents before them with very little hope for improvement.

For the few villagers who were more daring, there was a glimmer of hope. Stories had filtered to Serednica about the wealth to be made in America where it was said the roads were paved with gold. And wasn't Ivan Bechkowiak proof? True, Ivan did not tell of finding gold on the roads, but he and his wife, Amelia, had returned with a son born in America, and look what Ivan was able to do.

Even in Serednica there were social distinctions. Families with two or three rooms to the house, who had more than one cow, or a horse and cart were considered to be people of property. Ivan was now a man of property. He had horses and cows and a house with wooden floors. He had done very well by going to America.

By contrast, most village homes were little more than huts. Often it was just one room with a dirt floor and perhaps a loft for sleeping. Poorest of all, was a one room hut without even a chimney for the stove. It was called a *kurna halupa,* literally a "smoke house." The effect of this was that even with light from candles or a lantern, sewing or spinning or cobbling during long winter evenings became more difficult while eyes were smarting and tearing from the smoke.

Anastasia Molohoskey was my grandmother. Her husband, Basil, died and left his widow and their five children, a small plot of land and a *kurna halupa.* Unlikely as it may seem, it happened that the already mentioned man of property, Ivan Bechkowiak's American born son, Joseph, and the widow Anastasia's daughter, Julia, made their way to America as a married couple. Julia and Joseph were my parents. Theirs was not a do-it-yourself romance. Oh my no! It was a roundabout effort that involved the loyalty and promises of two sisters, the loyalty and promises of a son and brother, considerable making of deals by a budding patriarch, and much cooperation from everyone concerned. It is a "coming to America" story with a cast of characters whose stories deserve to be recorded.

Chapter 2
SISTERS

The story must begin with Anastasia. She was my grandmother. It was through her and because of her that everything else in the family history developed.

She was one of three sisters. Her older sister was Barbara who married Basil Molohoskey. In Serednica, it was not uncommon that as a young girl, Anastasia went to live with her married sister. Anastasia was eighteen years old when Barbara died of unknown causes and left a very young daughter, named Mary. Anastasia conveniently assumed care for the infant as well as other household duties. In due time, Basil married Anastasia. Together they had one son and three daughters.

As with most of the villagers, the family's security depended on whatever harvest resulted from their hard labor. Basil and Anastasia as well as the children worked the land, but when the man of the house died unexpectedly, the family's circumstances changed drastically for the worse. Anastasia was left with five children, and no husband to take on the hardest physical work.

Fortunately, step-daughter Mary was sixteen years old and had already been able to occasionally earn money by hiring out as a servant or as a worker in the fields. Elias, the only son, was fourteen years old. He had been given the privilege of going to school for a very few years. He developed beautiful penmanship and had learned enough to serve as a scribe for those who could not read or write. Indeed, even at his young age, he was acquiring a reputation that he could be consulted on many matters that required interpretation of the written word. There were three other daughters: Barbara, Julia and Hanya.

Very little else is known about this period in their lives. Whether it was through the charity of their neighbors or the church, or what they managed to grow on the small plot of land, or whatever the children could earn to contribute to the family, or most likely the combination of all their efforts, the six of them did survive. To her credit, never then or in later years did Anastasia complain about the hardships she and her children had endured. Rather, she developed her own unusual method of coping. During her life in the village and after she came to live with her son in America, periodically she would threaten to die. It was a form of escape (and control) that worked quite well for her until she died many years later.

Anna was Anastasia's more adventuresome youngest sister. She had a child whose name was Agnes. The child's father, Josef Bralek, had already gone to America. As was expected of her, Anna waited for a year or so, but hers was not a patient nature. As communication from Josef dwindled, Anna became restless. Her thoughts were often concentrated on how she could possibly manage to follow Josef.

Josef had occasionally sent money to Anna. She was frugal with it as well as what little she was able to earn. The money for ship passage for herself was almost enough. But there was also her daughter to consider. It was not just the expense of taking the child with her. What concerned Anna more were the uncertainties she would be facing that would be complicated by traveling with a child. Anna confided her thoughts and fears to Anastasia.

Together the sisters gnawed at the problem until they came up with a solution that might benefit both of them. The agreement they reached was that Anastasia would assume care for Agnes while Anna made her way to America to join Josef. Anna's part of the deal was that as soon as she possibly could, she would send for her daughter, and also that she would provide for Elias, Anastasia's son, the opportunity to go to America.

This verbal agreement between the two sisters was honored by both of them. Anastasia cared for Agnes just as she did for her own daughters. Several years later, when Anna sent passage money for Agnes, there was also money for Elias. The sisters' trust in each other became a turning point in the history of the family.

Chapter 3
ELIAS, THE BUDDING PATRIARCH

Elias was seventeen years old and Agnes was seven when they arrived at her mother's home. Anna worked as a hotel maid in Wilkes-Barre. The mines of Pennsylvania were magnets for immigrants from all over Europe. Towns like Latrobe, Altoona, and Hastings sprouted up all over the hillsides surrounding the mines. Dirty and dangerous as mining was, there was work to be found. There may have been some who were disillusioned that there was no easy gold on the streets of America, but for most, money in the pocket at the end of the work week was a welcome difference from the uncertainties of the past. The hardships in the mines did not seem much greater than what they had known before.

Elias did work in the coal mines for a short time, but soon chose another path. He was more than willing to work, but not at hard physical labor breathing coal dust and covered with it. He set about not only to speak the language of America, but also to read it and to write it, and always in his own elegant script. English classes were provided for immigrants. He may have enrolled in them, but most accounts indicate that he learned on his own. Remarkably before long, just as in Serednica, he learned enough to become advisor and guide to those who were less literate, this time in English. At the same time he was working if not exactly at white collar jobs, neither did he work in the coal dust of the mines.

The boy developed into a presentable young man, quite handsome, tall, and erect. It can be excused if a boy approaching manhood was not always as frugal as he might have been. Very early he recognized the importance of appearance and indulged himself with decent clothes. But it was his dignified posture and his self assurance that gave him an aura of authority that people responded to. He became the "go to" man in immigrant communities wherever he happened to be.

Elias was the cherished son among a family of women. It is doubtful that any demands were put on him as to his responsibilities to his mother and sisters who were still in the old country. It was enough that Anastasia could say she had a son in America, and that he wrote to them to tell them he was doing well. When he also sent money, the whole village knew of it.

Archduke Ferdinand was assassinated in 1914. His death triggered World War I which lasted for four years. Cities as well as the countryside in Europe were devastated. Serednica was too small to ever become a part of world news, but it was in the path of Austrian and Russian armies. The village suffered not just the horrors of propaganda, but the reality of invasion by soldiers of both sides. Elias could do very little to help his family during this time. Letters or packages may or may not arrive for them.

America did become involved in the war. It sent thousands of troops to Europe. Many died, but otherwise the country itself did not suffer. Rather, industry mushroomed as steel plants and rubber factories were put in operation to provide the equipment for war.

In the process of finding work and making a life in this new world, very little importance was placed on romance and love. Of course couples married, but often the marriages were arranged by go-betweens and just as often for very practical reasons. No doubt a personable, ambitious young man like Elias had opportunities, but there is no known alliance until he came to Akron, Ohio and got work at the Firestone Tire and Rubber Co. At about that same time and quite by accident, he saw a personals ad in the paper put in by Mary Prystach, a pretty young woman from Reading, Pennsylvania. Whether on a dare, just for adventure, or seriously, Mary described herself and hinted that marriage was a possibility.

Elias saw Mary's ad and picture in the paper. The novelty of her approach appealed to him. Why not? Besides, she was good-looking. He wrote to her, she answered, and they agreed to meet. It was enough. A spark was ignited. It was as if each one had been waiting for the other. They married soon after. Those who knew how they met, took pleasure in their story. It was reassuring that romance and love could be found, if not for everybody, at least for some.

Part of the measure of success in America, was to have a steady job and to own a home. The years of struggle were paying off. Elias was promoted to Foreman at the factory, and he bought a three story house at 14 East Wilbeth Road that very sensibly was just three blocks from his work.

It was not very long before Elias and Mary had a daughter and a son. During those early years, they also developed into an enviable team that lasted throughout their marriage. Elias continued to gather relatives and friends who were always invited to his home. Mary fed them and also housed them if necessary. Her easy good nature made guests feel welcome no matter how inconvenient their visit.

It was not that Elias forgot about his family in Poland. Rather he was occupied with other essentials of life. The years had gone by so quickly. How could it be that the war had been over for nine years, and that it was sixteen years since he had come to America? He had good reason to be proud of what he had accomplished. He had a good wife, two attractive children, a comfortable home and a comfortable life, and no fear that if he took leave from work that he would lose his job. Most important, he had savings. The time had come to see what he could do for his family in the old country. He also had the self assurance of his own success. He had no doubt whatsoever that he would make satisfactory arrangements for his three sisters and his mother. He returned to Serednica fully prepared to do just that.

Anastasia's oldest daughter was named Barbara, after the sister who died so young. (Mary, the step-daughter, was by now on her own.) When Elias returned to Serednica, Barbara was already married. She had obligations to her husband, his family, and her own young son. Whatever plans Elias may have made for Barbara, he did understand that major changes in her life had already taken place, and that she was not unhappy in her life.

Hanya, the youngest sister, was a different matter. She out and out rejected any of her brother's suggestions for her future. She had a good job as a servant with a kind family in Lesko, a nearby city. She let it be known in no uncertain terms that she had no wish either to go to America or to marry. This bold stand by a young girl surprised and annoyed Elias. He accepted her decision reluctantly, but it was quite satisfying to him when neighbors agreed that since she was the youngest, she was no doubt spoiled by Anastasia and allowed to go her own way too long. She just didn't appreciate his efforts.

Hanya never married and remained a servant all her life. Her American family knew her through her letters. She was not at all shy about long distance scolding of nieces and nephews and in-laws for whatever strange American behavior of theirs she may have heard about third hand.

Julia, the middle sister, on the other hand, welcomed Elias's concern. Arrangements for her were involved and required Elias's best efforts. Her story begins the American story and comes a little later.

As for Elias's mother, it was a given that she would go to America with him. No one questioned the wisdom of that decision at the time. But Anastasia was in her fifties, not an easy age to be uprooted from the familiar into a totally different way of life.

She lived with Elias and Mary on Wilbeth Road for the rest of her life. If those who knew her in Serednica had a glimpse of her life in America, they would have marveled at her good fortune and envied what her son had provided. In his house there were eight rooms. All of them had wood floors, and some even had a soft covering that was meant to be walked on. Water did not have to be carried into the house in pails. It came into the house in pipes, and just by turning a handle, hot water came if you wanted it. Best of all, no one had to go outside to the toilet. There was a special room in the house! There were no smoky oil lamps. When darkness came, there was a button to push on the wall or on the lamp, and magically there was light. Why even the cellar had a hard floor that was not dirt, and at the very top of the house, there was space that was just used to store what wasn't used. Truly she was fortunate. But as some who knew her well may have suspected, for Anastasia it was not enough.

From her first days in America, no one called Anastasia by her name again. Those who could have were peers she left behind in the village. Instead, she was immediately called *"Babcha"* by her two grandchildren. It means grandmother and grew more appropriate as Elias and Mary had four more children. The wonder, to Anastasia's neighbors in Serenica had they known, was that in spite of a house full of six children and assorted visitors, Elias always honored his mother with the room of her own. What's more, the room was almost as large as the family hut in the village.

Nevertheless, whether Anastasia could have identified her dissatisfaction or not, there were two causes for irritation. In the past she had respect as a widow who raised five children alone. She had made life decisions for herself and for them. In America it was obvious she had no role and no status. It was her daughter-in-law who had the status and made the decisions. In the old country, Mary would have entered Anastasia's household as the lowly daughter-in-law. Maybe with more thought, if Anastasia put a name to it, there was only one cause for dissatisfaction -- Mary.

There was never anything as crude as an obvious battle between the two women. For her part, easy-going Mary mostly ignored her mother-in-law while Anastasia resorted to every wily, undermining, subtle and not-so-subtle trick she could devise. Through the years she proved to be resourceful, creative, and disruptive.

Babcha in America

CHAPTER 4
BABCHA

How to write about our grandmother? It's not an easy thing to do. Babcha (it means grandmother) died in 1963. Almost fifty years later when remaining family members get together and start to reminisce, inevitably we end up telling stories about Babcha. It's not meant as disrespect or mockery. It's just that she was such an unforgettable character and such a presence in our lives. What follows are some of the stories we have shared.

In no way did Babcha fit anyone's image of a grandmother. She was not plump with rosy cheeks, white hair, and twinkling blue eyes. Quite the opposite. We once saw an 8mm film about Siberia, that vast expanse of eastern Russia that's mostly in Asia. In it was a peasant woman who could have been Babcha's sister. Her body was slim to skinny. She looked ancient, with a wizened, deeply lined face and very few teeth. On her head was a colorful scarf called a babushka (comes from the word for grandmother). What could be seen of her hair was dark, as was Babcha's hair that had only a very few strands of gray throughout her life. She always wore a print house dress and stockings and sometimes a cardigan sweater.

Babcha offered no cookies to grandchildren or anyone else, because she was never known to bake anything, or for that matter, to cook a meal. During the almost forty years she lived in the house on Wilbeth Road, while her daughter-in-law, Mary had four more children in addition to the first two, and all the responsibility of a busy household, Babcha was never known to wash a load of clothes or to do any cleaning in the house. She would occasionally wash the dishes or wipe the wooden steps to the upstairs, usually when there were visitors who noticed and commented on how helpful she was to Mary.

Anything American was suspect, ignored, or condemned. (That might explain why she never touched the vacuum cleaner or washing machine.) She refused to learn the English language. All the grandchildren had to speak to her *po nashimo.* However, some twenty years after she came to America, when the Molohoskeys were among the first to get a telephone, the family got reports from friends that when none of the family was home, Babcha would answer the phone in understandable English. For many years, none of us knew she could, or would, do this.

Babcha had never seen a play in her life or been to a movie, but she had a definite talent for theatrics. In many of her habits, she was a drama queen of the highest order. One of her daily routines was morning prayers. They were not spoken quietly to God in the privacy of her room. Oh no! She prayed out loud, *po nashimo,* up and down the stairs and from room to room. Should there happen to be visitors, either adult or friends of grandchildren as sleepovers, her prayers seemed to be louder. That could be just that we were more aware when visitors were present. To the family's credit, if anyone asked about this, the answer was a simple, "Babcha is praying," as if this were a common practice in every house.

Nothing about the rituals and traditions of the Orthodox Church are casual. Most of them require serious commitment. The Church was a very important part of our lives. I'll tell more about some of the customs on other pages, but this is about Babcha. Easter is the Holiest Orthodox holiday with forty days of serious fasting leading to it. Although she did not attend church regularly, Babcha usually attended at least one Easter service. She favored the midnight service before Easter Sunday when all members of the congregation who were able were required to kneel before a replica of the Tomb of Christ. Babcha would be in line with all the other kneelers. When it came to her turn, Babcha went one better. At sixty and seventy years of age, she prostrated herself before the Tomb with arms extended at the shoulders so her body formed a cross. Applause, of course, was not appropriate, but there was a definite hum of approval from the pews.

Sunday was a Holy day. No work was to be done. It should be reserved for church, rest and prayer.

My youngest sister, Vicky tells of an incident that happened in later years. The Molohoskeys were on vacation. Babcha was staying at Mom's house. She was resting in the bedroom where the treadle sewing machine was. Vicky came in intending to finish something that had to be done for sewing class. She made the mistake of going to the sewing machine and making motions to sew. Babcha did not take this as a teaching opportunity. Instead, still lying on the bed, she put her fist to her mouth and began a soft "yoi, yoi, yoi" that Vicky didn't hear. She continued to peddle the treadle. Babcha's "yoi, yoi" gained crescendo. Mom heard the ruckus. In those days, if she got upset, her head would move from side to side in a continual "no." Her head shaking uncontrollably, she got Vicky's attention. The treadle stopped, but Babcha didn't. She was thoroughly agitated. There was no stopping her now. Mom and Vicky were both frightened enough to call cousin Nancy. A few minutes later Nancy came, picked Babcha up bodily and pointedly said, "We have her all year, and you can't take her for even a week!" and carried Babcha out to her car. Not then or any other time was there sewing or other work done on Sunday when Babcha was around.

I don't ever remember being directly scolded by Babcha, but neither was there praise or a compliment. As with Vicky, there was however, no doubt about her disapproval. I also got the treatment from Babcha because of a lack of courtesy. So did my mother because of me.

Po nashimo there are two different words for you: *ti* when you speak to one person or an equal; *vi* is the plural you, but it is also used as a sign of respect for status or for age. Babcha overheard me say *ti* to my mother, which to Babcha was showing disrespect. Not to me, but to Mom, she said, "You allow your daughter to say *ti* to you? Shame!"

You have to give credit for masterful. In one simple sentence she managed to criticize both of us. Mom told me it didn't matter so much to her, but when Babcha could hear, I was to say *vi* to Mom, and always, always *vi* to Babcha.

Weather permitting, Babcha walked and walked, always with a babushka on her head and her hands clasped behind her back. The entire neighborhood knew who she was. In spring and summer, she walked to the lot that Elias bought for a vegetable garden, more than a mile from the house. They, and sometimes the children, farmed the plot together. Babcha weeded and hoed and then brought fresh tomatoes, corn and other vegetables as they came in. She did not object to a ride in whatever car Elias had at the time, if he offered.

It's hard not to think that much of what Babcha chose to do was for the effect. One example is the wood she brought home in full view of the neighborhood. The Wilbeth Road house had a furnace for central heating. Elias or the oldest son, Walter, would stoke the furnace and add coal as necessary. The furnace would also burn wood. To be helpful, somewhere and somehow, during her walks Babcha would find and bring to the house on her shoulders, substantial pieces of lumber. The neighbors saw her carry the wood. They let the family know, to their embarrassment, that they shouldn't let this nice little old lady do such hard work. The lumber accumulated in the basement. For some unknown reason it was never burned. Years later when the coal furnace was converted to gas, Elias had to pay to have Babcha's wood removed from the basement.

No one is quite sure when Babcha started dying, but my mother remembered as a child when she first had the experience. Something displeased her mother, and Babcha started moaning, "Yoi, yoi" and then crying, "Call the priest! I'm dying!" It was frightening to Mom. She ran out of the house in tears, barefoot in the snow, to get the neighbor. The woman did not rush to help. Apparently this was not an emergency to her. She said to Mom, "Hush, hush child. Don't be afraid. Your mother isn't going to die."

The priest wasn't called, and Babcha didn't die.

There were other incidents in America of Babcha's imminent death. Several times the priest was called and came to administer Last Rites. The obvious question is, didn't anyone in the family realize what Babcha was doing? Easy to ask after it was over, but there was enough time between incidents that the family tended to forget. Besides, who could take a chance? Babcha was elderly. It could very well be that she might be dying. It took a long time for family members to catch on, but it happened just once too often.

Elias took his wife and family on a vacation to her family in Reading. Babcha was left alone in the house--in the house, but others of her family lived very near by. Her daughter was just four blocks away, and step-daughter and sister were each within a mile. If Babcha admitted to being afraid or lonely, she could have stayed with any of them for the week that her son and his family were gone. Whether it was by choice or some kind of a neurotic compulsion, or for real, Babcha started to die. Her daughters and sister and a doctor were called to try to ease her suffering. Nothing worked. Babcha was dying so convincingly that Elias was called and the family returned. And wouldn't you know, Babcha miraculously recovered. After that, news of Babcha's approaching death was passed around the family with a nonchalant, "Babcha's dying again."

Babcha never went to a dentist or a doctor's office or to a hospital. She died peacefully, without drama, in her room on Wilbeth Road when she was 92 years old.

CHAPTER 5
JULIA, THE MIDDLE SISTER

Every little girl wants to be pretty. It's not that Julia's teeth protruded like "buck" teeth. Rather as often happens, when front baby teeth are replaced by permanent teeth, the new teeth appear to be too big for the child's face. Julia was about eight years old when she overheard a village woman say, "That Julia would be a pretty girl if she didn't have those big teeth."

Julia decided to do something about her defect. She gave thought to different possibilities and came to a solution. In the village there was a mill where wheat was ground into flour. It had a huge stone grinding wheel with a rough surface that Julia decided would do the job. She waited for an opportunity when no one was around. While the wheel was moving. Julia bent her head and placed her teeth on the rough surface of the stone expecting that the stone would file down her big teeth to a more acceptable size. Instead, her head started bouncing. When her teeth did connect with the moving wheel, it was a shock that hurt enough to be downright unpleasant. The bouncing head did it. Julia at that moment, decided she was willing to wait until a more comfortable solution presented itself.

Julia's teeth story was an example, even as a child, of the practical way she approached life. If there was a problem, try to fix it. If it didn't work, at least you gave it a try.

Julia was born in 1904. World War I lasted from 1914 to 1918. As was mentioned, Serednica was in the path of the Austrian army as it advanced east against the Russians and again when the Austrians were driven west by the Russians. Her memory was very clear about huddling against the inside wall of their hut as they heard the "pook, pook, pook" (Mom's words) of bullets against the outside of the house. She also remembered women and children covering their heads with a featherbed (like a huge feather comforter) and scurrying to the safety of the root cellar (where onion, carrots, and potatoes were stored during the winter). A soldier saw this futility and said with pity, "Poor, foolish women that you think feathers will protect you from bullets."

There were also the terrible stories being circulated about the cruelties of both armies. Julia especially remembered what the Austrians said about the Russians-- that they cut off the breasts of women and worse. When the Russians did come, everyone in the village expected unspeakable horrors.

It was even worse when Anastasia and her daughters were ordered to billet a Russian soldier. The first time he entered their hut, they were terrified.

There are enough common words between Ukrainian and Russian that the women understood when he spoke to them, "Don't be afraid *rebyatki* (little fish). I'm not going to hurt you." He stayed with them for a short time and Julia remembered kindness from him.

By the time Elias returned to Serednica from America, Julia had grown into her large teeth that fortunately were not damaged. She was a small woman, almost petite...not exactly pretty in a conventional sense, but attractive in her own way. No one knew of her best feature because her dark, wavy hair was always in a thick braid down her back or with braids wound around her head. She also had intelligence, a sharp sense of humor and a gift for wicked mimicry. Of course, none of these qualities were particularly welcome in a young woman, especially if she had no prospect for property. Everyone in the village knew the circumstances of Anastasia's three daughters, even if their brother was in America.

Julia did on occasion find work with families who could afford to pay her. With them she got some insight into a better way of life that awakened something in her. Maybe she didn't have to be resigned to what seemed to be her lot. Maybe to have a better life, a person needed to take risks. Isn't that what her brother had done?

When Elias, this impressive personage came back into her life and then took time to ask Julia what she wanted for herself, she was more than grateful. No one before had been particularly interested in anything she had to say, and certainly not in her ideas or dreams. With some insight and a little prodding, Elias asked if there was anyone in whom Julia was interested. Shyly and almost reluctantly, Julia produced the name of Joseph Bechkowiak and immediately was shocked at her own audacity. What developed from this conversation was altogether improbable. It came about through arrangements made by Elias before he returned to America.

Joseph in his Polish Army uniform

CHAPTER 6
JOSEPH

The status of the Bechkowiaks was considered to be far above Julia's. As a marriage prospect Joseph, the oldest son, was very desirable. Never mind that he had four brothers who would be sharing the family property. Besides, he was handsome, a good dancer, popular with the girls, and in general, a definite asset at village festivities. People couldn't understand why he wasn't already married, although everyone knew he was enjoying himself and certainly in no hurry.

As soon as Julia spoke Joseph's name, she started providing obstacles to her own suggestion. Elias calmed her. He knew of the family. He would call on them to see what he could learn. If there was any interest at all in a possible alliance, he could persuade. He knew very well how to use *solotki slowa* (sweet words).

By now Elias was eager to return to America. He wasted no time. He knew that Ivan Bechkowiak had lived in America. When Elias went to speak to him and to his son, he learned two other important pieces of information. The son had been born in America and was therefore an American citizen and, he had also served in the Polish army for two years.

Joseph had been a young child when he and his parents came back to Serednica. He didn't know the importance of his American birth, and it meant nothing to his father. When the Polish army conscripted young men into service, Joseph went as required without ever realizing his American citizenship should have provided an easy out.

It was just the kind of problem that appealed to Elias. It also gave him a bargaining advantage. He assumed his most proper authoritative posture and suggested to Joseph that he, Elias, was the best person to guide him through the uncertainties of restoring his American citizenship. After all, he did write and speak both languages (English with a strong accent). When he returned to America, he would be willing to work especially hard and would spare no expense if he knew he was working for the benefit of a relative, for example, like a brother-in-law.

Joseph understood. He knew Julia. She was not exactly what he would choose for himself, but she wasn't so bad either. The promise of America, however, was the greater inducement. With a little more negotiation, Joseph agreed to the arrangement. Elias set about immediately to get "ahfeedayvitz" from Polish officials stating that Joseph was coerced into the Polish army.

Elias and his mother sailed for America in 1927. Soon after he arrived, he made contact with a "Pheeladelfia lawyer" to legalize Joseph's American citizenship. Julia and Joseph were married in 1927. Their daughter, Olga, named after Elias's oldest girl, was born 18 months later. Six months after Olga's birth, Joseph left his newly pregnant wife and his infant daughter in the home of his parents while he went to America on an American passport.

Joseph came to the house on Wilbeth Road, but stayed with his brother-in-law only a short time. Very soon he found work at the

Holub Iron and Steel Company in Akron. But this was 1929, the beginning of the Great Depression. It took him three years to acquire enough passage money for his wife and daughter. There was only one child. The second one, a little boy, died soon after he was born.

Passport Photo of Olga and her Mother

CHAPTER 7
ARRIVING IN AMERICA

(Julia Molohoskey Bechkowiak's name is on the Immigrant Wall of Honor at Ellis Island because of arrangements made by her second daughter, my sister, Mary Anne Smith.
The story of how it came about is at the end of these pages.
Should you have an opportunity to visit, the setting on the Island as well as the Wall and Museum, are all worth seeing.)

At last Julia was leaving the ship that had caused her misery. She had been seasick for most of the thirteen days it took to cross the ocean between Europe and America. Now her fear was that in her weakened condition, her trembling legs would not hold her and she would collapse. Julia had heard that sick people were sometimes turned back. Then what would become of her and her daughter? She looked with pride at her little girl. Not many three-and-a-half year olds could have managed among strangers on the ship as well as Olga had while the mother was feeling so wretched most of the time.

She clung to Olga's hand as the passengers were herded toward the building where who knows what she would have to do, and what if she couldn't understand what was said to her? She checked again to make sure she had the necessary papers and the passports. She glanced at the others waiting in lines. They seemed just as fearful and uncertain as she was. They had good reason. Only a few of them knew it at the time, but they were on Ellis Island, the gateway to America.

Julia looked at the building they were approaching. She had caught glimpses of large buildings in cities on her way from Serednica to the ship in Hamburg, Germany. They were just structures with no connection to her. This one was personal. It was impressive, solid, beautiful, and frightening all at once. Inside this building were the officials who would decide whether or not she and her daughter could stay in America.

She had waited almost five years for this. She was here already. The thought of returning to her father-in-law's house with those four rowdy young men who were her husband's brothers, was unbearable. It was not that her in-laws were unkind. It was just that she longed for her own home. She forced herself to be strong and visibly straightened her back. No one should recognize her fears.

Olga's attention was taken with other waiting children. Julia could concentrate on pushing doubts from her mind. It was remarkable that she had come as far as she had. It wouldn't have happened at all of it weren't for Elias. Through her brother's efforts, Olga also had an American passport. Since Joseph was born in America, their little girl was already an American citizen. The officials wouldn't refuse to admit an American child, would they? But what about the mother? No! She would not allow these fears.

And then they were standing in front of a table. A man smiled at them and spoke to her in Polish, asked her for passports and other papers they were required to have. They were pointed toward another door where a man in a white coat examined their heads and ears and mouths. It did take some time, but it was not nearly as bad as she had imagined. The passports were returned to her and she was given the result. They could stay in America. She sat down on the nearest bench and then realized her whole body was shaking.

CHAPTER 8
THE EARLY YEARS

Nothing brought home the reality of what Mom faced until I visited Ellis Island in 2005. Until then our arrival in America was a story. But at Ellis Island, what I knew of Serednica, and what Mom would have seen as the majesty of the administration building on Ellis became a stark contrast. It was then that the empathy kicked in full force. She had been seasick during the crossing. She had a small child. She didn't speak the language. There were trunks to see to. Most fearful of all, she had to get to Akron. Did someone meet her, or did she do it on her own? Unfortunately, the questions didn't occur to me when I could have gotten the answers. Whatever way it did come about, we did get to Wilbeth Road in Akron.

We didn't stay long. It was already a crowded household. Elias and Mary just had their second set of two children, Vera and Nancy, who were my age. There were three years difference in our ages. I was the oldest. The three of us pretty much grew up together, because when my parents moved, it was only four blocks away.

For a short time we rented a bedroom with basement cooking privileges from neighbors who were not that tolerant of a child. I left a doll on the back porch. Our landlady was annoyed at the clutter and threw the doll into the grass. It rained and the doll was ruined. There had been other incidents. Mom had been hinting, then pleading for a place of our own all along. The doll gave her reason for a full-blown campaign, and we moved again.

I'll have to explain a little about the circumstances of the times. It's very hard for anyone today to understand what was common then.

The year was 1933, the heart of the Great Depression. Today there are pockets of poverty all over the country that most of us don't see. Back then poverty was blatant.

Unemployment was a 25% with very few jobs available and no safety nets like Unemployment Compensation, or Social Security.

There were people who lived comfortably during this time, but the ordinary working person who depended on a weekly pay, had no cushion at all if the job was lost. There was a terrible need for a Welfare program. Some kind of aid called Relief was just being instituted, but it was considered to be charity and frowned on even by those who needed it most. Electricity and inside plumbing were mostly luxuries. Very few could afford to go to a doctor or a dentist. Health care was advice from the local pharmacist who might or might not give credit if an over-the-counter medicine was necessary. A vegetable garden and canning the vegetables in glass jars (no freezers) and keeping chickens even in the city could mean the difference between survival or hunger.

About two blocks from our landlady, there was an enclave of three little houses. Two of the houses had one landlord. We rented the "little house." It had four very small rooms and stairs outside that went up to two more slope-walled rooms with no heat. Those upstairs rooms were a plus since we also took in renters at different times. The house had no electricity, and no running water. It did have open land around it for a garden and maybe chickens. Best of all, it was a place of our own.

The other house of the set was the "big house." It had five rooms that were larger and a cement floor basement that was converted to living quarters at different times as the need arose. Mr. And Mrs. Stecyk lived in the big house. They had nine children although most of them were married or lived on their own. When anyone of the Stecyk family or its in-laws had troubles, financial or otherwise, they always found a place in the big house. The Stecyks were our neighbors for fifteen years.

In those days, outhouses (outside toilets) were quite common. Our set of two houses had an outhouse. Once after I was an adult and "treasure" hunting in junk shops, I saw a small, 24 page booklet of outhouse pictures. Of course I got the booklet. There were pictures of many different styles, but none like the one that came with our house. To go with our set of two houses, our outhouse was a duplex. It made practical sense. Construction lumber could be saved by one wall of the duplex being shared. But our duplex outhouse also had another unique feature. Each side of the duplex was a two-seater. Now I have to admit, during all the time my family lived there, we never questioned the logic of the two-seater. Maybe distance provides perspective or maybe objectivity. Whatever triggered the question, it finally came, "What kind of mind conceived the idea that a two-seater might be desirable?"

The unheated outhouses were in use through all kinds of weather during winter and summer. The funny thing is I don't ever remember my fanny freezing or of being frightened. Probably it was selective memory.

Mr. And Mrs. Kulka owned the third house. It had three small rooms, and they had their own outhouse. When we first became neighbors, they had two children. Eventually they had two more. The Kulkas were our neighbors for some forty years. We still visit back and forth.

Our three houses had two sources for water. Very common in those days was a barrel placed under a gutter at the corner of a house to catch the rain water. Appropriately, it was called a rain barrel. That water was used for laundry and for washing. Not very far from the houses was a well or cistern. Mom would put a barrel on a child's wagon, and she and I would go to the well. She would fill the barrel with buckets of water. The path for the wagon was uneven ground. Mom would have to steady the barrel to keep it from tipping. That water was used for cooking. It was never tested for purity, but nobody got sick from its use.

My brother, Russell, who is six years younger than I, and my sister, Mary Anne, nine years younger, were both born in the little house. Victoria, my youngest sister, was the only one born in a hospital. I was fourteen years old at the time. We still lived in the little house. Ours was an absentee landlord who lived in Cleveland. He was a decent person who did before long bring electricity and running water into the house. It was always an event when he came to visit (and to collect the rent).

The Stecyks moved eventually. It was then that my father bought both houses. We moved into the big house and rented the little one.

Julia as a young mother in America

CHAPTER 9
ALVIN C. VORIS
SCHOOL AND READING

Alvin C. Voris Elementary School was a new school built six ears before I started. School was a major change in my life.

Somehow Mom found out the date for school registration. She put on her one decent house dress, shoes and stockings, took me by the hand, and we set off on paths across open fields for about a mile. Those fields are now filled with houses.

Even though we spoke only *po nashimo* at home, I had managed to pick up some English, but apparently not enough to take care of important business. There was no kindergarten. First grade was a half day either in the morning or the afternoon. Mom wanted me to go in the afternoon. I was to translate this request when it was necessary.

We arrived at Voris School and waited our turn until we got to Miss Darkow who was going to be my first grade teacher. Mom motioned to me that I was to explain that Mom wanted me to go in the afternoon. I did my best, but my six-year-old English vocabulary wasn't up to the job. The lady could not understand what I was trying to explain. Mom took over. Somehow between her limited English and Miss Darkow's patience, I was registered for afternoon first grade. Mom was so grateful to Miss Darkow for taking the trouble to try to understand her that after that she always referred to my teacher with the greatest respect and said she was a good lady.

I learned to read and discovered the wonder of books. They really were a magic carpet to me. With school I learned about the library that let you take out books to borrow for free! True, during the school year I could only take out two books at a time, but after school was over in the summer, I could get four books at once. My treat on the last day of school in June was to go to the library for my four books and then read into the night until my eyes blurred and teared from the light of the kerosene lamp. My books were never overdue because I returned them before the two week limit. I couldn't wait. There were more books waiting for me.

In about the fourth or fifth grade, one assignment was to write a poem. About all I can claim is that my verse rhymes, and it is about books. Here it is anyway:

Oh, for a book in a shady nook, and someone to turn the pages.
'Twould be pleasant indeed, if one could but read,
With all the flies in the world in cages.

The Firestone Company complex of buildings was on Firestone Parkway that was a straight walk to the library about a half mile away. The different plants of the complex were fenced in with tiny guardhouses with a security guard at each plant gate. I walked back and forth to the library often enough that the guards got to know me. On occasion, we had conversations that were interesting, at least to me. I remember one conversation with a favorite guard. Somehow we got into a discussion about money. I, in my ten-year-old wisdom, quoted, "Money is the root of all evil." The guard corrected me, "It's not money that's evil. It's the *love* of money. That's what it says in the Bible." That impressed me no end, especially when I found out he was right. I make the same correction whenever I get a chance, and sometimes think of that guard, and the impression he made on me without knowing that he did.

You've probably noticed how often Firestone was used in naming places. Wait till you read the next two paragraphs. That's because Harvey S. Firestone, the founder of his company, built Firestone Park in South Akron as a community for his employees. His plans offered 17 different house styles, from the basic to the more elaborate that would be more suitable for mid-level managers. Executives of the company mostly lived in West Akron that was, and still is, the wealthier part of the city. The house I live in now just happens to be on North Firestone Boulevard. There is also a South Firestone Boulevard. In those days Firestone Park was a very desirable neighborhood. It is still stable with well-maintained homes, but not nearly as prosperous as it was once considered to be.

Those who lived in the heart of Firestone Park went, of course, to Firestone Park School. Alvin C. Voris School was built just on the outskirts of Firestone Park mostly to accommodate Firestone employees who lived on South Firestone Boulevard and other nearby streets. It developed that Voris School had three very distinct groups of students. Mostly there were the children of Firestone employees who were at least comfortable if not well off. There were also the "bus kids." Many lived on farms far enough away that they could not walk to school. For some reason, the "bus kids" don't play a major part in my memories of Voris.

And then there was our neighborhood that was not actually in Firestone Park, but close enough that the kids could walk to school. There weren't any railroad tracks, but if there had been, we would certainly have been on the wrong side of them. We were a mix of immigrant nationalities as well as migrants from the South who had come to Akron to find jobs, found them, lost them, and were trying to survive hard times. When the kids were outside playing, and barefoot in the summer, we all looked pretty much the same. When we went to school with the other kids of Firestone Park, the differences were obvious.

There were no junior high schools. Elementary school went through eighth grade, and then you went to high school. My brother and sisters and I couldn't have got a better basic education that we got at Voris. Standards were high in learning and in behavior. Running in the halls was considered to be disobedience, and excellence was encouraged. Of course, I don't know what my teachers thought privately, but my memories of my teachers are that they were kind and fair, except for one or two very minor instances.

Miss Storing was the principal. She set the standards and maintained them. She looked the epitome of an old-timey teacher: tall with erect posture, hair in a tight bun at the back of her head, conservative dresses or suits, and sensible oxford style shoes. When I see pictures of her now, her face seems pleasant, and she certainly wasn't old, but during Voris years, to know that she was watching was enough to squelch any behavior, even if it was just the fidgets.

Once when I was in second grade, Miss Tugend (more about her later) chose me...ME for the privilege of taking a note to another teacher. I was beyond happy. The room door closed behind me. There were the gray metal lockers on each side of the walls, and the long polished floor. Not a soul was around. It was total freedom. I ran!

The worst possible happened. Who should be coming through the double doors at the end of the hall but Miss Storing. She didn't have to say a word. She just looked at me. I froze. I wanted to vanish from the face of the earth, but it was too late. I was caught running in the hall.

If Voris teachers had first names, I didn't know they did until I was in the upper grades. They were always Miss Piazza, Mrs. Crawford, Miss Brownstein, etc. Some of them I liked better than others, but all of them had a strong influence on my education and on me.

It's possible that I was more naïve than the other kids, but in my mind, a teacher's life was only in the classroom. It was beyond my realm of imagination to picture any of them in their homes, with problems, or children or pets, or with any kind of private life. There was an incident that made me start to think otherwise.

Some of the bus kids got to school earlier in the morning than the rest of us. They were the ones who saw it as it happened. By the time I got to school, everyone was excited and buzzing about this fairy tale story. It was a rainy day. A man drove Miss Tugend to school...a man! He wasn't her brother or anyone like that. The kids knew he was her boyfriend. How they knew it for sure was that he picked her up and carried her across a puddle! Yes he did. It really happened. He carried her!

I will always have a special place in my heart for Miss Tugend and her boyfriend. (I'm going to skip ahead to when I was in high school, because these two people belong together.)

When I went to Garfield High, the assistant principal was George Kidder. Everyone called him "Pop" Kidder. By then I knew. He was the one who was Miss Tugend's boyfriend. They were married now and lived on North Firestone right across the street from Garfield just five houses from where I live now. It was probably my sophomore year. The Depression was over. World War II, that had created so many jobs, was almost over. It was 1945 when Pop Kidder called me into the office, and asked me to come to his house to talk to his wife. Of course I went.

They asked me if I would be willing to do light housework like vacuuming and dusting once a week for pay. When I told my parents, they considered it to be an honor that I was asked. Needless to say, I accepted. Through them, I also got baby-sitting jobs which was another source for earning money. They told me where there was a key to the house, but best of all, sometimes we talked like real people, not like teacher and student. Occasionally, Miss Tugend (I always had a hard time saying Mrs. Kidder) and I talked about Voris. She was the one who told me that the kids weren't the only ones who jumped when Miss Storing was around. The teachers did, too. That was certainly a perspective that I hadn't considered.

Miss Tugend was also the one who told me how it was for the teachers during the Depression. It happened more than once that they would work sometimes for two months and not get paid. When the checks finally came through, Miss Storing would deliver them herself. Miss Tugend giggled and said it was the only time she was glad to see her.

Pop Kidder talked to me not as an adult to a student, but as a person. He had a twinkle in his eye and a sense of humor. I have to say it. He was a kidder. Just by being himself, I got from him an indefinable something that I cherish.

At Garfield, the first day of school was always a pain for me, both annoying and embarrassing. In each class, the teacher called the attendance roll. In those days, ethnic names were far less common than they are now. It went something like this: Adams. Here. Baker. Here. Beachy. Here. "Betcha... Betcha...Olga, how do you pronounce your name?" Those were the kinder ones. Other teachers would mangle my name.

Maybe he was just in a kidding mood, or maybe it was insight on his part, but one day in his kitchen at home, Pop said to me for no reason at all, "You know, my name is such a harsh name, George Kidder." And when he said it, he deepened his voice and made it sound clipped and harsh, but Ol-ga Bech-kov-i-ak" and he moved one hand in a curvy motion as he said each syllable, "Ol-ga Bech-kov-i-ak has such music to it!"

I loved that man. I worked for the Kidders for two years. When my mother died twenty years later, Pop Kidder came to the calling hours.

I'm sure they must have known that I cared for them, but I wish I had in more ways than I did, let these two wonderful people know how much they meant to me.

The teachers at Voris gave me opportunities, but for me, some of them were challenges, too. My Mother, who went to school in Europe probably about two years, did everything she could to support and encourage me. Countless times she got involved and came through to help me do whatever was needed. If it was for school, it would get done somehow.

In third grade we were studying Plains Indians. Each of us had to bring in something that represented Indian life. My little brother was almost two now. Even so, we had very few toys. I have no idea why there was a miniature wooden horse around, but there he was. I wanted to use it to attach two wooden sticks (like poles) from the back of the horse and put a bundle at the end of it to show how Indians moved their possessions from camp to camp. I didn't know how to attach the sticks to the horse. I don't remember how Mom did it, but she did. I took my horse with the bundle attached to the two sticks to school, and Mrs. Worth praised my work to the whole class.

Harder (and more expensive) was when I was to be in the Thanksgiving play for the whole school. I had to have a Pilgrim costume. Mom knew nothing about Pilgrims, so I had to explain what the dress looked like. I don't know why I didn't bring home a picture of a Pilgrim from school or the library. Instead I drew a picture with two white rectangle collars hanging from each side of the neck. Mom took it from there. It sounds simple, but it wasn't. There was the black material that had to be bought or donated. Then the material had to be cut to the right size and shape and then sewn. Mom had no pattern or sewing machine. Somehow she did manage to do it. The neckline was cut a little bit too low, but it did have the white rectangle collar. It was a Pilgrim costume.

You've probably seen multi-colored Ukrainian/Russian Easter eggs. The designs are applied with a tool called a *kystka* that is dipped in hot candle wax. The colors are achieved by re-dipping the egg into several different colors and then applying parts of the design in candle wax on any particular color. It takes skill and experience to learn the process, because you're drawing on a curved surface. The designs can go from crude, to intricate and beautiful, depending on the skill and creativity of the artist. All of them are colorful. The decorated eggs are included in the basket of food that is brought to church on Easter Eve to be blessed by the priest. After the blessing, the tradition is that the eggs are exchanged among family and friends.

Mom and other women of the family would get together of an evening during Easter Lent and decorate eggs. Their tools were all homemade. When times were hard, they made their own dyes: yellow from onion skins, red from beet juice, and purple or blue from whatever berry was available. The eggs were hard boiled first so that if any were ruined they could be eaten. Children could watch, but were not allowed to have an egg just to experiment. Eventually when we were allowed to try, it was almost an apprenticeship. We could do only certain basic things on a grownup's egg.

Mom's egg designs were more simple, but I thought they were just beautiful. I coaxed her to make me a few for school. Of course, the best one was for my teacher, and then a few more for special friends. Mom decorated six eggs for me. I carried them in an egg carton very carefully to school. When I presented the eggs, the teacher admired how pretty they were. All of them thanked me, but they had no idea what was involved. The eggs were entirely new to them.

One egg went to Del, a Firestone Park kid. I'm not sure why because he wasn't even a particular friend. Maybe it was because he played the piano beautifully. Otherwise he was a little bit odd. Our school desk tops lifted up. He used to hide behind his desk during class and eat food he had stashed.

Del walked home across the fields on the same paths I walked. On the way home, I saw some bright pieces of color on the ground. I looked closer and recognized Mom's egg shell pieces. Del had eaten the egg I gave him. I didn't tell Mom, but in the future I was very sparing with the eggs I did give.

The last two years at Voris were a new experience. In preparation for high school, we moved from room to room with different teachers for different subjects. It was Miss Brown for literature; Miss Petley for geography and history; Mrs. Thompson for English; and Miss Witthoff for science and math. Maybe because I was older and could remember more, these women are still vivid characters to me.

For the most part, Miss Brown was a good teacher, and the literature we were assigned to read was tolerable to interesting. That is, until we spent hours in class reading and analyzing that dull, dull poem, "Snowbound." I didn't know then that required reading was decided by a Curriculum Committee. I thought it was Miss Brown's decision. It annoys me that I still remember one line from the poem. It was the description of a cat on a rug "like a couchant tiger." Miss Brown made us look up the definition of couchant. It was the perfect word for the description of the cat. I wouldn't mind giving Miss Brown credit for my interest in words, but I'd hate to give it to "Snowbound." Besides, what are the chances of couchant coming up in conversation, or anywhere else for that matter?

Mrs. Thompson was older, heavyset, and seriously corseted. Her English classes were repetitive and boring. We diagrammed and parsed sentences. These are old fashioned sentence analyzing techniques that were outdated even when I went to school. Mrs. Thompson gave us complex sentences to analyze. They were a challenge, but it was the same thing day after day after day. What I really hate to admit is that even now I may picture a diagram in my mind if I'm not sure where to place a clause or a phrase. Mrs. Thompson would love to know that, but I wouldn't want her to have the satisfaction. English is a wonderful language. She did nothing to make her students appreciate the versatility and beauty of it.

Miss Storing really didn't need an enforcer, but she had one. It was Miss Witthoff who was over six feet tall with a solid muscular figure and white hair in a mannish cut. In those days, if your grades were bad, you repeated the year in school. The result was that there were nearly grown fifteen year olds just biding their time until they could quit school at sixteen. A myth spread that Miss Witthoff picked up one of these good-sized, boys who had done something un-acceptable to her, by the nape of his shirt and hung him on hook in the cloakroom. I'm not at all sure this really happened, but I did have a personal experience with her that reinforced the myth.

A few days after we came into her class for the first time in seventh grade, she gave the class an assignment, told us to keep working, not to waste time by talking, and that she would be back shortly. She left and closed the door. What an opportunity! Immediately a buzz started as everyone talked. After a short while the door opened. Miss Witthoff came in and said nothing for a bit. The tension mounted. Then she said, "Those who were talking while I was out, please stand." Most of the class did stand, although hesitantly. I was among them. I looked around for a kind of group support and saw some that I knew had talked who were not standing.

There were any number of ways Miss Witthoff could have handled the situation. She could have praised those who were standing for their honesty and dropped it at that. She could have assigned a short essay on not wasting time or being trustworthy. She could also have asked questions of those who were not standing. Instead, what she did do was start down each row of desks to give a swat on the behind to each student who was standing. I was one of the first. This was not a perfunctory pat. It was a substantial swat with the strength of a fresh arm. Whether or not it was just a pat or a serious swat, it was demeaning. Worse, it was unjust. Worst of all, it condoned "getting away with it" and punished those who were honest. She did accomplish her purpose. In future, we did "behave," according to her standards, that is. But for the two years I had her for science and math, at best, I tolerated her.

Miss Petley was the first teacher to allow us to work in teams. This was a revolutionary concept even to teachers at that time, but more so to students. Our assignment was a unit on the history of Ohio. We were allowed to talk to each other during class as we worked on projects. This freedom took some adjusting since it required self discipline, but the work did get done.

Miss Petley had actual conversations with her students. Because of that, she knew family circumstances and genealogies. Best of all, she had a sense of humor and seemed to get a kick out of what her students came up with and laughed with them. I also have a vague memory of visiting her class when I was in the first grade. Miss Petley stood behind me and let me stand on a desk. As a foreign born child, I was probably a novelty at Voris, but I can't imagine that with my limited English at that time, that I could have said anything that might have interested her students. In those days, though, any diversion was welcome. Anyhow, Miss Petley was my favorite teacher in the last two years. It could be just because of a general feeling of acceptance. That's a nice feeling to get from anyone.

Minnie Bower was our music teacher. I usually refer to her with her full name or sometimes just as Minnie, not because of any disrespect. She wasn't as colorful a personality as other teachers, but I credit her with introducing me to good music of every variety. It wasn't that I got any special attention. It was because to me the music was all new. We didn't even have a radio for some of those years, although there was always the *a capella* choir at church, and always group singing at family celebrations. I guess the foundation for appreciation was there, but Minnie Bower broadened the scope to classical music and everything else (except jazz) for me and all her students. She brought records for us to listen to. I never was able to picture the baby deer cavorting in "Afternoon of a Faun" as she suggested. Rather it was the sounds I liked, although for my taste "Afternoon..." could have been livelier. Another thing she did was that she didn't limit us to the approved grade level music text.

Years later in a box at a garage sale, I spotted a thin little paper-bound brown book that looked familiar. It was "Twice 55 Plus," the supplementary music book that Miss Bower used. I didn't know how much I loved that book until I found it in that garage like a lost treasure. I still have it and use it. It has everything from rounds, to spirituals, to the "Triumphal March from 'Aida,'" to songs from WW I. It also has what I consider to be one of the truly most beautiful love songs ever, "Believe Me If All Those Endearing Young Charms." It's not so much the music as it is the words. Minnie Bower told us the composer wrote that song for his wife when he learned she was in a carriage accident. I remember the words 60 years later. Honest!

Believe me, if all those endearing young charms,
which I gaze on so fondly today,
Were to change by tomorrow and fleet from my arms,
like fairy gifts fading away,
Thou wouldst still be adored, as this moment thou art,
let thy loveliness fade as it will;
And around the dear ruin, each wish of my heart
would entwine itself verdantly still.

It was a really big day when the WPA Orchestra came to Voris and the whole school got to hear them in the auditorium. As part of the program to relieve unemployment, the Work Projects Administration was formed to hire skilled and unskilled people in all kinds of fields including art and music. Musicians were hired for the local WPA Orchestra. Part of its mission was to go to schools and present live concerts. When they came to Voris, I remember sitting on the edge of my seat absolutely *commanding* them mentally to play a Strauss waltz. Believe it or not, they did play "the Blue Danube." I'm sure it was because of Miss Bower that I even knew there was a Strauss and that he composed music.

All through my school years and then some, I did have a pretty soprano voice. I sang in the church and the high school choirs. I also sang walking down Wilbeth Road on my way home from Voris School. My movie heroines were Deanna Durbin, Jane Powell, and Kathryn Grayson, all wonderful sopranos. My fantasy was that I, too, might be discovered. It didn't happen, but Virginia Brand, who didn't know me at all, but lived in one of the houses I passed, for no reason unexpectedly one day, presented me with the *The Music Lovers Encyclopedia.* I treasure that book.

Also for a time, Mom managed to scrape together the money for me to take voice lessons from Marie Arend MacPhee. It was through her that I came the closest to fame in a very roundabout way. (I love to tell this story.) In the 1930s there was a movie about the life of Johann Strauss called "The Great Waltz." The female lead in the movie was lovely Melitsa Korjus, a great soprano. I am proud to say that Miss Korjus and I both had Mrs. MacPhee for voice teacher. How about that for a near claim to fame?

My own children now mock me when I mention my pretty soprano voice. They mostly know my singing as it is now, sort of a one-octave *basso profundo*. Never mind. I still love to belt out the words at any chance I get. I don't even pay attention when my dear children say, "Don't sing Mom."

There was one other area where I got no fame even in a roundabout way. Maybe because of the WPA orchestra, but I decided I wanted to play the violin. Mr. Saladin, also a part of the WPA program, came to Voris once a week to give instrument lessons. Word was passed among family friends who loaned me a violin, and I was on my way. By seventh grade, I was skilled enough to be concertmistress of the

Voris orchestra. There were three violinists. Then a new girl named Martha came to Voris. She was only in the fourth grade, but tried out for the orchestra and displaced me. That was a blow, you can bet! It sure made me regret that I hadn't practiced more, but it was too late. A fourth grader deposed me from my position as First Violin of the Voris Elementary School Orchestra.

There's just one more little tidbit to my violin experience. One day I was wiping the rosin off the violin. The light was just right, and I could see letters inside the carving of the body. I thought for sure I could see in a faint elegant script *Stradivarius*. The owner of the violin was recently from Europe. My imagination took off! I couldn't wait to show my great discovery to Mr. Saladin. When I brought it in to show him, he just shook his head without saying a word. At the time, I thought he should have paid a least a little more attention to my treasure. When I recall the look on his face though, he probably made his evaluation on the basis of the sounds I had produced with that instrument.

Back then, the schools in Akron developed a wonderful music program called the May Festival. From about the 7th grade and up, each school sent a few of its best music students in voice and instruments, to the Festival. A director, Guy Fraser Harrison, was imported. I was privileged to have this experience (for voice, not for violin) several years, thanks to Minnie. One year Mr. Harrison worked with us on a four part Welsh lullaby, "All Through the Night." He had us repeat singing a phrase over and over until he got what he wanted. When we got it, we knew it. We recognized the beauty of what he worked to have us achieve.

Eventually I taught sixth grade in the West Seneca, New York school system for six years and substitute taught for a few years, also. I tried to be as good a teacher as I could be. I should say that I reacted to both good and bad practices of teachers that I had.

I'm sure Miss Bower would love to know that my garage sale copy of "Twice 55 Plus" was put to use again. In connection with the study of Europe in my Social Studies class, I would teach a song from "Twice" that represented the music of the country: For Spain it was

"In Old Madrid"; and "Funiculi Funicula" for Italy. With England, the kids loved the nonsense song "A Capital Ship for an Ocean Trip."

* * * *

This is kind of a post script. I thought I had finished writing about my Voris School Teachers, but for some reason, Minnie Bower kept milling around in my mind. I never considered her to be as much of an influence as the other teachers, but unexpectedly she kept popping into my thoughts. I started wondering why that was. It led me to try to analyze what it was about one teacher that made her memorable some sixty years later. It took some delving.

Besides introducing us to different genres of music, she also taught us important musical concepts like reading music and determining musical keys. It was all probably part of the required curriculum, but hardly stimulating material for many students, so that in retrospect, what amazed me more than anything else (probably because I had been a teacher) is that I did not remember that she ever raised her voice, scolded, or was harsh to any of us. Considering we went to music class once a week right through eighth grade, that is quite an accomplishment for any teacher. It was also so hard to believe, that I began to doubt my own memories. I needed back-up.

I first spoke to Mary Anne, my sister, who followed me in school nine years later and also had Minnie as a teacher. Her memories were very much like mine. Minnie Bower taught us in depth about the world of music, and she did it in a quiet, unassuming, kind manner. Mary Anne also remembered a detail that was an important part of Minnie's equipment. To draw the five line music staff on the blackboard, Minnie had a five chalk tool that drew the five lines in one swipe. Watching her work with that, impressed my sister no end.

My brother Russ, who came six years after me, had a perception of Minnie so different from ours that it shocked me. When I explained that Mary Anne and I both gave Minnie lots of credit for her teaching, and further, that neither of us can remember scolding or unkindness from her, he scoffed. "Well sure. That's because she didn't pay attention. When she had her back turned and drawing on the board with that five chalk thing, Jack (his buddy) and I would do all kinds of stuff that she never saw or heard. Minnie Bower didn't teach me much. Most of the time I was bored and just goofed off."

An Aside:
Russ' Voris buddy was Jack Lengyel who as an adult became a well-known football coach. After the entire football team and other personnel (more than forty) of Marshall College in Huntington, West Virginia were tragically killed in a plane crash, Jack was hired as football coach to rebuild the team. "We Are Marshall" is a movie made about that story.

There you have it. When I hear discussions about the condition of our public school systems, it's very easy to talk about merit pay for good teachers or weeding out the poor teachers. Just of the few examples I've given here about teachers I've had, I ask myself which ones should receive merit pay, and which ones should be let go? Besides, it took sixty some years for me to fully appreciate Minnie Bower. That's a long time to wait for merit pay. Of course, as you can see, if I were making the decisions, I would be objective. What if others weren't? What criteria would they use to decide? It seems to me that test scores can't tell the whole story. Or, what if the powers that be had consulted Russ?

For sure, judging teacher quality is a dilemma.

CHAPTER 10
THE RUSSIAN ORTHODOX CHURCH

Some of the happiest memories of childhood were the ones associated with holidays. If you think it's because of Santa Claus or the Easter Bunny, you'd be wrong. What I remember with much affection are the traditions of our family. They had almost nothing to do with gifts or candy and everything to do with St. Nicholas, the Russian Orthodox Church that we attended in Akron

I'm not in any way qualified to try to explain the religious basis of these practices. However, should you be interested, I've included a very little about the history of Eastern Orthodoxy at the end of these pages. What you're going to get here, are some of the teachings and customs as my family followed them, and as I remember.

What little Americans know about the Orthodox Church comes mostly from snippets they see in the papers or on TV, usually during major holidays. That's because many Orthodox (not all) follow the old Gregorian calendar that is about two weeks behind the newer Julian calendar that most Christians follow now. So then Orthodox Christmas falls on January 7, and Easter varies from year to year. What is shown on TV as news, mostly because of the date differences, seems gaudy, ritualistic, and even mysterious. No doubt about it, the Church is all of these and fundamentalist as well. But for me, there was also beauty as well as emotional ties.

I was married at St. Nicholas to a lapsed Catholic. Neither of us wanted to convert to the church of the other. Instead, we took what we thought was a very rational path. We joined the Unitarian/Universalist Church. It is about as unfundamental as you can get. At the U/U Church, we heard some of the very best sermons on social and moral topics. They were truly inspiring. I loved that part of it, but, I never felt like I was in church. It took me a while to realize that I missed the pageantry of Orthodoxy.

It may be hard to understand. To an outside observer, the rituals may seem almost alien. I hope I can adequately explain why I would miss the ceremony and color by taking the lazy way with a quotation.

Some years ago, I wrote *Crazy Spider,* a historical novel about the Russian Revolution. One of the narrators was Jim Hercules, an African-American. He was a real person who worked in the palaces of two tsars of Russia. He described his visit to a Christmas Orthodox church service through my eyes.

The church was overflowin', but my host led us into the church like he owned it, and people made room for us.

First off, all at once, my ears and eyes and nose told me this was a special place. I heard human singin' from somewhere that sounded the way angels would sound. My nose got the smell of a pleasant, heavy perfume in the air. When I could see, everywhere I looked were flickerin' candles and bright-colored pictures. Then, the priest, in what looked like a gold cape, started the service in a sing-song kind of chant with those heavenly voices answerin'. It was a glory surroundin' me in every way.

The altar part at the front of the church was the most decorated with fancy stands holdin' many lit candles and almost a wall of pictures. I saw there was more than one priest. While one was chantin', another took what looked like a small bowl on a long chain, swung and aimed the bowl at different parts of the church. I saw smoke comin' from the bowl and realized this was where the perfume was comin' from. I got to thinkin' the incense was like the presence of the Spirit. It was a comfortin' thought.

We were standin' for quite a while so I got used to the strangeness a bit and started lookin' around, mostly hopin' for a place to sit. Onliest place I saw was a few benches against the wall where the oldest or crippled were sittin'. Everyone else, young, old, and in between was standin', some singin' and everyone bowin' their heads at times and makin' the sign of the cross all through the service. The people cross themselves a lot.

The service that Jim Hercules attended lasted four hours, which was not unusual in Russia. At St. Nicholas, the usual Sunday service was well over an hour. If it was a saint's day or some other holy day, a two hour service was common. Those Sundays weren't rare either. Children were a part of the congregation. Some allowance was made for the patience of two and three year olds. Older children were expected to behave no matter how long the service. In the tradition of "it takes a village..." there was always some Babcha to frown on misbehavior or tap a shoulder and shake her head in disapproval.

After the second and third generation in immigrant families, St. Nicholas was gradually Americanized to some extent in superficial ways. Instead of every service being conducted in Russian, it was changed to only once a month in Russian. Lately it amounts to a hymn or two at most. Christmas is now celebrated on December 25 with other Christians. Easter is on different days sometimes.

The first church we attended, had benches only along the walls as Hercules described. A place for everyone to sit seemed like a good idea. In the next church, pews were provided, but the disadvantages weren't discussed. An open space in the center of the church allows freedom of movement for adults and children, and an informality that is still common in Russia. With the addition of pews, the setting became more formal. It was very obvious when you rose from a pew. Children, and adults as well, were hard put to find purposeful reasons to wander during long services.

Nothing contributes to the atmosphere of the Orthodox church for me like the music of the Liturgy. Some denominations of Orthodoxy like Serbian or Greek have a piano or organ to accompany the choir that sings the responses. The Russians rely on the human voice. The choir is out of sight in a loft. Depending on the size of the congregation, there is always at least one excellent soprano and several good altos and sopranos. If the church is lucky, there may be one good tenor who can hit the high notes without straining. And there always do seem to be good male voices as well as one basso whose low notes resonate in your body. The priest chants the order of service. The choir sings the responses as well as several traditional hymns in varied arrangements. Except for the sermon, there is music throughout the service. The choir at St. Nicholas did not always achieve angelic, as described in the quotation, but it did often enough produce sounds that were quite beautiful and inspired reverence.

I did one time attend a service at a very small Orthodox church. There were only three voices singing the responses, and one of the male voices was hardly bearable. I don't know how the congregation could tolerate his sounds. That is not the kind of service you would want to hear. In no way did those voices do justice to what the liturgy could be.

Trying to live up to the tenets of Orthodoxy is not for the faint of heart. In our family we memorized prayers and psalms in Russian and repeated one or more of them morning and night. There were also holy days and saints' days that had to be honored by some degree of fasting, or extra prayers or services. Always there were meatless Fridays and, of course, the long church service. Most families did the best they could in meeting these obligations, but in addition, there were two forty day periods of Lent, one before Christmas and one before Easter.

Orthodox Lent was not simply giving up one favorite food or some favorite activity. Lent was (and is still now) intended to be a serious period of prayer and reflection. Lent meant no movies, dancing, weddings, or anything else that could be considered entertainment. (In Russian novels, the social season at court ended before Easter Lent. Nobles, or others who could afford it, went to Paris, Vienna, or the Riviera rather than stay and observe the strictures of Lent in Russia.)

Probably Orthodox believers would accuse me of heresy, but in spite of all the restrictions, I think there is a kind of casualness to Othodoxy that keeps it from being as dogmatic as it sounds…sort of an acceptance of human weakness. It's as if we know God understands that we try to do the best we can.

In our family, Christmas Lent was not as carefully observed, but Easter Lent, that I'll describe later, was serious. Yet during my growing up years, I have no memory of resentment toward our customs, or objecting to them. That's just the way it was. Rather, just as with my feeling for the music of the Liturgy, the observance of Lent and fasting has maintained a special place in my memory. When Lent was over, even as a child, I remember a hard to define feeling. Whether it was a sense of pride or virtue or accomplishment, it was definitely a release. And my goodness, everything seemed to taste so much better!

Christmas Day was January 7, and our celebration was on Christmas Eve. In the earliest days we were at Uncle Elias' house where there was hay on the linoleum floor to remind us of the manger. Several times a Santa with white beard and red suit did arrive to our wonder. He threw some coins into the hay. My cousins and I had the fun of scrambling for the coins. That was enough. No other gifts were expected or given. It wasn't until we heard at school what Santa brought to others that presents became important, or that a decorated tree was essential.

When Christmas Eve was at our house, Mom did everything she could to make it special for us. Presents were still rare, but we did have a tree. The problem was that for some of those years, we had no electricity. Mom tied small candles on the tree limbs for decoration. We also had hay on the floor until one year the tree with lit candles fell over. Luckily the candles flickered out as the tree fell, but that ended the hay on the floor. We did however, always have straw on the table.

The rest of the emphasis was on food. It was a Lenten meal. The custom was to have 12 meatless dishes in honor of the twelve Disciples. Some skimpy years Mom and I would count the bread, butter and garlic to get the required twelve dishes. We didn't count the vodka that was also on the table.

The food always included Mom's golden loaves of homemade bread. The biggest one, baked in an oval pan, was decorated with either a braid of dough or an Orthodox cross unique to Russia that has two bars at the top and one slanted bar toward the bottom.

The rest of the menu consisted of split pea and sauerkraut soup that tastes much better than it sounds. There were *pirohi* (you may know them as *pirogi*) some filled with mashed potatoes and sauerkraut and some filled with prunes or cheese. They were served with a butter/ sautéed onion sauce or sour cream or both. Cabbage rolls are usually filled with hamburger, rice, and onions and baked with tomatoes.

During Lent Mom substituted barley grain for the hamburger, but these just didn't have the flavor.

As we got older, we invited friends for Christmas Eve. After dinner we all went to midnight service at St. Nicholas. The candles, incense, music, pageantry, chanting, and strange Byzantine art everywhere were new experiences for our guests.

Christmas Eve dinner is one of my happiest memories. Even during my adult, non-Orthodox years, I continued the tradition of Lenten foods for Christmas Eve dinner. I did manage to bake my own bread that looked like Mom's, but to me it just didn't taste as good as hers did. I don't know how Mom managed all the different dishes. I made the split pea soup and two kinds of pirohi. That was enough for me. That food takes work!

When I moved back to Akron with my two kids, my sisters and I (all living close by) started having Christmas Eve dinner together. Vicky's husband was Slovak. His side of the family had mushroom instead of split pea soup. We ended up with both soups.

At first it was the immediate families. Eventually more and more people came so that there might be from thirty to sixty people. Those who could, came in the afternoon to help make the *pirohi*. Our kids grew into the jobs of mixing and rolling the dough. Everyone helped. Some people added the fillings and some pinched the edges to seal the fillings into the dough. We all sang Christmas carols in English except for one that we remembered in Russian. One year we made 800 some *pirohi*. Group work made it a lot easier and more fun. I often thought how much more Mom would have enjoyed this than working on her own as she did.

It was a sight to see so many adults and children together at the table set for dinner. Before we sat, we said the Lord's Prayer twice. Once from cards where the Russian words were written in phonetic English, and the second time the Prayer was repeated in English. Most everybody, even the older children, tried to pronounce the Russian words, which was fun (and gratifying, too).

The whole afternoon and evening had a kind of magic. Cousins who saw each other once a year or less were getting reacquainted and having fun together. Friends were participating in every way with food and customs that were unfamiliar to them. There was lots of laughter, and I don't remember hearing the kind of bickering that happens in families or even among friends. It was a boisterous gathering, but full of good cheer and good will.

I think Mom would be very happy with the legacy she helped to create for her children, grandchildren, and yes, great-grandchildren.

Easter Lent is far more solemn. It is a period of mourning for the death of Jesus as well as preparation for the Resurrection. The forty days of Lent are filled with extras of prayers, fasting, and services, but much more is concentrated the week before Easter. Wonderful aromas of Mom's cooking and baking were wafting through the house while the family dipped pumpernickel bread into white sauce for dinner. It tasted good, but it didn't take the place of the smells of ham and sausage. That week, Uncle Elias was known to observe a "black fast," tea and toast only.

Every Orthodox is obligated to receive Communion at least once during the year. It is the most sacred rite of Orthodoxy. To be prepared for Communion, Confession was required. This obligation brought many unfamiliar faces during Lent. Every year, men with heavy mustaches, boots, and bright shirts, and women with colorful skirts and many bracelets and beads came to St. Nicholas. We never saw these strangers anywhere else or at other times, but the congregation knew them to be Gypsies who always appeared before Easter.

The day of Communion, nothing, not even a sip of water must pass the lips (except for medicine).

As the choir sings, the communicants line up. The priest holds a chalice that contains blessed wine and bread, and administers it to adults and children with a spoon.

Communion is a mystical experience that defies explanation. As bacteria conscious as we are, Communion is given to everyone with the same spoon. It is true that the spoon rarely touches the mouth and only by accident, but still it would seem that this practice would invite epidemics. None have been reported anywhere.

At another Orthodox church I visited, it was almost a shock to see the priest pause and go back to the altar to replenish the chalice. Father John Mason, my favorite priest at St. Nicholas, never had to refill the Communion cup. On the busiest Sunday of Lent, no matter how many people appeared to receive Communion, Father Mason preserved the mysticism. In his hands, the Communion chalice was bottomless. None of us were ever able to explain how he managed this.

Finally, it was time for the Easter Eve midnight service. Lent was almost over.

We arrived about 11:00 to a hushed church lit only by candles. In front of the altar was a replica of Christ's tomb. As people came in, they knelt before the tomb and crossed themselves. (This is when Babcha prostrated herself.) The church began to fill to overflowing. The priest conducted a short service. Candles in holders were distributed to everyone except the smallest children. People turned to light their candles from other candles. Men went to the icons and icon banners that could be removed and lined up holding them. It was the beginning of a dramatic pageant with a full cast of extras.

The priests and the deacons in their resplendent robes led the procession out of the church. (For this most important service of the year, there were usually visiting priests and deacons.) Altar boys came after, and they were followed by the men carrying the icons and banners. The choir was next and the entire congregation followed them. As the choir sang dirgelike music, everyone walked outside around the church three times. The walk was symbolic of searching for the tomb of Jesus. Many people in the neighborhood lined the sidewalks to watch this ritual.

At the end of the walk, the priest stood in front of the doors at the top of the church steps and three times triumphantly proclaimed, *"Xristos Voskres!"* (Christ is risen!) Each time everyone responded with, *"Vo Esteno Voskres!"* (Indeed He has risen!) The choir, joined by everyone, burst into joyous music, and the huge church bell was ringing as we re-entered the church. The tomb replica was gone. The church was bright with lights. It was like a happy awakening.

Even though we faced at least two more hours of service, in my mind, the best was yet to come.

It was the blessing of the baskets that didn't happen until the very end.

As families arrived for the Easter Eve service, most of them carried baskets covered with colorful embroidered cloths. In the baskets were representative foods like, bread, butter, sausage, ham, salt, hard cooked eggs, grated horseradish with beets, and of course, the decorated eggs...all the kinds of good food that Mom had been preparing and that we were smelling while fasting during Holy Week.

If the weather was poor, the baskets were blessed in the basement of the church. If it was a pleasant night, the blessing took place on the church lawn. Mothers removed the cloths and placed a lit candle in the basket. The priest carried a bowl with Holy water and a whisk brush to sprinkle the baskets. Finally, after the long, long wait of the service and the blessing, we were free to find our friends, compare the decorated eggs and exchange them. Then at two or three o'clock in the morning, it was home or to someone's house where we could break the fast at last.

I still try to observe meatless Fridays, mostly because I associate fasting with Mom and with family memories.

CHAPTER 11
ELECTRICITY

We could probably get a good discussion going as to what invention or technology (cars, television, computers, etc.) had the most effect on our lives. In my opinion, the one that had the most impact was electricity. We were living in the little house when electricity became a part of our lives. Almost overnight we went from pampering kerosene lamps to a light bulb that took no attention at all. But for me still in elementary school, the real wonder of electricity was radio. Just as with books, radio opened a whole new world to me. When Minnie Bower played "The William Tell Overture" in music class, and the boys at their desks started imitating riding cowboys, we all knew it was the theme music from the program, "The Lone Ranger."

It seemed to me that everyone had a radio before we did, so I nagged until arrangements were made so that I could go to Frances Jakich's house, our first landlady. She was more tolerant now that I was older and no longer a nuisance live-in. She and her husband were kind enough to let me come on Sunday evening to listen to their radio. Some houses had a small set that sat on a table. The Jakiches had a handsome, wooden, stand-alone that was a marvel to me. I remember peeking behind it to see if there were little people hidden back there. I wondered where the voices could come from.

My favorite programs were comedy shows like "Fibber McGee and Molly" and "The Jack Benny Show." There was also the ventriloquist, Edgar Bergen and his dummy, Charlie McCarthy. Charlie got the laughs with his wisecracks and putdowns as he got the better of every guest who appeared on the program. Edgar's daughter is Candace Bergen who is an actress and comedienne now. Candace admitted in an interview that at times she thought Charlie was her brother. Many of their fans thought so, too.

After we did get a radio, I also tuned in to Major Bowes, an amateur talent show, and "Phil Spitalny and His All Girl Orchestra." There were pictures of the girls posed in virginal white gowns. I thought they were just beautiful.

One night, Pop and Mr. Kulka, our neighbor who rarely visited inside our house, were sitting at the table while I was listening to a music program. A soprano hit a high note that I felt compelled to see if I could match. I burst out with the same note and surprised myself as well as the two men. Mr. Kulka reacted with something like "That's nice, Olja," (He did pronounce my name with a "j" sound.) Pop just shook his head. I can still see the look of incomprehension on his face.

The Molohoskey house on Wilbeth Road was the gathering place for the neighborhood. Olga and Walter were the older teenagers with their entourage. Vera and Nancy and I and some other girls were a few years younger. It didn't happen often, but for a short time the two groups interacted. A pattern of listening to scary radio programs developed. We would turn off the lights and huddle during programs like "The Shadow," "Arch Obler, " or "The Mystery Theater." The bad part for me was that I had to walk home in the dark and alone. Of course that didn't keep me from staying after dark. In a nostalgia shop once, I bought tapes of a few of these programs just to see if they were as scary as I remembered. Some were and some weren't. If you've never heard Agnes Moorhead do her monologue called "Sorry, Wrong Number," you should hear it, if possible. It's amazing the emotions that one speaking voice can evoke. Just don't listen to it with the lights off and alone.

The radio did bring the world closer to all of us. It was a Sunday when I was walking home down Wilbeth Road, when I heard a loud, strident voice blaring from one of the houses. I stopped to listen only because it was so unusual. It was a radio announcement about the Japanese attack on Pearl Harbor. I was twelve years old. That day I didn't understand what a profound effect this would have on the country. It was the beginning of World War II. I'll tell more about that time in another chapter.

When electricity was brought into homes, there were changes that made everyday life so much easier. Some of these changes for various reasons, were evolutionary. There were intermediate steps. I would put washing machines, refrigerators, and probably central heating in that group. Other changes were immediate. Lighting and ironing clothes were among these, but you have to know a little about what came before in order to understand how much of a change it really was.

Before electricity there were three main sources of light: candles, kerosene lamps, and gaslights. Usually only wealthier homes had gaslights, because gas had to be brought through pipes to wherever the lamps were. This was expensive to install. Most homes had kerosene lamps and candles that could be carried to wherever light was needed. Both had wicks. The lamps did give more light, but everything about them had to be babied and handled with care.

There was a small, bowl-size base at the bottom of the lamp that was made either of metal or glass. This had to be filled almost daily with smelly kerosene. Above the base was a clear glass globe that narrowed toward the top. From the kerosene to the globe was a cotton wick that carried the fuel when the wick was lit. The purpose of the globe was to shield the temperamental flame of the wick from any gusts of air that could be caused by a moving body, an open door, or a wick either not trimmed right or that was turned up just a bit too high. This moving air caused a whiff of black smoke to settle on the inside of the globe. It was my job to clean the globes. Wouldn't you know, the smoke always settled into the narrower part that was harder to reach. Mom said it was easier for me because my hands were smaller. True, but my fingers were also shorter, the smoke was hard to clean, and my frustration built.

I can tell you when electricity came, even a naked bulb hanging from the ceiling with a pull chain was a wondrous improvement. Not only was there better light, there were no messy chores to do.

Sad irons, used for ironing clothes, were well named. They were cast iron small ovals or triangles, usually with a handle that could re-clamp onto a set of two or three irons. They came in sets because while using one, the others could be reheating on the stove.

Almost every item of clothing was made of cotton. If a woman wanted her family to be presentable, clothes had to be ironed. That meant that even during the heat and humidity of summer, she and her ironing board had to be near the stove so the irons could stay hot. That's where the "sad" comes from. It might look like the lady was crying (and sometimes she probably was) but it could have been perspiration, too.

I learned to iron with sad irons. With Mom it was an apprenticeship on easy, flat things like handkerchiefs and pillowcases till I worked my way up to shirts, pleats, and ruffled trims. Besides burning myself with an iron, there was another hazard that I learned about the hard way. A too hot iron could leave a suntan shade scorched oval on whatever was being ironed. If that happened, nothing could be done to disguise the scorch. The item was a goner unless the scorch was on the tail of a shirt that could be hidden in the trousers.

What wonderful freedom it was when a woman could just plug in the cord from a neat little iron into the electrical socket, and the iron produced whatever temperature was necessary.

Before there were refrigerators, there were iceboxes to help keep perishables cold. Iceboxes were wooden rectangles, smaller than a refrigerator, with shelves and a metal box inside that held the ice. As the ice melted, there was a pan under the icebox to catch the water. The pan could not be ignored. It had to be emptied daily or else there was the floor to mop.

Milk was quick to spoil, so it was delivered every day. To keep the milk cold, ice had to be brought in at least every other day and more often in the summer. These deliveries were made by the iceman and the milkman.

The milkman came very early in the morning and left milk on the stoop in a quart size milk bottle that was narrower at the top. The wider bottom held white milk while cream settled about two inches at the top. It was obviously cream because it was the right color. The bottle could be shaken to make "whole" milk, but most families poured off the cream for special uses. Empty bottles were picked up by the milkman sometimes with notes in them for other orders like butter, cheese, and eggs.

Since the iceman came during the day, he was much more a part of our lives. He carried a 12-14 inch cube of ice into the house with large tongs that dug into two sides. In the summer when the neighborhood kids saw the truck, they would gather around and ask for ice chips. The nicer icemen would chip off a mouthful for each of us. That sliver of ice was a treat on a hot day. What was better was if we were lucky enough to get a nickel for a Popsickle. Popsickles were then just what they are now, fruit flavored twins of ice on two sticks. They were wonderful even if you had to share half with your little brother.

Sometimes on a Popsickle stick you would find the word "FREE." That meant you could present the stick at the store and get a free Popsickle. Then you could brag to the other kids, but it sure didn't happen very often.

The milkman and iceman were casualties of electricity. Their jobs were eliminated, but gradually, probably because electric refrigerators were quite expensive. Families had to save to make bigger investments like for refrigerators and washing machines. There were no credit cards. Making payments on anything was rare for most working people.

Electricity eventually brought the development of automatic washers and dryers, but it was a slow, gradual process over many years. In these days of full automation, it's almost beyond comprehension to understand the hard physical and tedious labor that women had to do just for the family laundry. The basic steps for getting the laundry done (usually once a week) went something like this:
- Two round, metal tubs (No.3) were on a bench, one for hot, soapy water and one for rinsing.
- Water was heated on the stove and brought by buckets to the tub.
- Clothes were put into hot water, light colors first.
- Each piece was scrubbed by hand on a metal scrub board placed inside the tub.
- Soapy water was wrung out by hand and items were put in the

rinse water tub.
- Items were wrung out by hand from the rinse water and put in a basket.
- Shirts, dresses, tablecloths and such went through an extra step of starching (stiffening).
- Each item was pinned to dry onto a clothesline.
- Each item individually was removed from the clothesline, folded and put away, or further prepared for ironing, which had its own separate steps.

Every item in this laundry routine is manually handled at least six times. This would include work clothes, play clothes, underwear, socks, dress up clothes, other sundries for people, and then household items like sheets, towels, pillowcases, etc. A conservative estimate on quantities for a family of four might be something like this: Mom = 25; Dad = 35 (goes out to work); Boy = 45 (shirt and pants); Girl = 35 (dresses). That comes to about 140 pieces. Add to that the household items and it is probably about 200 pieces, each of them handled six times. Of course, larger families had more laundry, and that much more labor. On laundry days, having fewer clothes was an advantage.

When a hand-cranked wringer was available to add between the washtubs, to squeeze out the soapy water or rinse water, the work eased a little, but it was electricity that brought partial automation with the first washing machines. This was a tub standing on its own legs with a central agitator (instead of scrubbing), an attached wringer, and both powered by electricity. Each item being laundered had to be fed by hand through the wringer both out of the tub and out of the rinse water, but it could be done while standing rather than stooped over the wash tubs.

An unexpected benefit from this new machine was that it also had a hose from the tub that could empty directly into a drain. No engineers (who I might add were all men) ever thought to design wash tubs with a drain hose. The tubs had to be emptied with buckets.

Hanging the laundry outside to dry on warm, sunny days was almost pleasant. In the winter though, it meant cold, raw, red chapped hands. Or if she misjudged the day, and it started to rain before the clothes were dry, she had to hustle and adapt to whatever developed. It wasn't unusual at all to come home from school and to see wet clothes hanging on lines in various rooms (if the house had various rooms, that is). If not, for the kids, it got to be a game of ducking so as not to feel a cold, damp towel against your face. Mom didn't see it as a game. These were serious threats that could ruin her day's work.

These days to control the heat (or cool) in my house, all I have to do is turn the knob on an electric thermostat on the wall, and very soon the temperature in the house responds. Not every time I turn that knob, but especially on cold days, I remind myself to be grateful for this wonderful convenience. I can remember when it wasn't always so easy. Heat didn't come from one main source that was spread throughout the house as it does now. There were sources of heat, but the farther you moved away from them, the colder you were. Air conditioning was unknown.

From earliest days, the open fireplace was the source for heat. Then Ben Franklin, that wonderful man whose curiosity took him in every direction including identifying electricity (his kite experiment), applied science to better control heat from a fireplace. He developed what came to be called the Franklin Stove. It wasn't really a stove, but those principles helped to develop more efficient stoves.

When we moved into the little house, there were two stoves: a kitchen stove that had an oven for baking and a flat top for cooking and heating water. In the living room was a taller, narrow, round stove that was wider in the middle that made it look like a pot belly, and that's what it was called. It was used mostly for heat, but it did have a flat space on top big enough for one pot.

For fuel, both stoves used wood and coal that had to be brought into the house. Also, the ashes that were the result, had to be disposed of. Neither of these jobs was neat. Wood left splinters or chips of bark wherever it was, and coal is black and leaves sooty marks on whatever it touches. Burning either of these caused ashes that couldn't be disturbed without creating dust.

The kitchen was comfortably warm in winter, but in order to cook or bake in summer, the same fire had to be made no matter how hot a day it was. Sometimes Mom waited for cooler days to bake, but that was chancy. Mostly, cooking, baking, or ironing meant sauna-like heat for all of us.

The heat from the potbelly in the living room didn't travel far. (Apparently it had none of Franklin's science.) In winter, the bedroom right next to it was downright cold. Often we took a flat rubber flask filled with hot water (called a hot water bottle), or a hot brick wrapped in a towel to warm the sheets, and then put either one by our feet to warm them.

By morning, the house could be icy cold. Mom or Pop had a fire going in the potbelly by the time we got up. We ran to it as quick as bare feet on a cold floor could take us so we could dress by the warmth. There was a problem. Only the side facing the stove got warm. We had to keep turning.

Heating finally became centralized when furnaces were installed. A furnace was a major household investment because it was huge and because of the work that had to be done. It was a cylinder about six feet tall and about three feet in diameter with large tubes leading from it to rooms that were to receive heat. Stoves were black with shiny, chrome-like trim and were attractive. Furnaces were basically huge stoves, and were not the least bit attractive. They were more like monsters with tentacles reaching out. They were rightfully placed out of sight, usually in the basement.

Furnaces also used coal (and some wood) but in much larger quantities. Houses during that time had an outside opening that led to the coal bin. The bin was a windowless space about the size of a small room. The outside opening was called a "cellar door," but it didn't at all look like an upright door. It looked more like a lid that lifted up on a slanted box. This opening was made especially for coal that was delivered by the ton or the half-ton. The coal truck came to the house. The driver opened the cellar door, put a chute from the truck into the coal bin, and the coal was shoveled down the chute. A ton of coal almost filled the bin.

Furnaces had to be tended manually just like stoves. The fire had to be started, fuel added regularly, and ashes removed. Like with fireplaces and stoves, there was an art to banking the embers so that they lasted till morning. It was a little trickier with furnaces because they were out of sight. The furnace tender, usually the man, had to develop almost an inner clock to add fuel just when it was needed.

With electricity, families could use fans for cooling. In time, coal furnaces could be converted to gas. Eventually air conditioning was added, and at last there was a thermostat to control heating and cooling.

I have a fireplace in my house now. Granted, it is pleasant and cozy to sit in front of a fire, but I rarely start one for myself. I can get just as cozy with the thermostat. And that doesn't make ashes or dust. Yes indeedy, cars and computers have changed our lives, but marvelous electricity made life easier.

CHAPTER 12
THE GREAT DEPRESSION

Shirley Temple was a delightful, talented, beautiful little girl with teeny dimples at the corners of her mouth, and bouncy, sausage-size curls. She was a Hollywood movie star before she was old enough to start school. If a frown crossed her brow, it was in sympathy with someone else's problem. From the beginning of the Depression, she tap-danced, sang, and smiled her way into becoming the darling of America. She glowed with good health and good cheer. Every little girl who was lucky enough to get a nickel to go to the movies, wanted Shirley's curls as well as her magical life that was portrayed in everything that could be sold.

Not so long ago, it hit me that babies and children these days were so much better looking than they used to be back then. As I recall, there were skinny kids with dull, stringy hair, crooked teeth, and runny noses. Their bodies may not have been as skeletal as starving children in other parts of the world, but the eyes that I remember had the same haunted look. Poverty was pervasive, certainly not like Shirley Temple's fantasy world. Most of us lived in the reality of the Depression.

- Scottie, our neighborhood pharmacist, was the medical advisor, and often he provided over-the- counter medicine on a running tab. A doctor was consulted only as a last resort after all home remedies were exhausted.

- Dentist checkups were unknown. A green film at the top of teeth was not unusual. If teeth hurt, they were usually pulled, by a dentist if the family could afford it, or just pulled.

- Common practice was one pair of shoes a year for school and barefoot in the summer. If a shoe developed a hole before June, cereal box tops or cardboard were put inside the shoe to cover the hole and make the shoe last.

- Clothes for children were bought bigger so they could be worn longer. Hand-me-down clothes from anywhere were welcome. Matching the clothes to the size of the child was secondary. In a family of several children, clothes were passed down until they were threadbare.
- String and rubber bands were saved on doorknobs or chair posts. Wrappers from store bought bread were reused for sandwich wraps.
- Rips on clothes were sewn or patched; holes in socks were darned (weaving thread over the hole).
- There were no plastics and no synthetic material for clothes. All sheets were flat, cotton, rectangles that got the most wear in the center. Thrifty women would cut the sheet down the center and sew them "sides to middle" for longer wear. Cuffs and collars on men's shirts frayed first. Again, women would unstitch the three pieces, turn them to the unfrayed side, and re-sew them.
- Even in the city, families tried to have vegetable gardens or kept chickens or rabbits. A fruit tree in the yard was an added benefit.
- Toothpaste and toilet paper were luxuries.
- Unemployment was 25% in the whole country and much higher in some areas like the Dust Bowl in Oklahoma. *The Grapes of Wrath* was written by John Steinbeck. It is an excellent book about one family trying to cope with that devastation. It was also made into an equally good movie.

The situation in the country was so desperate, that some caring government officials were willing to try just about anything. President Franklin Delano Roosevelt instigated and Congress passed many programs intended to help working people through that unemployment crisis. Some of these were labeled artificial "make work" programs. Maybe they were, but I especially remember some of them for the good they did.

My father came to America in 1929 at the beginning of the Depression. Mom and I came in 1932 as conditions became steadily worse. Most of the time Pop did have work at the Holub Iron and Steel Co. junkyard where he cut scrap metal with massive ten foot long scissors with thick steel jaws. For some period though, he was out of work. I was six or seven years old, too young to understand how frightening this was for the adults until Pop was called to work by the WPA, the Work Project Administration (the same program that brought the orchestra to Voris). He worked on filling ruts and holes on roads with shovels of dirt and gravel. He was allowed to work only two or three days a week, but for our family, it was at least some money coming in. It eased the worst of the threats hanging over us.

As young as I was, I remember that our news spread to the neighbors and relatives. I sensed a sort of lightening of spirit among them. Someone did get work. Things might get better. There was hope.

What the WPA did for our family, it did for millions of other workers all over the country. Nearly every community had a school or park or bridge built by the WPA. Many of them like La Guardia Airport in New York City, or Camp David, the presidential retreat outside of Washington, D.C., or Doubleday Field, the baseball memorial in Cooperstown are important landmarks today. Besides building projects, the WPA encouraged and funded prize winning authors of books and plays and composers of the period. At the opposite end, it developed literacy programs for the undereducated.

I knew about the CC Camps because of our neighbor, Edward Kulka, who joined the Civilian Conservation Corps two different times. Years later as adults, he told me just a very little about his experiences. On one assignment, he went to Utah and the second time to Washington state. He was eligible for the camps because he was an unemployed young man. What stayed with me was that he said it was one of the best experiences of his life. I couldn't write about the Depression without including a little about the CCC, but before I wrote, I thought I'd better get my facts straight and did some research. What I learned was better than what I remembered.

President Roosevelt, was inaugurated on March 4, 1933 (not January 20th as it is now). He and members of his cabinet and staff knew they had major unemployment problems to try to solve. One of the hardest hit groups, then as now, were inexperienced or undereducated young men who could not find work. All that volatile energy was roaming the streets with nothing constructive to do. Wise minds realized here were seeds for trouble. They devised plans to harness this energy in conservation projects. Almost every department of government was involved in some part of the solution to make the plans work.

The first enrollee in CCC was assigned on April 7, not six months or a year after inauguration. No. It was in fact, just 37 days after the President took office. Apparently it was not a "say no" Congress.

The young men would be sent wherever they were needed. They would be given uniforms and board and room in barrack style accommodations. Medical care, necessary training, and literacy (if needed) would be provided. They would also receive $30.00 a month in pay. What's hard for us today to believe, $25.00 of his money was to be sent home to the family. The young man had $5.00 a month left to fritter away on anything he liked. To be sure, 80 years ago, $5.00 bought a lot more than it does now, but the $25.00 contribution to his family deserves recognition for its unselfishness.

Of all the "alphabet" programs that were tried during the Depression, probably the most popular were the CC Camps because the money filtered down into the home communities as well as those near the camps. The CCC lasted until the beginning of World War II. Among its many contributions in every state and U.S. possession, the young men developed 800 state parks, worked on 4000 historic restorations, built 13,000 miles of hiking trails, and worked on countless campgrounds.

According to Edward, there were personal benefits to him. He had an opportunity to see more of the country, got the satisfaction of working at useful projects, got some training, met people and made friends, and also was able to help his family.

The CCC seems to me to have been a win/win/win/win/win deal.

My brother-in-law, Theodore Smith, worked on another program that was not as well known. It was the NYA (National Youth Administration). This was "day work." The boys went home after work. He drove a truck hauling dirt to help build our own Derby Downs in Akron. He was allowed to work several days a week, and got $18.00 a month. The Downs is an Akron landmark. Kids from all over the country come to compete with their own homemade race cars in the National Soapbox Derby.

There have always been people who try to avoid work or try to get something for nothing. I'm sure they were present in the WPA, the CCC, the NYA, or any other of the alphabet programs of the Great Depression, as they would be today. Freeloaders will probably always be present. The best society can do is put safeguards in place to help keep them at a minimum. Even then, those so inclined will find a way.

There are critics who use freeloaders as an excuse. Some of these critics referred to the WPA as "We Poke Along." Whatever their reasons, whether sanctimonious virtue, bootstrap philosophy, "nobody ever helped me" mentality, or politics, they are willing to condemn entire worthwhile projects on the basis of one or two personal experiences, or worse, second hand anecdotes.

These people will always be around, too. We should not allow either group to sidetrack us from the greater good.

CHAPTER 13
DUMBEST CREATURES

For the thirty years that Johnny Carson was host of the Tonight Show, I watched him whenever I possibly could. Occasionally, Johnny and Ed McMahon (or a guest) would argue about whether a pig or a horse was dumber. I could hardly contain myself from talking back at my 12" TV screen, "You guys just don't know!" I did know. I had intimate experience with dumbest animals.

For most of my growing up years, we kept chickens and rabbits. They were not pets. They were food. There was however, a big difference between them not just in appearance, but in what they required. Rabbits were much more docile. They stayed in their cages and propagated. Chickens, however, took more space and attention from the time they first arrived.

Mom ordered day old chicks from the Sears Roebuck Catalog. That is, each of us three girls grew into the job of filling in the order blank and sending the Money Order from the Post Office. (You had to have money in the bank to be able to write a check.) She usually ordered baby chicks in batches of 25 or 50. They were adorable, teeny, soft, fuzzy little things when they arrived, but each of us was fooled only once by their golden baby cuteness. We learned soon enough.

Mom prided herself on the survival rate of her baby chicks. The premature death of one was acceptable. If more than one died, it was a financial loss as well as a reflection on her care. Mom rarely lost more than one chick. She would accept no commercial chick feed for her babies. Rather she hard boiled chicken eggs for them. (Somehow that just doesn't seem decent, does it?) It was Mary Anne's job to chop the eggs. She would chop, show the result to Mom who always said, "Chop smaller," until Mary Anne would feel like throwing the eggs or smothering the chicks.

But the chicks thrived and started growing feathers and showing other signs of chicken puberty that involved the law of averages. One could assume that in any batch of chicks, half of them would likely be females and half likely to be males. This is all well and good for averages, but bad for Mom. There was an adolescent period with chickens when many males were testing their maleness where there was only a limited number of females. Furthermore, the males were too scrawny to be useful even for the cooking pot. No doubt about it, from Mom's viewpoint, averages be damned. Females were more desirable, but this stage of chickenhood had to be tolerated.

Our father (we always called him Pop) was not a handyman by any measure. He built a makeshift, boxy structure out of pieces of metal and wood and whatever was available. He surrounded it and a few square yards of ground with a wire fence. This was their home, the chicken coop and its yard. It gave the chickens space to roost and to move around a little. Outside of their yard they could forage for bugs and seeds that saved on buying chicken feed. Every day the chickens were let out of their yard to roam. I was assigned the job to herd them back into the yard for the night. I have not forgotten that first time.

I did what I heard Mom do, "Cluck, cluck, cluck" to call the chickens. They did respond to my call which encouraged me. One end of the fenced yard was a gate that I opened. I assumed the chickens would willingly enter the wide open gate. After all, it was their yard, their home, and they had been out and busy all day. No such luck. No sirree! The chickens sauntered right past the open gate and clucked conversationally to each other as if they were sight-seeing in new territory.

I stood there unwilling to accept what was happening. I wanted this chore to be done! I went into action and started shooing the chickens toward the gate. The more I shooed the chickens, the more excited they got, running wildly around the fence with wings spread and squawking the whole time as if the sky were falling, with me in useless pursuit. All of us went round and round the fence, and always right past that yawning gate. I have tried to thread needles with teeny eyes with the same frustration.

I hated that job with a passion. No doubt about it, if I had had the opportunity, I would have told Johnny Carson or Ed, with no uncertainty whatsoever, as to which animal was the dumbest.

Roosters are different. For those of you who have had limited interaction with chickens, roosters are male chickens. Roosters swagger. They have kind of a hesitation step that they couple with a belligerent stare that makes you pay attention. I once saw a male baboon in a cage at the zoo. He may have been in a cage, but he had that air of assurance as if to say, "This is my domain. I rule here. Wanna challenge me?" Like the alpha male he was, he looked you right in the eyes till you were the one who blinked. Same with roosters, They're protective. Most of them however, will recognize a force bigger and stronger than themselves and back off after putting on a loud, aggressive show of strutting and squawking.

All of us in the family remember one particular rooster who didn't bluster. He acted. He allowed no trespass anywhere near his harem of hens. It didn't matter what size man or beast, if it approached his turf, this rooster went into attack mode. He was just plain mean, and the older he got, the meaner he got. Mom normally wouldn't have tolerated him as long as she did, but the hens cackled contentedly, and the eggs were plentiful. Anyhow, she tended to overlook the rooster's evil nature until one day he could no longer be ignored.

As usual, when the fence gate was opened, the rooster and his harem could roam. The old bird never stayed in the fenced yard. There was no reason for Mom to suppose anything else. With no hesitation whatsoever, she sent Mary Anne to gather eggs from the coop. Mary Anne was probably about eight years old at the time. Her experience with chickens was mincing boiled eggs for the chicks and occasionally strewing chicken feed in the fenced yard. By some twist of Fate, that day the old bird was still in the coop yard. To him, Mary Anne was a threat invading his turf. He went through his usual repertoire of evil stares, ruffling of feathers, squawking, and threatening poses. Unfortunately Mary Anne didn't recognize his warnings. She didn't retreat. Her presence was a direct challenge that infuriated the old bird. He attacked. He flew to the top of her head and held on, the whole time screeching and flapping his wings while Mary Anne, poor kid, was screaming in terror.

The uproar was so severe that Mom knew that whatever it was, it was serious. She grabbed a broom as a possible weapon on her way out the door and ran to the rescue. The rooster was no match for her broom. He flew off Mary Anne's head and out of the fence. Poor Mary Anne was still trembling and sobbing.

It was then that Mom fully realized how much of a menace the rooster had become. She comforted Mary Anne with all kinds of soothing words. But what seemed to give Mary Anne the most comfort was when Mom said, "No more! No more that *diabol kohut!*" (devil rooster). His time had come. It was just a question of when and how.

I can't say that Mom and I actually had a discussion, but there was no doubt that the rooster was a problem for her. Mom would have liked nothing better than to have the bird disappear, but that would go against her nature. It would be wasteful. Still, even for soup, he would take hours of cooking and probably be tough and stringy anyhow. Whether she talked aloud to herself, or to me, I, the reader of everything that came into my sight, was inspired to remember something I read that might be useful.

In those days, there were always articles in newspapers and magazines on ways to take short cuts and to save. There were patterns in the paper for making dresses and all kinds of household hints including various ways to use patterned flour sacks. Women baked their own bread. They bought flour in 10 and 25 pound sacks that were sold in material with pretty prints that could be made into pillow cases or children's clothes. Somewhere in articles like those, I had read and filed away in my mind, the hint that old birds of any kind could be tenderized with a shot of whiskey before they were executed.

It made sense to me. One of our family cures for the common cold was to drink about a half cup of hot wine sweetened with sugar. Medicine nowadays recommends treating a cold with plenty of rest. The hot, sugared wine sure helped me sleep. The next day I woke up feeling just fine. My colds never lasted more than a day or two. Honest! Anyhow I told Mom what I had read, and she decided it was worth a try. There was nothing to lose.

I don't think Mom had any idea what to expect. I certainly didn't, but a confined space did seem appropriate. By now the little bedroom off the kitchen was the bathroom. The plan was that she would sit on the commode, hold the bird and pry open his beak, and I would pour from a cup a couple spoonsful of booze. Mom brought that old rooster into the house, squawking and screeching and furious. It took all of her strength and concentration, because he was putting up a real fight, but Mom held on to that bird between her knees and somehow managed to keep open his beak with her hands. For my part, even though my hands were shaking, I got the cup near the open beak and poured.

You never saw anything like it. That bird exploded from Mom's lap and became a creature from hell. He tore around that little room, wings flapping, thumping hard from wall to bathtub to wall, and all the time screaming hellish sounds. We couldn't get out of that room fast enough and slammed the door, afraid the crazed rooster might get out.

It's hard to measure time under those circumstances. Mom and I waited on the safe side of the door until gradually the wild thumping and horrible sounds slowed down to no sounds at all. Mom opened the door very slowly, suspicious that the rooster might be lying in wait. He was there, but splayed out in a corner like a Skid Row bum.

It sure would be nice to say the old bird wasn't as tough as we thought, and that he did make a tasty stew. The truth is that none of us can remember how he finally did meet his end. We didn't ask, and Mom didn't say.

CHAPTER 14
ENTERTAINMENT

The Molohoskey house was on East Wilbeth Road right behind Scottie's Drug Store that was on Main Street. It was the gathering place for most everything we did as kids, partly because of its location, partly because of the house itself, partly because of the age groups of the Molohoskey kids. But mostly, when I look back, it was because of Aunt Mary's patience and indulgence. In spite of the fact that kids of all ages were constantly traipsing through and disrupting her home, I don't remember that she ever seriously scolded any of us. The most we ever got from her was a half-hearted, "Girls, that's not nice." It was directed at her two middle girls, Vera, the younger Nancy, and me. There was a three year difference in our ages with me being oldest.

The two oldest Molohoskeys were Olga and Walter who were six to eight years older than the three of us. They were old enough to be interesting because we could annoy them, their friends, and mess with their belongings. Olga got the worst of it. We loved her high heeled shoes and her lipstick. Ten-year-old feet can play havoc on the arches of high heels. Olga protested, but in vain. We got into her stuff at every opportunity because we played at "dress up" which meant long dresses, heels, and lipstick. The two youngest Molohoskeys were Sandy and Sergei who were around Vicky's age. They came along later and were not a part of our activities.

From the outside, there was nothing unusual about the Molohoskey house. It was a common, three-story rectangle with a porch across the front. It had four bedrooms upstairs with one bathroom for the house, and downstairs the usual living and dining rooms and kitchen. But the house had some unusual features that appealed to our imaginations in different ways at different times. Off the dining room was a room that we called the den. It had a sofa, a treadle sewing machine, and a radio. That's where we listened to the scary programs. The room also had a sliding door that disappeared into the wall. We used it as a pretend elevator door. That was in the days when elevators were operated by people. The sliding door was a novelty for all of us.

Upstairs, the big attractions were the bathroom (of course) and Olga's room. The laundry chute was another novelty. I do think we tried to use the chute as an intercom system, but the sound went only to the basement, and nothing interesting went on there. Babcha's and Walter's rooms were off limits. Aunt Mary and Uncle Elias's room weren't exactly off limits, but we knew better than to disturb anything of theirs. The stairs to the attic were in their closet. The attic was our favorite place. It was exactly what an attic should be: full of no longer used or dated furniture or other items. It was dusty, dimly lit, with several trunks filled with vintage clothes starting with the 1920s. The attic is where we went to play "house" and "dress-up." Besides that, nobody in our group of kids bought costumes for Halloween Trick or Treat. (It was called Begger's Night in those days.) In the Molohoskey attic, we could become hoboes or ghosts or Flappers or gangsters. We did just that for many years right through high school. I think I may even have skipped a night school class at Akron U one year to dress up for Beggar's Night.

In our early teens, Vera, Nancy, and I entered a contest because of the attic. Loews was _the_ movie theater in Akron. If a date took you there, it was big time stuff. The décor was sort of a medieval rococo. Everything was gaudy and ornate, but it also had a wonderful organ as well as a ceiling with clouds and stars that moved across the blue sky. (The interior has been cleaned and restored and is quite beautiful in its own gaudy way. It is now called The Civic Theater and is a community showplace.)

At that time, Loews was promoting a Marx Brothers movie by sponsoring a look-alike contest for Groucho, Chico, and Harpo. There were three of them and three of us. Why not give it a try? It was decided that Vera would be Groucho, Nancy as Harpo, and I as Chico. We found appropriate jackets and trousers in the attic, and even the platinum wig for Harpo and Chico's Alpine-looking hat for me. I believe Vera used a coloring pencil for Groucho's black rectangle mustache. With no hesitation at all, we took the electric trolley to downtown, giggling the whole time.

Our turn came to go up on Loew's stage. We were totally unprepared when the announcer asked us to perform. We did some silly impromptu Marx Brothers' imitations. Vera was the best by imitating Groucho's stooped walk and brandishing his cigar. We won the first prize that was $25.00.

For full disclosure I have to admit there were only two other contestants, but we really were better.

Diagonally across from the Molohoskey house was the Firestone Baseball Diamond. I don't believe that we ever went there to see even one game. We went to play on the bleachers. When no one was there we could be stage stars. Our voice reverberated so that it sounded like we had a microphone. Or, we went there to play cops and robbers or cowboys and Indians. The ball field was at the bottom of a hill in sort of a hollow. The Main Street side was an eroded hillside not unlike the hard formations and colors of cowboy country. There were perfect kid-size crevices and crannies to ambush the opposition. We didn't have toy guns or arrows, just our fingers to point and say, "Bang, you're dead!" Then we'd argue about whether the shot was a good one or not.

Years later when I came back to Akron for a visit, our hillside at the ball diamond was terraced and covered with green grass. As an adult I could appreciate how much more attractive it was. But there was a part of me that mourned. I felt sorry that another generation of kids wouldn't have the fun of that wonderful, eroded hillside.

The Firestone Research Laboratory was built on the land directly across the street from the Molohoskey house. When we were kids, that land was empty until the Barnum and Bailey Circus came to town. The arrival of the circus was such a major highlight of summer that some of us spent the night at the house because that's when the circus came. Aunt Mary and Uncle Elias's bedroom windows faced the circus grounds. The sounds of the animals, the trucks, and the tent pegs being pounded, woke us up before dawn. We didn't care whether the adults were sleeping or not. From their windows we could watch the whole setting-up process.

The circus was usually there for a weekend. We rarely had money to spend on games, or shows, or souvenirs, but we spent hours there anyway. Occasionally we had a dime or a quarter for cotton candy or a candy apple. I loved the anticipation of watching the sugar being spun for the cotton candy. With no money at all, we spent hours watching people trying to win prizes at the games, listening to the Sideshow spiels about the Tattooed Lady or the Snake Lady or the Sword Swallower. If we waited long enough, once in a while one of them would be paraded on the small platform in front of the tent. It would be worth the wait.

The best part was the animals. I felt the power of the tiger as he paced in his cage. Or, even when the lion was in a couchant pose (Ha! Miss Brown would be proud.), and when the lion yawned, his teeth seemed huge and fierce. Once on a close-up, the lion roared. It was enough to send a shiver and make me back away fast.

I loved to watch the elephants work. They lifted heavy tent poles with their trunks or pushed large equipment with their foreheads. It was as if they understood the language. They followed all directions given to them. They were so huge and yet seemed so gentle.

One summer by carrying buckets of water for the elephants, Russ earned a ticket to the Big Show. He gave the ticket to me. Because of my little tag-a-long brother that I tolerated for years, I got to see the Big Tent Show for the first time. I was sixteen. That was a status change that took me off guard.

We were always outside in the summer, bike riding, skipping rope, or making up games with friends. Water in any form was welcome. When we were very young, Mom would fill a No.3 tub so that we could "swim." When we were older, we could walk to the wading pool in Firestone Park. It also had slides and swings. When still older, we walked the half mile or so to the Canal to swim there. The bottom was so mucky that it was slippery between your toes, but it was good for an afternoon of splashing on a hot day. Sometimes when it rained, Mom would just let us run in the rain in our clothes.

Another major event of summer was Three Cent Day at Summit Beach Park after school was out. There were all kinds of rides at the

Park including the Rollercoaster. Normally the Park was out of our price range, but Three Cent Day was possible. That was something we scrounged pennies for and tried to earn money any way we could, and still never seemed to have enough. We tried to go on as many rides as we possibly could, but an awful lot of time was spent standing in lines. For Vera, Nancy and me, it was a day well spent. We left for home only after we were good and hungry. Money spent on food meant fewer rides.

Movies were entertainment all year round. The bigger movie theaters downtown were more expensive, but the neighborhood movie houses cost five cents for kids. Close enough for us to walk was the Circle in Firestone Park, and a little farther away on Main Street was the Majestic. I don't remember anyone ever mentioning movie times. We just went in any time and stayed as long as parents allowed. For the nickel, you got to see a feature like Tarzan or Roy Rogers, a cartoon, and a bit of news. There was also a serial that was a different episode each week, and of course, it stopped at the most exciting part. Some of the kids went to the movies every week. I envied them because in the preview to each episode, they knew when to cheer for the good guys and when to boo the bad ones. I didn't go often enough to know who was who. Poor me. Who knows what kind of a mark that can leave on a kid.

It was a Sunday. Mom and Pop were going to visit Aunt Mary, Babcha's step-daughter, on Grant Street. The Southern Theater was on the way, and I knew "Snow White" would be showing there. Not only did they allow me to go, I got the usual nickel and, a very rare nickel more "to spend." This time I went alone. My parents dropped me off and drove away. At the window, I was told the movie was ten cents. For an instant it was fear and then great relief. I realized I had the necessary money, and that I would get to see the movie. That's when I decided I had a guardian angel. I've only seen that movie once, but scenes of the dwarfs, beautiful Snow White, the songs, and the Wicked Witch are vivid. Once when I was doing the usual housekeeping chores as an adult, I started singing "Whistle While

You Work." I'm sorry to say no animals and birds came to help out like they did in the movie.

During the late 1930s, Pop was hired at the Firestone Tire and Rubber Company and conditions improved for us. Pop was able to buy a used car. It was a sedan, but we all knew it was not a family car. It was Pop's car. A big treat for us was a Sunday drive, but it didn't happen very often and only after serious negotiation and coaxing. When we did go for a ride, occasionally, certainly not often, Pop might stop at Isaly's Dairy store. It had every flavor of ice cream and featured a unique cone where the ice cream dip was cone-shaped and as tall as the cone itself. Each of us would get a cone. My favorite was rainbow. I figured I got a taste of everything that way. A ride in the car and an ice cream cone was a wonderful day.

After one of our drives, I bragged that we went all the way to Wayne County (probably about 15 miles). Wayne County didn't look much different, but the sign "Entering Wayne County" made it seem like another country. I felt like we had been somewhere.

Most kids in our neighborhood weren't big on outside activities in the winter. We did sled ride down Dartmore Hill when conditions were right. Real sleds had wooden slats to lie on, and steel runners. They also had handles that helped to steer. On our hill you could see just about anything that would move on snow: old tires, cardboard, and even tubs, as well as the occasional sled. Our first choice wasn't playing in the cold. I do wonder though, how Mom could tolerate two, three, and four kids in the winter in the confined space of the little house. The funny part is I have no memories either of squabbles or of what we did to amuse ourselves. Maybe we were just glad to be inside and warm.

As for the adults, social activities were mostly church related. Pop and some other men of the church did belong to the Russian-American Citizens Club. The Club had a building, but that was mostly a place for the men to gather and play cards. It was also available to members for weddings, or other celebrations, so families were included in that way.

Weddings and Baptisms were major social events. There was always plentiful food and drinks, some kind of music, and usually impromptu singing, with or without music. Children were included. As long as they did nothing outlandish, they were considered to be a part of the company, but were expected to find their own amusement. When the adults danced, the kids "danced" too, around the edges of the room. We were underfoot everywhere, but no one seemed to mind.

Funerals were also important social events. The obvious reason was to pay respects to the deceased and to their family. This was not done at an impersonal funeral home. Rather, the body in the casket was brought to the family's house where visitors were welcome. Visitors did arrive, some of them from out of state. Nobody went to hotels. A place for them to stay was always made available. As far as the kids were concerned, funerals were excuses for sleeping on the floor or four to a bed "feet to middle" to make room for visitors. Relatives or friends were also generous with casseroles and whatever food and drink were necessary. There may not have been the obvious merrymaking (although sometimes there was). It was an opportunity for people to reconnect even though the occasion was more solemn.

Again, children were a part of the scene. No attempt was made to shield them from reality. The message from adult attitudes was that Death wasn't weird or frightening. It was a part of life.

There is a scene that I have in my head of a neighborhood party. I was describing it to our neighbor, Helen Kulka (now Lindner) and she added more information. Between the two of us, we conjured up what happened more than once, and that neither of us forgot. It was neighbors making do during hard times and having fun doing it.

Stecyks still lived in the big house. Their living room was the biggest indoor space, and that's where the party took place. Of course there were drinks, and during Prohibition, too. The floor had a linoleum cover, but at one end, it was bare wood. That was Mr. Kulka's place. He had an old-fashioned kitchen broom over his shoulder with the wooden end rubbing the bare floor to make the vroom, vroom of the beat. Mr. Stecyk had a metal tub turned bottom up and was making drum sounds. Someone else was smacking a set of spoons against hand and thigh for another percussion sound. That was the basic ensemble whenever the spirit moved them. Sometimes word got around enough ahead of time that real musicians showed up: a violin, accordion, or harmonica. These were the best, because someone could carry the melody. If none of them came, there was always someone who would volunteer to "play the comb." He, or heavens sometimes a she, would lay a thin cigarette paper (people often rolled their own cigarettes) over the teeth of a comb and sang into the paper. It tickled the lips, but with a sound like a bumble bee, the melody came through. Whatever way music was made, it was a good time for all.

Whether the entertainment was for adults or children, there was imagination and improvisation. Now we have possessions. I'm inclined to think we may have lost something in the trade.

CHAPTER 15
EARNING BIG BUCKS

There were ways that kids in our neighborhood could earn money. A neighbor, Veda Granados, whose kitchen window looked out at our house, called. This was a voice call since we had no phone. She proposed that I come to wash dishes by hand for her at ten cents a sinkful. I was ten years old and felt quite grown up that someone was willing to pay me for work. Mom agreed. Next thing, Veda offered 25 cents to wash her kitchen floor, not with a mop, but with a bucket and cloth on my knees.

I'm not sure how long I worked for Veda, but I was proud of earning money. Mom and I started talking about what could be done with my savings.

A part of every household in those days was a big dictionary-size Sears Roebuck Catalog that was indispensable for making any wish list. I pored through that catalog many times and finally decided. It wasn't a pretty dress or a toy, but of all things, a desk.

In a small house with, at that time, five people, there was very little personal space for storage or privacy. I was never very neat, and I thought a desk of my own would help with "a place for everything etc…" Of course we realized that the rich, dark wood desks were too expensive. The catalog offered unfinished furniture that was shipped unassembled. We decided one of those would do very nicely.

Every nickel or dime was means to some kind of treat. Much as I'd like to tout my own virtue, I'm sure I didn't save everything I earned. Mom must have added something to make my desk possible. She also asked a friend to assemble and varnish (a pre-acrylic finish) it, so that when the desk was finished it looked almost as good as the catalog picture. Now I had my own space. It would be nice to say that now "everything was in its place." It didn't happen then, and I'm still untidy now.

Probably about this same time, we also started working at Koroncai's truck farm in Copley. This was summer work that started with strawberries in early June and, as other produce began to ripen, going through tomatoes and other fall vegetables.

Pop would drive us to Koroncai's before he went to work in the morning and pick us up after work. Mom was really the hired worker, but the Koroncais tolerated whichever of her kids were old enough to do at least some work. We picked strawberries into a carrier that had six little one-quart baskets in it. When the quarts were filled, we took the carrier to the truck where Mr. K. kept a tally of everything we picked. We were paid three cents a quart, although that increased a little in the eight or so summers we worked there. I tried to compete with Mom and always lost. She would have picked twelve quarts to my three. I improved with time, but never matched her speed.

Each of us kids had a few summers of working at that farm. Mr. and Mrs. K were Hungarians who spoke English with a thick accent. They were not unkind, but not warm either. Mom brought sandwiches for us for lunch, but occasionally Mrs. K would cook fresh, but so much over-ripe corn-on-the-cob that it stuck to the teeth. Mom said it was field corn, the kind you grow for animals. Sometimes Mrs. K. also made coffee that she served half milk. She always commented, "My coffee gude!" Each of us all these years later still use that phrase with that first cup in the morning.

Mr. K. drove his produce before dawn the next day to the Farmer's Market in Akron. The produce that looked the nicest got the best prices. We had to separate the tomatoes with blemishes and then wipe any dirt off every acceptable one. A table was set up in the shade under the kitchen window. Mrs. K. had a radio on the windowsill and let me listen to soap operas. I suppose we cleaned all kinds of vegetables, but I remember the tomatoes.

Kalman's truck farm was walking distance from our house. Russ, my brother, started working there in the summer when he was nine years old. So did most of the kids in the neighborhood summer after summer. Whether it was planting or weeding, the pay was ten cents a row. Russ says the rows seemed like they were a mile and a half long.

One of Kalman's crops was horseradish, a root vegetable. When it was ready for harvesting, Mr. Kalman would drive a machine down the rows to loosen the soil around the plant to make it easier to pull the horseradish root out. Russ says he tried to do that work, too, but the roots were so imbedded, he wasn't strong enough to pull the plant even with the soil loosened.

One of my jobs was working for a young woman who had a severe case of poliomyelitis. Before the Salk vaccine, contracting crippling polio was the great health fear during my growing up years. One of my classmates, Lee, got it. For fear of its spread, Lee was quarantined in his home and our class was kept out of school it seems to me for about two weeks. When Lee came back to school, he had no visible effects. He was lucky. Others ended up with braces to help them walk. President Roosevelt also had polio. He was left with paralyzed legs, although most of the country didn't know that while he was in office.

The result for my young woman was even worse. She had to spend hours every day in an "iron lung." It was a big machine like a cocoon that encased the whole body so only the head was exposed. She wasn't in our neighborhood, but close enough that we knew of her. A friend passed the word that she wanted to see me. When I went to her apartment, the iron lung took up a good amount of space. What surprised me was that the lady was sitting in a chair. She was a pretty, petite woman, smiling, and friendly. She asked me to do ironing for her and her husband on an "as needed" basis.

It would be nice if I had a record of beginning and ending dates for these jobs and what I earned from them, but I don't. In this case, I don't even remember the lady's name. What I do remember is that even in her circumstances, she was kind and cheerful. She had a teasing sense of humor toward me and about herself. We even laughed about her iron lung. Once in her ironing basket was an extra fancy blouse. After I ironed it, she said I rescued it so that she could wear it to go dancing.

My best and most constant source for earning money was baby sitting. It wasn't that I earned so much. It was that the work was always available both within walking distance and by bus. It never occurred to me to bargain for money. I took whatever they gave me and was glad to get it. Several times I took a bus to Cuyahoga Falls which meant a transfer, stayed overnight and took buses home. I still got a dollar and no bus fare money. I finally did realize this was not a profitable deal.

One of my steadiest families was the Trouts. They had a boy who was five and a girl who was three. Usually it was a dollar for an evening. I worked for them for two or more years. The duties were simple. The kids usually had the evening meal. Sometimes they were dressed for bed. If not, I helped them change clothes, brush teeth, etc. There was no television as yet. Sometimes I played games with the kids or read stories to them. Then it was bedtime. I usually picked up after the kids were in bed. If there were dishes in the sink, I'd wash them, but once the kids were in bed, I could do homework or read or just goof off.

Two doors from the Kidders house, I babysat for Rev. Will, his wife and their three children. I don't know what they paid me, but the kids listened very well, and I had no difficulty. Mrs. Will was pregnant with her fourth child. Of course they had all the necessary baby equipment and clothes. Instead of a baby shower, the women of the congregation organized a "mending party" to repair clothes and equipment. I always thought that was such a practical as well as a thoughtful idea.

I started babysitting when I was about twelve and continued with it all through high school. I suppose what helped me get baby sitting jobs was that I was mostly available. I didn't start dating till I was seventeen. I hasten to add, a boy did ask me to go to the movies when I was fourteen. Mom thought I was too young, and refused. Probably, if either of us had known that it would be another three years before I got a second offer, neither of us would have been so quick with refusing. For the record just so you know, I will say that when I did begin to date, I made up for lost time.

Looking back, two things seem remarkable. The first is that in the six years or so that I babysat, nothing traumatic happened with the children in the way of accidents or in their behavior.

The second remarkable thing is that sometimes (though not often), whether it was 11:00 or the wee hours of the morning, I would walk home alone. Only once did a car slow down as if to accost me. Thankfully I was passing houses with lights on, and I knocked on a door. When the door opened to let me in, the car drove away. It seemed to be a party in the house. When I explained why I knocked, there was no sign of sympathy, welcome, or reassurance. I felt to be the intruder. I stayed a few minutes and left, alone. No one asked me where I lived, and no one offered to drive me home.

CHAPTER 16
WORLD WAR II

It was Sunday, December 7, 1941. I was walking down Wilbeth Road and heard a radio blaring from a car that was pulled over by the curb. That was so unusual, that without thinking, I stopped to listen. It was something about the Japanese bombing Pearl Harbor. I didn't know where Pearl Harbor was, but neither did the rest of the country. In the course of that momentous day, we all learned that Pearl Harbor was in Hawaii, and more important, that Hawaii was an American territory (not a state at that time). The Japanese had dared to do the unthinkable. They pulled a cowardly, sneak attack on an American possession. That day the mindset of people in our country changed.

Of course, there were people in America who knew very well the turmoil that was going on in Europe, but it was in Europe. They watched with concern the dictatorial powers that Adolph Hitler and the Nazi party were assuming in Germany. Their concern continued to grow as Germany invaded Czechoslovakia in 1938. Then during 1939 and 1940, country after country: Poland, Belgium, Denmark, Norway, each of them surrendered to the Germans within a few days or a few weeks. News filtered out of Europe that Jews in these countries were being resettled and confined into Jewish ghettoes. Other stories of mistreatment and even atrocities that were too hard to believe seeped out in dribs and drabs, but that came later in the course of the war.

Here in America, the official government policy of neutrality was fostered by a general complacency and isolationism. Feelings in the country were that countries of Europe had always had their wars. They were on the other side of the world. Why should we get involved with their problems? Even when newsreels showed the destruction caused by German planes continually dropping bombs on the cities of our good friend, England, the United States remained neutral. However, when the Japanese attacked Pearl Harbor, it was as if the whole country was galvanized into an angry, "Now they've really gone and done it!" The next day the U.S. and Britain declared war on Japan, and three days later the Nazis declared war on the United States. Till now, it was a war in Europe. From now on it was World War II.

I was twelve years old, in sixth grade at Voris School, and not at all aware of battles and victories and losses. What I remember are the mundane, insignificant details that directly affected me. But those details would have no meaning without the context of the times. Much of what follows is a combination of memory and information I've learned since the actual events.

Everyone was encouraged to buy War Bonds. They could be bought in various denominations. Whatever money was raised would be used for the war effort. Celebrities sponsored War Bond fund drives where millions were raised. At school we brought dimes to give to the teacher. She gave us a stamp that we pasted in our $25.00 War Bond book. It was the smallest bond where the dimes eventually added up to $18.00. After I believe twenty years, the Bond would be worth $25.00. It was an investment in the future of the country. Every dime was showing patriotism.

Frequently with the school as a pickup place, there were recycling drives for paper, tin cans, and scrap metal. Many times I didn't feel as though my family was doing its part. We didn't subscribe to a newspaper or magazine, so what little paper I brought was a pittance compared to what others could bring. It was the same with tin cans. Mom canned our fruits and vegetable in glass quarts. We bought very few cans of anything. The labels and both ends of the tins had to be removed and the cans flattened. Mom told me if I wanted to take cans to school, I would have to cut off the second end of the can. I did it, but with lots of effort. It's much harder to cut off the other end when one end is already cut. What I did wonder about was why the few cans I brought had such jagged rims, while the cans from the other kids had smooth and even rims. It wasn't until I was older that I saw better can openers that could make that nice, smooth cut.

Certain foods that were either imported from other countries (like coffee and sugar) became harder to get. Supplies like gasoline and meat were needed for the troops. Before too long, a system of rationing was put into effect. Every family had coupon books that were allotted by the size of the family. There were stamps for different items. Mom took care of our books, so I don't know much more about them. Cousin Olga got married during the War. Aunt Mary did much stamp trading with family and friends to get enough meat for the reception and for sugar for the cake.

After Pearl Harbor, it was no longer an abstract "them" causing turmoil in Europe. It was the evil Nazis of Germany and now the horrible Japs in a cowardly attack on us. The feeling in the country was that it was our moral right not only to defend ourselves, but to keep the Fascism (a dictatorial, military government where the individual was less important than the state) of the Nazis, Japs, and Italians from spreading. Most important, we had to preserve democracy for ourselves and our friends. Isolationism disappeared. The country was caught up in a patriotic fervor.

My attitude during most of the war years was influenced by that fervor. As an example, Mom must have told me she was expecting a baby. She asked me for ideas for names. I thought Victoria would be nice, not because of Queen Victoria or because Vicky was a cute version of the name. I suggested Victoria for "victory. " Yep. That's how my baby sister got her name. (Probably if she had been a boy, he would have been Victor.)

Thousands of men began to voluntarily enlist into every service. Later, a compulsory draft was instituted. All men eighteen years and older were required to register and then to be assigned a draft status. "One A" was the most eligible and the first to be called. "Four F" was exempt. General health, eyesight, hearing, importance of work toward the war effort, and number of dependents were among the considerations in assigning draft status. Every community had a Draft Board made up of local citizens who interviewed the men and made the decisions. Once in a while, someone would be accused of trying to influence the Draft Board, but for the most part, the system was remarkably free of corruption.

Allowances were made for Conscientious Objectors. They were people who opposed violence either for moral or religious reasons.

The C.O. status was hard to get, but it was granted. These men were still drafted and then given non-battle assignments. They did not have an easy road. They were regarded with suspicion and sometimes labeled as cowards, during their service and even after they were discharged.

Relatives and young men of the neighborhood were going off to war. I felt sympathy for them and their families, but there was also a kind of detachment that I've tried to understand. Maybe it was because I was in my impressionable early teen years. Probably I was influenced by the romantic Hollywood versions of war. The men were bravely doing their duty fighting the Nazis and the Japs. Yes, there was gunfire, wounds, bombs, and dirt, but our guys were the heroes. They got through it all with courage and good deeds. Or maybe it was because I wasn't particularly close to any of the boys who served. Cousin Walter was in the Air Force, but he was a flyer. His role fell into the romantic Hollywood version.

Gold Stars did begin to appear in the windows of apartments and houses. Those were framed certificates from the Department of War that were awarded to families who had lost a young man who had given his life for his country. Those Gold Stars in the windows did make a person pause and think. Thankfully, nobody that I knew was seriously injured or killed. The United States was spared the destruction of war that Europe and the Pacific endured.

The war had been on for two years by the time I went to ninth grade at Garfield High School. During that time, the country had been undergoing profound changes. Almost every area of everyday life was affected.

In industry, everything was geared toward the war effort. Factories that had been producing cars or appliances for home use, were converting to weapon, tank, and plane production not just for our country, but also for our allies. Appliances and household machines became scarce. No new passenger cars were manufactured between 1942 and 1945. Of course there was grumbling about all kinds of scarcity, but for the most part, we surprised ourselves. The country was proud of how quickly we could adapt, and what we were capable of producing.

Economic conditions had been improving for several years before the war, and war production absolutely ended the Depression. Workers were needed for the factories. Akron made tires for everything that moved. It became known as "The Rubber Capital of the World." Thousands of people from Pennsylvania, West Virginia, and states farther south came to find jobs in the factories of Akron and Detroit and other cities, and found them. Housing became scarce, and schools overcrowded.

CHAPTER 17
GARFIELD HIGH SCHOOL

My grades in elementary school were usually As and Bs, but I was never "the best" in any subject.

We all knew who the stars were. However, sometime in the eighth grade I think, all students were required to take a national achievement test. Toward the end of that school year, I came into one of the classrooms to see listed on the board, the subjects of the tests we had taken. Under each subject were names of the three highest scores in that subject. There were of course the usual names that I expected. The big surprise to me, and probably to my classmates and teachers, was that I ranked the highest in English and was one of the top three in in two other subjects that I can't remember for some reason. Those results may have given me a different perspective on my status as a student.

When we entered high school, we were expected to choose a path of study. Three were offered: College Course which was preparation for college; Commercial which was office skills like typing and shorthand; Industrial which was vocational study like carpentry or machinery. There were no counselors to give us guidance on what course would be appropriate. Nor did it occur to me to talk to others who had made the choice. I may have talked it over with Mom. Anyhow, it was my decision to take the College Course path. It turned out to be an excellent decision, but I'm not sure whether it was nerve or ignorance.

Because of the war, there had been such an influx of workers to Akron that city high schools were put on double sessions because of added students as well as fewer teachers. Morning session was from 7:30 to 12:00 and afternoon session from 12:00 to 4:30. I went in the morning which meant my afternoons were free. It allowed me to get involved in so many things. And I did.

Since there was no need for a lunch period, extracurricular activities like choir and band were scheduled between the two sessions so that both sets of students could participate either by staying later or coming early. One of the best things I did was try out for the choir. I was accepted and sang with it for three years.

J. Benson Collins was the music director. He introduced us to every variety of choral music. I certainly wasn't his best soprano, but I sure was an appreciative one. Besides Mr. Collins had music connections all over Akron including that he scheduled ushers for musical performances at the Akron Armory. This was a huge brick building that did have a stage and ample seating, but as a concert hall, it had all the warmth and charm of a gymnasium. Choir members could volunteer to usher. I volunteered every chance I could. Organizations like the Tuesday Musical Club, then as well as now, managed to persuade top-notch talent to perform in Akron, and are still doing so. I saw performers I would have never gotten to see or hear: Yehudi Menuhin, a world renown violinist, whose autograph I got; opera singers like Lauritz Melchior, Robert Merrill, and Melitza Korjus, my fellow student (ha!); and the original Broadway cast of "Porgy and Bess." I still belt out "It Aint Necessarily So" every now and then, mostly when I'm alone, but on occasion just for the effect. The lyrics are fun!

The Garfield choir was featured at a Sunrise Service at the Rubber Bowl one Easter. We sang the "Hallelujah Chorus" and made a decent job of it, if I do say so. I've been known to break out with an irreverent "Hallelujah!" as a reward for something unexpected that my kids did. Handel probably would not be pleased. Neither were my kids, but I did it anyhow. I just can't help myself. There is so much music to suit different occasions.

Alexander Wilson taught English and directed school plays and musicals. He also had a farm with a large, clean barn outside of Akron where he produced and directed summer stock plays. Vera, Nancy, and I tried out for several of them and each of us got parts. One was "January Thaw," a light comedy-mystery. It was in Mr. Wilson's barn that I discovered that stage fright was a small price to pay for having your name on the program and to be on stage. I also learned to project my voice so that now it carries even when it doesn't need to. I have wondered on more than one occasion if that makes the difference between amateurs and professionals. Professionals learn to control the voice for the occasion.

During those four years at Garfield, although I can't give duration or dates, it seems to me I made good use of those afternoons. I did my class assignments and made the National Honor Society. I worked at the Kidders and also at the school paper, at that time appropriately named "The President." There was choir practice at Garfield and also at St. Nicholas in the evening. And then I tried to get a real job.

At that time when kids turned fourteen, they could apply for a working permit. You had to have proof of age. I had no birth certificate. The only proof of my existence and citizenship status was my American passport that I took with me. Somewhere during the application process I lost the passport. It was a catastrophe that was downright frightening. I'm not sure whether I talked to people or figured it out for myself that the U.S. State Department was the place to go to get help. In the proper business letter format that I learned at Voris, and in my very best penmanship, I wrote describing my problem and asked for some kind of proof of birth and citizenship. It took some weeks, but the answer came. On State Department letterhead and with the official U. S. Seal, there was a letter verifying who I was and my birth date. Also included was a copy of the law that declared that children born overseas to American citizens are also citizens. It was certainly a relief, but most gratifying to me, a fifteen year old, was that someone in the government in the State Department in Washington sent a response. Of course I still have the letter and the law.

After that scare, I did get my working permit, applied at Scott's 5 & 10 Cent Store. Scott's was on Main at the corner of State Street next to O'Neils, Akron's major department store. Scott's was torn down to make room for the Aero's Stadium. I was hired for a few afternoons a week at 32 cents an hour. I worked mostly at the cosmetic counter. In time I was promoted. I got a 2 cent raise and a title, Head Counter Girl.

This was my first experience in a formal work environment. We punched a time clock and were docked if we were late. I took my duties seriously. Everything at my counter was teeny: lipsticks, nail polish, powder, combs, hairnets, and all kinds of other stuff advertised to be necessary for beautification whether it worked or not. This little stuff was usually in order on top of the counter. But should a customer ask for something not displayed, there was no system or order to the supplies on the shelves underneath. I set out to cure that problem. Little by little, I alphabetized supply boxes in different sections. It worked fine for a few days, but by the time I got to the fifth or sixth section, the first ones were back in a mess. It was here I learned that some systems work and some don't. Title or no title, here was a losing battle.

At that time at Scott's, most of the employees were women and girls. There may have been a cook at the lunch counter or a janitor who was a man. That's about all except, of course, for the store manager who was a clean cut, pleasant looking young man, probably in his middle or late twenties. I remember watching his tour through the store as though he was a prince among his harem. Not so much women, but the girls seemed to materialize in his path. There was no need for bangles or beads. Little gestures or smiles were enough. The message was, "Notice me! Notice me!" Something turned me away from the sight without understanding what it was that bothered me.

It was that same young manager who went among the counters at Scott's on April 12, 1945 to tell us that President Roosevelt died in Warm Springs, Georgia from a cerebral hemorrhage. The President who had been such an important part of our lives, did not live to see the surrender of Japan on September 2, just four months later.

Every now and then if we're lucky, there appear in history charismatic political figures. Whether it's persuasive speech skills, personality, style, smarts, political savvy, or a combination, people want to believe in such people and follow their lead. Handsome President John Kennedy and his lovely wife Jacqueline were such a couple. Their time was too short. More recently, it seems President Barack and Michelle Obama have those qualities, but it's too soon to make that conclusion.

Franklin Delano Roosevelt however, was our President for three terms and had just been elected to a fourth time. He had guided us through the Great Depression and through four years of war, and always with a reassuring confidence, good humor, and a jaunty style that included a cigarette in a long holder that somehow, for him, seemed right. He came from wealth, as did the Kennedys. Yet people responded to what they felt was understanding and compassion from these men. Their wives, who had very much the same qualities, contributed to the mystique.

Photographs of Eleanor Roosevelt, Franklin's wife, aren't flattering at all. She was a large woman with no particular sense of style. Miss Keener, our Speech and Debate teacher at Garfield, went to hear Mrs. R. speak in person. She brought back to class a professional critique, describing the First Lady as one of the best speakers she had ever heard who had such "expressive hands."

Mrs. Roosevelt was the first First Lady to take a *public* interest in the affairs of the country. Among many other causes, she was a strong supporter of women's rights as well as all human rights. Both Franklin and Eleanor did what they thought needed to be done to accomplish their purpose. In the process, they made enemies. There were those who, for several reasons, thought the President was assuming too much power, but especially when he was elected for the third and fourth term. They couldn't do much about Eleanor, but it's because of him that we have a two term limit on the Presidency.

In spite of criticisms from his detractors, Franklin Roosevelt was highly regarded for service to his country. When the train carrying his body from Warm Springs to Washington, D.C. passed by, thousands of people gathered all along the way to pay their respects and to mourn. For many, it was hard to imagine how the country could possibly manage without his leadership.

As a former teacher, it would give me much pleasure to know that in some way I had an influence on a student. I suspect I'm not the only teacher who feels that way. As a kind of tribute, I'm going to describe a few other teachers I had at Garfield. First in general, I must say that all the teachers I had were knowledgeable in their fields. I may not have had a personal connection with all of them, but they knew the subject matter.

The second thing is that none of them tolerated disorder or disrespect. It was an atmosphere that was encouraged and maintained throughout the school. Once after a football game, word got back to the administration that someone from a bus of Garfield students had spit out the window at opposing team hecklers. Mind you, this was not vandalism, or a fight, or foul language. It was spit, which is bad enough if you're on the receiving end. The next day a school assembly was called. Pop Kidder was assistant principal. He gave such an impassioned lecture about what is acceptable behavior from Garfield students, that he fell off the stage.

This gives me a nice opening to a controversial subject, discipline.

My very firm belief is that anything...anything at all that is worthwhile takes discipline: football, playing an instrument, learning a part for a play, or space travel. When I see champions in any field, I admire them for their abilities, but I also think of the thousands of hours they must have spent in boring, repetitive exercises to acquire their skills. Yet teachers, in a society with every conceivable distraction, are expected to teach captive students when the teachers have been deprived of almost all authority and certainly have no clout.

In the late1950s when I had a regular classroom, teachers were expected to maintain order, and there was very little interference from parents or administration as to methods. Substitute teaching is I believe, even under ideal conditions, one of the hardest jobs in the world. Ten years later when teacher authority had eroded considerably, I did some substitute teaching. I had an experience that a little earlier, would have been considered unacceptable.

I was called to sub in a fifth grade class. I introduced myself, explained that the teacher had left directions for a test, and asked the students to clear their desk tops. Simple enough. Generally speaking, fifth graders are pre-teen and relatively docile. Not this group. In unison, as if by prearrangement, they picked up whatever was on the desk and at shoulder height, dropped the load, books and all, to the floor.

I was told later that my anger could be heard all over that floor. I believe it. I was appalled that mere children that young dared to defy what should be an authority figure. I was also told, "Good for you!" The day before for another sub, these same kids had thrown art paint around the room. The shame is that this class experienced no repercussions for their behavior. Too bad. It seems to me that students, parents, schools, education, and indeed all of society could benefit from someone like Pop Kidder to set standards and preserve them, in that school, any others like it, and by golly, in homes too.

Eton, that prestigious school in England that educates royalty and the elite, still permits caning. I'm not talking sadism. I'm talking discipline. Some behavior deserves caning. If discipline doesn't come from within, some other means may be necessary to make a greater impression.

I just re-read this Garfield part. Two things were obvious. I digressed from the topic, and a person could assume that I have a bias for teachers. Usually people tend to deny a bias. In this case there's no doubt at all on both counts. It's true. Since I've gone this far, I may as well continue with my biases. Teachers need all the support they can get.

Recently a group of us were discussing a proposed school tax that was coming to a vote for Akron. One of the women (who works for a charter school, wouldn't you know) laid the tax square on teacher pay. She claimed that teachers get paid plenty for the six hours a day and 180 days a year they work. Of course I knew she was wrong. I explained the extra hours I spent in making lesson plans and grading papers. She dismissed that with, "But that's you. What about all those teachers who don't?" This left me with "Teachers do so work hard," which is admittedly a very weak argument. To back up my opinions, I needed something much stronger.

A few days later, my niece Julie called and asked me to babysit their two children. She said, "Not for free. It would be $6.00 an hour from 7:00 in the evening to probably 1:00."

It had been a long time since I paid a sitter. "That comes to $30.00. Not bad. Are you giving me a special auntie rate?"

"No ma'am. The going rate is $4.00 base and a dollar more for each child."

I went. The kids watched some TV, had snacks, I read them a story, and off they went to bed.

Just for fun, I started doodling some babysitter numbers: $4.00 base and a dollar more for each of, say 27 kids, comes to $30.00 an hour. Multiply that by 6 hours = $180.00 a day. Multiply that by 180 school days and it comes to $32,400 a year. That's what a babysitter would get paid pretty much just for being there and, hopefully being nice to the kids.

In contrast, think what a teacher has to do. Every parent knows how the dynamics change when there are two or three children. Imagine what happens when there are 27 (or more) children in a confined room, all with different interests, different abilities, different attention spans, and different standards of behavior. A teacher has to keep the kids busy for six hours of the day, not just with fun and games, she has to try to meet all those varied needs as well as to teach the required subject matter. Besides, how many creative ways are there to make multiplication tables less than boring? And suppose she really does have that perfect, stimulating lesson prepared, and some kid, for whatever reason, disrupts that first important introduction. That behavior cannot be ignored, so there go the best laid plans. Worse, what if the kid gets nasty? Teachers confront these situations every day. What do they get paid? Next thing, I was calling the Akron Board of Education. I couldn't believe it myself. Beginning pay for teachers is $32,400. Honest!

Four years of college, loans to repay, caring for the safety of a roomful of children, trying to teach them something to prepare them for life, defending a necessary profession from constant critics, explaining to parents or the principal why a student had to take consequences for bad behavior, trying to stay cool and be reasonably pleasant the whole time, and my goodness, beginning teachers earn the same as untrained babysitters!

Something seems to be a wee bit warped here.

What a nice segue. I wanted to continue writing about some memorable teachers at Garfield before I got sidetracked. I think Miss Thelma Allen would have been pleased with my defense of teachers. She was a small, dynamic little woman who got me interested in politics and current events in her ninth grade Civics class. I've usually maintained that interest ever since. She forced us to think. Early in our first days with her, we found listed on the board some ten different forms of government. About half were variations of democracy. She asked the class which one we liked best. The kicker was that we had to defend our answer. We learned very soon that platitudes were no-noes. Till then, most of us had no idea that many of our opinions were platitudes. Each night for homework, a row of desks was assigned to tell about news from the paper. No crimes or sensationalism, please. It got so that just about every class ended up in a lively discussion. There were even a few radicals who did research, not because it was assigned, but just to prove someone else was wrong.

Mr. Griffith taught geometry. He practiced a unique grading system. His experience after many years of teaching was that it took some students longer to grasp geometry concepts. Therefore, he gave no grade in the first six week grading period. Then whatever we earned in the second six weeks became our grade for both periods. It seems sensible and compassionate, but I don't know of anyone before or since who used that system.

Two other favorite teachers were Lula Smith for English and Ludell Boyes for history. Miss Smith maintained high standards both for English composition as well as for required reading in literature. She wasn't as colorful a personality, but most of us prized a good mark or a favorable comment from her. She knew English and American authors and would often read passages of quality writing aloud which made us appreciate them more.

I can still see Mrs. Boyes sitting on the edge of her desk with one leg dangling. She had a lock of hair that fell across one eye that she brushed back with beautiful, manicured, expressive hands. History came alive as she told us stories. To her history was about real people, not just battles and dates. I can remember thinking as I listened, that I wish I knew as much as she did. Several years ago, I wrote a book called *Crazy Spider* about the Russian revolution. One of the narrators was Lula Boyes (composite of Lula and Ludell), a teacher who told stories. I hope both of them would be pleased.

During my last two years at Garfield, I started working at The Corral and the Spotless spot. They were both drive-in hamburger joints. The Spotless Spot is no longer there, but The Corral is still serving foot-long, chili hot dogs and "The Nightmare," a hamburger loaded with everything, both of them known by most of Akron. My job as a carhop was to go out to the car, take the order, and then deliver the order back to the car where the serving tray was fixed to the open driver side window. I also removed the tray when the customer blinked the lights on the car. It was here that I first learned the benefit of tips. Even on the evenings when tips were lean, there was always some money coming in, not just on paydays.

I was in my senior year at Garfield. Since my birthday is in March, I was seventeen most of that year. I had read both *Seventeen* and *Seventeenth Summer*. Both books were coming of age stories that included a first romance. I was dreamer enough to have hopes for my own romance. I'm sorry to say, January arrived and HE didn't, and the Senior Prom was in the very near future. I not only had no prospects for romance, what was worse, I had none for the Prom. HE wasn't showing up. Desperate may be too strong for what I was feeling, but I sure was very much aware that there was precious little time left for my seventeenth year romance. It happened in stories, why not for me?

AND THEN IT DID HAPPEN!

Russ Salvia asked me to go out! True, he was only a junior, and he wasn't what you could call handsome, although not bad-looking, either. The important part was, he appeared. The romance fantasy was alive. I was still seventeen, and besides, he had a car.

There followed a period of bliss. We went to movies, long drives, for hamburgers, and for the first time ever, I invited a boy to the Trouts while I babysat. My prom date was practically a done deal. It was better than stories. Just as I was convincing myself that it could be love, I got a call from Cousin Nancy. She wanted to speak to me privately. That in itself was unusual. What could be so important?

She didn't want to offend me or hurt my feelings. After some hesitation and hem-hawing, she came out with it. Russ had asked her for a date.

There was a pause while my brain absorbed this information. Could she possibly mean the very same Russ who was my only prospect for the Senior Prom?

On the outside was pride and a brave front. "Russ and I aren't going steady or anything. It's okay with me." On the inside I thought he was a mean, two-faced jerk, and probably stingy, too. I had noticed a practical side to Russ. Could he be avoiding the possible expense of a birthday and the prom, I asked myself? That was a more comforting rationale than to think he might like Nancy better.

I did go to the prom because I didn't want to miss anything. I had to ask a junior from choir to be my escort. The prom wasn't nearly as much fun as I thought it would be. I concluded that some things are better in the anticipation than in the real thing.

Nancy and Russ dated for a very short time. Luckily, it didn't interfere with the plans Nancy, Vera and I were making about a possible trip to New York City. I never saw Russ Salvia again.

It was 1947 when I graduated from high school. The war had been over for two years.

Chapter 18
AN INTERLUDE

It's funny how sometimes chit-chat conversations that seem unimportant at the time can have important consequences.

I was waiting for the bus at the corner of Main and Wilbeth when Rev. Pugh stopped and offered me a ride. He knew me because Vera, Nancy, and I used to attend Sunday school at his church. I guess our parents figured that getting some kind of religious teaching on Sunday was better than no teaching at all. Our parents couldn't take us to St. Nicholas on many Sundays. Probably what little I know about the Bible came mostly from those classes. (Bible stories were a part of sermons at St. Nicholas, but the sermons were in hard-for-us-to-understand Russian.)

During the ride to town, Rev. Pugh casually asked about school. When I told him I had just graduated, his next question of course was, "So what will you be doing?"

This was probably the beginning of summer. I didn't have to make a career choice immediately because I was still working at the drive-ins and had managed to save $80. That money was to be used for tuition as a full time student at Akron U in the fall. Rev. Pugh complimented me and thought it was a good idea. Then I'm not sure whether he asked a leading question, or whether I needed to talk, but I went on to say that Vera, Nancy and I had a chance to go to New York City. I wanted to go very badly, but if I went, I would have to spend the tuition money.

Most adults would have encouraged me to do the responsible thing and use the money for school. Rev. Pugh, this man that I knew mostly by sight and that morning met by chance, thought for a little bit, and then offered an alternative that I hadn't considered. "You could go to New York City and then take night school classes." His words were a whole new possibility. This kind man solved what was for me a real dilemma.

And that's what I did, but first came a memorable two weeks in New York City and in Reading, Pennsylvania.

There were no hotels included in our travel budgets. We were to stay with relatives and friends for free lodging. The rest of the expenses were up to us.

Train trips, rare as they are these days, are still my favorite way to travel. In those days it was porters, redcaps, polished brass, conductors, and an elegant dining car. All of that and a person could move around between the different cars. That's how we were able to see the dining car, with its snowy tablecloths and fresh flowers on the tables, and waiters in uniform with a towel over the arm. It all looked too posh for our pockets. We were glad we had brought food.

In NYC we took the ferry to Long Island where we stayed with friends. Vera took charge. Throughout that week, she seemed to have an aptitude that none of us had suspected, to interpret ferry, subway, and bus schedules and routes. If it had been up to Nancy and me, we would have wandered around in a fog.

Every morning Vera guided us from the house, to the ferry, to the subway in the city for our destination for the day, and then back again at night. Most of our "dining" was from street vendors. We did a lot of touristy kind of sight seeing, none of which I can remember except for one. That was our lunch on the 98th floor of the Empire State Building which was at that time the tallest building in the world. This was one of our very few meals at a table. I ordered a fruit plate that was very pretty. It had dark date-nut bread spread with cream cheese. The fruit was pineapple, strawberries, and blueberries. I remember the details because as far as I was concerned, the way it was served seemed so exotic, and the experience was the height of sophistication. Get it? Height? I must say though that without a doubt, it was a wonderful week.

Next we were going to Reading where we would stay with Vera and Nancy's Aunt Katie. She had no children. Yet three hormonal teenagers, one of them a near stranger, descended on her home for a week. She fed us, tolerated us, gave us the run of the house, and the whole time showed kindness, patience, and even a sense of humor. That woman is a candidate for sainthood. She did not however, have to entertain us. That developed on its own

Probably the first day at Aunt Katie's, we were sitting on the front porch swing. Soon two boys casually strolled by, and shortly after them, three more passed by going the other way. Obviously we were being sized up. In passing, one of them called out, "You visiting?" and another, "Where you from?"

We must have given acceptable answers. In a matter of minutes, they were draped on the steps and on the porch rail. That evening was the beginning for the days and evenings of our week in Reading: six, seven, or eight boys and the three of us. Not bad odds at all.

The center of activity was Aunt Katie's porch. The numbers of boys varied, but there were always enough for a lot of kidding back and forth and teasing. The boys had been pals for years. Whatever they did, they mostly did together. They told what seemed to be tall tales about their escapades, but if we doubted, one of them would add some colorful detail, the others backed him up, and we believed. Or one of them was the butt of a foolish story that was fun for all of us to hear. We three were a very receptive audience, and they entertained.

Somebody must have brought a portable record player because I remember a vinyl, 78 rpm record of the popular song "Near You." It became "our song" because by then Nancy and tall, dark, handsome Bobby Conrad were seen holding hands. I was petite at the time and Bobby Blessing wasn't very tall. It just happened that that we drifted together a lot. That was fine with me. Mind you, just for easy identification, "my" Bobby had blue eyes, sun bleached blond hair, a killer smile, and he was gorgeous.

Apparently the fashion in Reading was for the guys to wear their shirts unbuttoned. Then I didn't know they were abs, but he had them. Besides his good looks, he was fun and nice. I liked him a lot. There was talk between us that he might come to Akron to visit.

No one had a car. We didn't go roller skating or to the movies or even for ice cream. I do not remember that we did any sight-seeing of whatever there was in Reading to see, except a walk one afternoon to the abandoned coal mine. Maybe that's all there was. We might have missed something, but it didn't matter. That week in Reading was absolutely just plain fun with romance thrown in for good measure. It was wonderful.

I've never been a pessimist. However, I have noticed during my life that when too many things are going just right, something is bound to happen to keep it all from being perfect.

The night before we were to leave and after the boys had gone, Vera and Nancy said they had something to tell me. They just found out about it. As if to get it over, they told me quickly. They learned from one of the boys that Bobby Blessing, my Bobby, was fifteen years old.

Oh, my goodness. It couldn't be true! Usually a three year difference during a lifetime is no time at all. Three years between fifteen and eighteen *is* a lifetime. Inside I hurt bad, but didn't want Aunt Katie or anyone else to know just how much.

We took the train back to Akron the next day.

Sometime in the next couple of years, Bobby Blessing did come to Akron to see me. He was just as nice and good looking as I remembered, but by then I was a full-time working woman, and he was still in high school. Maybe the age difference at that particular time was too wide a gap to bridge. Or maybe Bobby was a "summer romance." Whatever it was, the week in NYC and especially the week in Reading was the best time in my life till then. And Bobby has a special place in that memory.

CHAPTER 19
FACING THE ADULT WORLD

Toward the end of that summer, what I was finding out the hard way, was that I had no marketable skills. There was a post-war boom. Jobs were plentiful, but the fields open to women were as teacher, nurse, librarian, or secretary. I wasn't qualified for any of them. Thankfully it didn't take too long till I got a job as sales clerk at Federman's Department Store in downtown Akron on Main Street. The job was nine to five, six days a week and paid about $25.00 a week plus commission. I was placed in the purse department. The best part of that job was the employee discount. We needed so many things at home, that it was a wonder I had any take home pay at all.

I took Rev. Pugh's suggestion and did enroll in a night class. It wasn't at Akron U. I figured the quickest route to getting skilled was clerical, so I signed up for a typing class at Hammel Business College. This was my first educational failure. Typing is a manual skill. Those around me were improving speed and accuracy with every class. I wasn't improving at all. It wasn't until I was married and had a typewriter to practice on my own, that I built up my speed to a whopping 35 words a minute, and that with two errors. Ever since then, even though I've done mountains of typing, I still plod along at that same speed. My fingers just don't go where I want them to. What I did learn at Hammel was that I would never make my fortune doing clerical work.

I worked at Federman's about a year when catastrophe struck. I was fired. Since I don't know exactly why, I've described what happened as best I could in the "Puzzles" chapter under "Napoleon."

There's no doubt that the country had to make a serious psychological adjustment after President Roosevelt died. In his role he had been authoritative, stately, and if not aristocratic, definitely presidential. The man who succeeded him, his Vice-President, Harry S. Truman, didn't seem to have any of these qualities. He was short, somewhat on the pudgy side, wore nondescript glasses, and worst of all had a Midwestern nasal twang to his speaking voice. He was an ordinary man from Missouri, proud of it, and never pretended to be anything else. After he became President, he continued to play poker with his Infantry buddies from WWI.

It's hard to comprehend that for most of American history, the Vice-President, who is a heartbeat away from being president, was a ceremonial figure who knew very little about the inner workings of the presidency. Most, if not all vice-presidents, were just not in the loop. Harry Truman was one of these. He had no knowledge of the secret work to develop the atomic bomb. Shortly after he became President, he was informed about the successful test of the most destructive weapon the world has ever known. He was the one who had to make the decision about whether or not to use the weapon against human beings. Maybe it was then that the small sign "THE BUCK STOPS HERE" appeared on his desk.

Franklin Roosevelt died and Harry Truman became President on April 12, 1945. Soon afterwards, he was informed about the successful test of the atomic bomb and its destructive power. Taken altogether, 1945 was a momentous year. At the end of July, Truman met with allies in Potsdam, and terms of surrender were offered to the Japanese, who did not know the capability of the new bomb and refused to surrender. Truman made the dreaded decision, and the first bomb was dropped on the city of Hiroshima August 6. The toll was 151,000 dead. Three days later another bomb was dropped on Nagasaki and 74,000 more died. Both cities were devastated. People all over the world recoiled at the horror, but Mr. Truman never made excuses for his decision. He felt it was necessary to save American lives. Japan surrendered on August 9, and accepted the Potsdam terms. The war was over.

Every morning it was his habit to walk on the streets around the White House. Presidents could do that then. Of course reporters followed him and fired questions. One day one of the questions was about something an opposition Republican had said. The President replied to the comment in salty, colorful language. Someone called out, "Give them hell, Harry!" The President responded with something like, "I just tell the truth, and they think it's hell." The "Give them hell, Harry!" stuck.

His wife, Bess, who he referred to as "The Boss" was a pleasant enough lady, but she was much different from Mrs. Roosevelt. She took far less interest in public affairs. Still as First Lady she got attention. The story went around that someone asked her why she didn't try to prevent her husband from using a coarse word like "manure." Mrs. Truman answered that she had enough trouble persuading him to use the word "manure."

What was much less obvious and certainly not publicized, was that he was a student of history as well as the Constitution that he had sworn to uphold. Also, it took the country years to discover that he didn't have to take the spotlight as long as the job got done. As to his staff and Cabinet, some were holdovers and some were his own appointees, but he surrounded himself with competent people, and very important work did get done.

One of their projects was the Marshall Plan. It was named after the Secretary of State, George Marshall, who was an outstanding general during the war. It could just as easily have been the Truman Plan. Setting ego aside, the President, who knew very well that he wasn't all that popular, thought the Plan would have easier acceptance in Congress and with the people if it carried the great general's name rather than his.

One of the hard lessons the world learned after WWI, was that countries devastated by war cannot be ignored. If they are, bad things can develop again, which is what led up to WWII. After the destruction of war, countries need help to rebuild and provide for their citizens. The Marshall Plan intended to do that throughout western Europe. The United States spent millions to help Europe restore itself. The Plan succeeded better than anyone had hoped. What's more, enough safeguards and oversights were incorporated that no charges of corruption ever arose throughout the years of the program and after.

The United States benefitted in several ways. One of them was that a reconstructed Europe needed American products that helped to boost our economy. Another was that for many years after the end of the Marshall Plan, wherever Americans went in Europe, they were welcomed and praised. The people of Europe remembered that the people of America had helped in countless ways when they needed help so badly.

The G.I. Bill also started under Truman. The country wanted to do as much as possible to repay the returning veterans for their years of service and sacrifice. The G.I. Bill had two far-reaching provisions. One of them was providing educational opportunity for those who wanted it. Books, tuition, and a small living stipend would be paid on a unit per service basis: so many months of service provided so many paid credits toward schooling; also, the more hardship in service, the more credits.

I was married a few years after the end of the war (more information in "Romance"). My husband, Frank, was one of the millions who benefitted. He spent two years in the Army Military Police as part of the Occupation Forces in Japan immediately after the end of the war. He completed his G.E.D. in the Army and then went on to get his B.S. and M.A. degrees on the G.I. Bill. Eventually he got an Ed.D., but that wasn't on the G.I. Bill. I suspect that if it hadn't been for that government help, he probably would never have continued his education.

The other major provision of the G.I. Bill was lower interest rates for home ownership. After the upheaval of the war years, there was a powerful urge for home, children, family, and a degree of comfort and peace. The Baby Boomers, who are now reaching retirement age, are the result of that urge for family. The urge for homes resulted in a building boom for housing both in cities and expansion into the suburbs. Open fields covered with trees and brush that we used to cross to and from school were being turned into modest homes in large developments.

However for many people, buying anything on credit was still a relatively new concept. There were those who preferred not going into debt even at low interest. They chose to build basement homes. You could easily identify one of them by the standing alone upright door that led to the basement. These homes were built and paid for in stages. Save money, dig a basement and make it livable, save more and add a first floor. Frank and I visited one of my high school friends in their basement home. It wasn't luxurious by a long shot, but it was cozy and practical. There was no rent or mortgage to pay.

Many economists and historians now believe that much of the stimulus for the growth of the middle class in America was the result of the G.I. Bill. Like the Marshall Plan, the G.I. Bill was remarkably free of corruption.

During those early Truman years, I was not at all politically informed or even politically aware. Most of my opinions, if I had any, were superficial. I repeated what I heard by chance with no thought given to the source. I was otherwise occupied with trying to make my way through the adult world.

It wasn't too long after the end of the Federman experience that I saw an ad in the paper for waitress. I applied and was hired. It was at the Garden Grille in downtown Akron on Main Street. At the time, it was one of the four or so best restaurants in town. I had a job. That was good, but first we went through a two week training period. There were about six girls hired at the same time. We were assigned to Blanche, a martinet who took her job seriously and didn't hesitate to make us fear. Her way was the right way. We either did it, or we were out.

Used silverware and dishes were put into assigned places in the dishpan so as to make the least clatter possible. Table conversation was not to be interrupted, and of course, all the other rules of proper service. In addition, since our uniforms were starched cotton, we were taught how to sit to minimize unsightly wrinkles. Honest! Blanche was tough, but we sure got the message about quality of service at the Garden Grille.

An aside, a "Sixth Degree of Separation" story:

Thirty years later when I had my own print shop, I hired a girl, Missy Villers, just out of high school who was very much like I was at that age. Missy needed strong direction that I was quick to provide ala Blanche. Missy complained to her mother about how mean I was.

Her mother told Missy about the strict woman who had trained her on her first job, and how much she had learned because of the training. She also asked Missy a few questions about me, and then added, "Her name doesn't happen to be Olga, does it?"

Missy's mother was Marcie who had trained with me under Blanche at the Garden Grille. We had worked together for about two years. I had attended Marcie's wedding shower and wedding, but then our lives took different paths. That's Akron for you. This kind of thing happens all the time.

The Garden Grille provided unexpected advantages. One of them again, was tips. Not only was I rarely out of money, but tips were considerably better than at the drive-ins. An unexpected benefit was desserts. Our pastry chef was Irene who produced the best cakes and pies ever. The GG practice was that employees could buy at discount any pastries that didn't sell. I brought home desserts that my family still remembers, like the wonderful walnut and pecan sticky buns or boysenberry pie that none of us have ever found to be as good anywhere else.

Another advantage was the split shift. The hours were 11:00 a.m. to 2:00 p.m. and 5:00 to 9:00 p.m. Not many liked this because those hours of work were a constant interference with just about everything. It worked for me. I generally took one class (or rarely two) at Akron U. in the morning before work, walked from AU to the Garden Grille, worked lunch, then found a quiet niche during the three hour break where I did school assignments (not the whole time) until the dinner stint.

This schedule sounds diligent and studious. It may be, but I wasn't. The work involved in one three hour credit class is not necessarily a hardship. My goal was not so much acquiring learning as it was acquiring credits. I did not aspire to scholarship. Besides, I was having fun. The girls at work planned all kinds of things to do. I was dating, not seriously, but often. There was always the lure of shopping on the break, with clothes and especially shoes being a priority. I was living at home, and indulged myself, or rather maybe Mom indulged me, since she was proud that her daughter was going to college. Of all the indulgences, one of them was the least logical and yet one of the most memorable decisions I ever made.

A lot of fourteen year old boys get interested in cars and motorcycles. My brother Russ was one of them. He had a paper route. Every day he passed a car that was for sale. The more he saw it, the more he dreamed. One day he caught up with me long enough to tell me about it. It wasn't a calm talk. He could hardly contain his excitement. If he wasn't out and out pleading, his eyes certainly were. "Just go and look at it! Just look at it!"

I'm not sure if I spoke the sensible, big sister questions or not, but it did cross my mind, "What will we do with it? You're too young for a license, and I don't know how to drive." But what the heck, we went to see the car.

There it was, a 1934 Ford convertible. The color was meant to attract. It was a bright, cheerful, aqua with red wire spoke wheels, and best of all, a rumble seat that was already open. It was beautiful! Russ went to get the owner while my imagination took off. No more buses or asking others for rides. I would travel whenever or wherever I wanted to go.

I tried to be nonchalant until the owner mentioned that it would be an investment. The car was already 15 years old. It could become a collector's item. He was letting it go for only $100.00. I was hooked.

At home I checked my stash and had just a little over $100.00. It was meant to be! Russ and I went right back and made the deal. Then we had to get our car home. We decided to take a chance. It was only five blocks, and there were same small side roads where Russ could drive and probably get away with it. We were sure everything would work out. It did. We were riding in my car on a sunny, summer day with the top down. Pure joy! It was such a high that the fact that the drive was all downhill didn't seem to be significant at all.

Around our house there were more small side roads. The plan was that Russ would teach me to drive. Countless times Russ would start the car with me beside him with just that intention. Starting the car was usually encouraging. Just when I would be ready to take the wheel though, our dream car would stall. This happened repeatedly one street or two streets away, or half way down the canal road. Russ tried everything, but rarely did the car start again. The two of us would end up having to turn the car around and then pushing it home. Sometimes in our optimism that this time it would be different, we took Vicky and Mary Anne, or maybe Tommy Kulka, or one of Russ' buddies for a "ride," and all of us would end up pushing.

For months Russ did his very best to try to correct the problems. Occasionally he got advice that worked for a time, like when a friend told him the battery was weak. After the battery was replaced, Russ and a buddy old enough to have a license, drove me right up to the front door of the Garden Grille. Never mind that the car wasn't running most of the time, I felt like a queen stepping out of my chariot.

Much later Russ told me what happened after the boys dropped me off. One of the streets was a slight upgrade. Russ took over driving since he knew how to baby the car. It was the five p.m. rush hour. Just in front of the main gate at Firestone, the traffic slowed to a stop. Russ pumped the brakes till he stood on them, but the Ford kept on going. Our car bumped the car ahead and scared the heck out of the boys. The other driver saw there was no damage, and to their huge relief, he didn't make a fuss, got in his car and drove away.

Russ was a teenage kid who could have used a lot more guidance than he got. I was no help at all. That car gave us mountains of trouble. My attention drifted away in time. Russ kept tinkering with it on and off for two years until he finally traded it in on a DeSoto. Yet, neither he nor I regret getting the car. We both loved it.

The GG had more formal white tablecloth dining areas for small groups of people and for families. It also had a separate room with about twenty or so stools for counter service that was more casual. I worked in both areas, but since I wasn't very tall, much of my time was at the counter which was a little lower than table height. Many of our customers were regulars who often came in alone, but there were couples, too. Pizza was relatively new in Akron. A very nice retired man who was responsible for installing many pizza ovens around

Akron was one of my regulars. When he ordered pie he said, "Apple pie without cheese is like a kiss without a squeeze." I always order cheese with apple pie and think of him. There were two brothers who came in separately and together that I could never tell apart. Some people we got to know by name, and some we identified by their eating habits like, "You know, the guy who always orders Brussels sprouts."

Some of these regulars wanted to talk. We got to know a little about them, and often they asked about us. When I mentioned that I was going part-time to Akron U, I usually got one of two responses, either an encouraging "Good for you," or a skeptical, "And how long do you think it will take you to get a degree?" I sensed a kind of put down with that one. My answer was a flippant "Oh, probably about ten years." That sort of got to be my goal. When it took me eleven years, the degree was almost an anticlimax. In between I must say, there were many changes and a lot of living.

CHAPTER 20
TURNING POINTS

Once when Mary Anne was in the hospital for some serious tests, I thought a little humor might lighten the mood for us and for the staff that was around. For no reason whatsoever I said, "You know you're dealing with two celebrities here." It got their attention. I went on to tell them about my near association with Melitza Korjus and "The Great Waltz." That claim either gets an odd look that seems to say "Does she really think that makes her a celebrity?" or an indulgent, pat-on-the-head smile. In this case, there seemed to be enough interest to a lead-in for our family's more genuine claim to fame.

The Akron Beacon Journal has for many years sponsored entry into the National Spelling Bee. In 1951, Mary Anne won the regional contest. Her prizes were a set of encyclopedias, a plane trip to the national bee in Washington, D.C. for her parents and teacher, as well as a wardrobe for the trip. Mom, Mrs. Houston, Mary Anne's spelling coach at Voris, and I went. Pop didn't go because he had to work.

The Beacon did it up right. There was coverage about Mary Anne in the paper before the trip, and just as much if not more, after. We were escorted by Bob Hollister from the Beacon and then met by Tom Haney, a Washington reporter. The two gentlemen from the Beacon couldn't have been more thoughtful, pleasant and fun. They really wanted us to have a good time. Their attitude probably made it easier for all of us to relax, but Mom became the star. In her broken English and heavy accent, she told stories and made quips, and had all of us, including Mrs. Houston who tended to be quite straight-laced, laughing the whole time.

The trip itself was a wonderful experience, but to top it all off very nicely, Mary Anne took third place in the nation. It was the best standing anyone from Ohio got till that time, and furthermore she held that record for a good many years after. We continue to follow the National Spelling Bee. The word that did Mary Anne in was "grosgrain," a kind of ribbon. Now the words seem to get more technical and more difficult, and the contestants more scholarly. "Grosgrain" would probably be too easy to be on the list. Of the words given to the spellers, Mary Anne always knows more than I do. If I know just the meaning, never mind the spelling, of one or two words of those pronounced, I consider myself lucky. In the 2010 Spelling Bee, a girl from North Royalton, Ohio (near Akron) won. Ohio holds the record of eight national winners.

Mary Anne's celebrity and our Washington trip was one big event that year, but I had also been doing some thinking about my future. In the four years since graduation, I had accumulated one year of basic credits at Akron University and made an appointment with an advisor to see what could be done with these hours. I was told that if I went to school full time for two semesters and the summer session, I could get a two year teaching certificate that in Ohio would allow me to teach. Becoming a teacher was not exactly a calling, but it did appeal to me. I talked it over with Mom who was delighted with the idea. She would have a "professorka" in the family, a respected position in her eyes. That's what I did. Beginning in September, I became a full time student at AU.

In all my reading, I had idealized college life, and part of that was a sorority. My intention was to fill this one year with everything I thought college life should be. I did manage to pretty well accomplish that in time, but first came three weeks or more of being an absolute "outsider," which is not an all a pleasant experience. Anybody from Garfield who might have gone to Akron U had just graduated. I knew no one on campus or anyone who had been a student who could have guided me or warned of pitfalls.

The Student Union and the cafeteria were of course where all the students congregated. What I didn't know was that sororities and fraternities sat at tables and at places that traditionally were considered "theirs." Unsuspectingly, I sat wherever. Those who were sitting at that table made no acknowledgment of my presence. It only took a few times of either unseeing, dismissive, or "You're invading our turf" looks from those at the table to realize I was where I didn't belong.

Another pitfall was the sorority "rushing" invitations all over campus. I went to several, fully expecting to have one or two sororities invite me into their fold. I waited for the acceptance letters. Instead it was one rejection after another. To me that's what it was, rejection. Those weeks were the loneliest of my life. I couldn't help asking myself if trying to be a full time college student was a mistake.

Then one day after one of my classes, an "older woman," probably in her thirties, asked me about an assignment. We talked as both of us were heading toward the cafeteria. Her manner was friendly and open. She was Claire Thomas, married, and a returning student. Next thing I knew, we were at a table where several people knew her. In a matter of minutes, I was included in the conversation. What a difference, and what a relief! Claire had brought me to the "Independents" table.

In those days, Independents were considered to be the unaffiliated campus radicals. Depending on class schedules, there could be a mix of every variety of student: ex G.I.s, returning students, a few serious students who to me seemed to know everything about everything, most of them in Liberal Arts, and Claire and I in Education. At any time there was discussion on any topic. It could be politics, ethics, current events, religion, old and new books, all sprinkled with literary quotations that impressed me no end, and always pros and cons on whatever the subject happened to be. Quite often opinions were expressed that I had never heard before, including criticism of sorority and fraternity practices. To be critical of them, had never occurred to me. A few days with the Independents and my doubts about college life were gone. A few weeks later, I was attending, Sociology, Psychology, Philosophy Club meetings, and Future Teachers of America. They weren't sororities, but there weren't membership fees either. Now at last was college as I had expected it to be.

An aside:

Try as I might, I could not remember how much I paid for part-time classes at Akron U. I thought it would be interesting to know. I made a few calls to administration offices with no results. I turned to two friends hoping they would remember more than I did. Milora

Beachy Van Antwerp and I knew each other from alphabetical seating back at Garfield High. I always thought Milora was such a pretty name. She and I had gone our separate ways, but had reconnected in the recent past. Grace Spears and her husband Jack, and Frank and I knew each other from the Independents table at Akron U and had remained friends. On a long shot, I called both Milora and Grace for help. Milora thought she had paid no tuition at all, and Grace, who lived outside city limits, thought she paid $77 a semester for 16 credit hours.

Thinking in today's terms, both of these sounded too good to be true. I thought I'd better try again to verify. Finally I contacted University of Akron Library Archives and was e-mailed official information from a 1950-51 college catalog.

Residents of Akron and veterans on the G.I. Bill paid **no tuition**. There were Maintenance, Building, Activity, and Library fees that amounted to a whopping $67.50 a semester. These fees were prorated for part-time students so that for three years, I paid even less than the $67.50.

Residents outside city limits, did pay $90 per semester tuition as well as the other fees. They paid less if they took fewer than 16 hours. Though both Milora and Grace weren't spot on in their recollections, they had the right idea, while to me these costs which now seem so minimal were a surprise. They kind of took the glow off the credit I gave myself for "working my way through college."~

CHAPTER 21
ROMANCE

During my carefree years, I had done a considerable amount of dating. There were some very decent young men that I remember with affection. But in the time shortly before full time at Akron U, there seemed to be a series of duds. On occasion, I have thought that maybe the system of parent selection or marriage brokers has some merit. The system we're using now seems so haphazard. Sometimes I think the stars have to be aligned just so for couples to find each other. So far in my case, the stars didn't seem to be cooperating. I was still unattached, and dangerously approaching spinsterhood. In those days for a girl to remain single was considered to be a serious flaw in her nature.

Lone Star was one of the fraternities on campus. One of its members often sat at our table. He was a quiet, slender young man, always neatly dressed in jacket and tie and a knife-sharp crease in his trousers. Just as most of us knew a little about each other, I knew he was Frank Kurtz, a veteran who was attending on the G.I. Bill. I knew he was a psych major because he was president of the Psychology Club. We had spoken a few times. One drizzly afternoon, he offered to drive me home.

He was pleasant, courteous, and easy to talk to for most of the way. Then for some reason, the windshield wipers stopped working. He had to stop the car periodically to clear the windshield. Besides, his car was an insignificant, older, Chevy coupe. The incident annoyed me. I was ready to class him with the other duds. Apparently I didn't show my irritation, because a few days later he asked me for a real date. I debated whether or not to go, and then decided the wipers weren't his fault. Anyhow he seemed nice. I'd give him another chance.

We went to Luigi's for pizza (my first time for both) and talked the whole time about books and school, and then to his apartment where we talked more and listened to music (really!) I think it was then that the stars started rearranging themselves. There was so much that we both liked and agreed about.

Early in the spring of 1952, Future Teachers of America was having its annual convention in Philadelphia. Four of us decided to go with our professor. It was over a weekend. I don't remember how we got there and back, but it was an eventful trip.

Frank and I had been dating regularly. There was no commitment, but we were doing almost everything as a couple. This three day proposed trip of mine was causing a disruption. I was getting strong hints about how much I would be missed, and that he would rather I didn't go. It did cross my mind that it was a big fuss for such a short time. I decided to go anyhow, even though it was flattering to feel so necessary. After we arrived in Philly, one of the girls on the trip received flowers from her fiancé. The rest of us were happy for her. It seemed so romantic. When I also got flowers from Frank the next day, I was touched and pleased. The stars were definitely realigning.

At the convention hall, there was an orientation session on Friday afternoon. Afterwards, the six of us went to a separate large room to look at new books being published that year for children. We were so caught up in the vast amount of textbooks and literature, that we didn't notice the rest of the building was emptying. When the stillness finally registered, we came out of the book room to a cavernous convention hall that was totally empty and dark. The only lights were the red exit signs. We went to the nearest one where the door was locked and with a chain across the door. The other exits all seemed to be miles away. There was not a soul around.

These were not the days with personal cell phones. We walked until we found a public phone. Fortunately, our instructor had coins. She called the operator who connected her to the police. They listened and asked a lot of questions. She had to explain our situation several times. I suppose the police wanted to make sure it was not a crank call. Considering the number of exits in that huge building, and that we could see nothing that would identify our location, it's a wonder the police found the right door to unlock and unchain. They did. We girls were giggling as we came out and explaining that we were really serious future teachers, while our professor tried hard to maintain her dignity.

Before the morning speaker the next day, an announcement was made about the future teachers who were so diligent, they were locked in the convention hall. Thankfully, no mention was made that they were from Akron.

Soon afterwards, Frank and I were engaged to be married. Frank had two more years toward his B.S. degree, and I would receive my two year teaching certificate after summer classes. Everything about that summer of 1952 was momentous. Besides completing certificate requirements, there were teaching job interviews. Jobs were plentiful. I interviewed at several school systems and signed a contract to teach fifth grade at Copley Elementary. My salary was to be $2200 for the school year.

We were looking for a place to rent when the people living in the little house where I grew up decided to move. It was convenient for us, and the rent was a good price. Part of the summer was spent painting and wallpapering and finding pieces of furniture we could afford.

There were also wedding preparations to make. Frank and I had set our wedding date for August 10. Getting married seemed simple enough, until we started talking about the actual plans. They took a lot of negotiating between my parents, Frank, and me.

Frank's family in America dated back to Revolutionary times. He was a lapsed Catholic whose family favored small, immediate family weddings. On my side, weddings first of all followed the rituals of the Orthodox Church, After the ceremony it became a major social event with much food, drink, and music in a general open house for just about anybody who cared to attend. Frank agreed to the Orthodox ceremony and celebration as a concession to my parents but reluctantly, and with the understanding that after we were married, we would choose our own way. We stayed busy all that summer as the wedding day approached.

The original St. Nicholas congregation was housed in a small, white, wooden building in south Akron. As the congregation and the church prospered, a larger, more elaborate, stone structure with the traditional gilt onion-shaped dome was built, also in south Akron.

On Sunday, August 10, 1952, Frank and I were the first couple to be married in the new church.

Each of us had three attendants. Frank's Best Man was an army buddy, Newton Haleblian. My brother, Russ, and Frank's brother, George, were groomsmen. Cousin Vera was my Maid of Honor with my sister, Mary Anne, and cousin Nancy as bridesmaids. Little sister Vicky, almost ten, was the flower girl. The men wore white tuxedos. The girls' gowns were sort of a smokey, olive green/taupe, layered net. The dresses were much prettier than the description sounds. My gown was a white bouffant that really did make me feel like a princess that day.

In the Orthodox faith, marriage is a Holy Sacrament. The ceremony is lengthy and heavy with symbolism, some of them unique to Orthodoxy.

During the time of three-day weddings, the Betrothal had a day of its own. Now, as Frank and I entered the church, we were met by the priest. The Betrothal was an exchange of rings, promises, and blessings by the priest. Next we were led by the priest to the steps leading to the altar where we knelt as the priest pronounced the marriage vows.

In front of the steps that lead to the altar is a Ceremonial Table. The priest led us back to the table where we were joined by Vera and Newt for the most significant part, the Order of the Crowning. The Best Man and Maid of Honor hold jeweled crowns over the heads of the bride and groom. The meaning of the crowns is that the couple is actually establishing their own little kingdom where they will rule with wisdom because they will be following God's laws. This is the longest part of the ceremony as the priest counsels, explains and prays. It can be hard on the Best Man and Maid of Honor. The crowns get heavier as (in those days) the two attendants held them suspended. Now I understand the crowns are placed on the heads which makes it easier on the attendants.

Next Frank and I were given a cup of wine. This is the Common Cup indicating a life of sharing joys and sorrows. The priest then led us three times around the Ceremonial Table in our first steps as a married couple in the teachings of the Orthodox Church.

Very often these days a written explanation of the symbolism of the wedding service is provided to the guests. At our wedding, there was no explanation, and the service was completely in Russian. Even so, an hour or so later, there was no doubt whatsoever that Frank and I were joined in wedlock. Optimistically, we faced the future together.

An aside:

In the movie "The Deer Hunter," there is a Russian wedding scene. Supposedly the wedding takes place in Pittsburgh, but the actual filming was done at St. Theodosius Cathedral in Cleveland. The priest who officiated at the film wedding was the Very Rev. T. Stephen Kopestonsky. Later Father Kopestonsky served as priest at our St. Nicholas Church in Akron for a number of years.

My niece, Michele Montgomery was married by Fr. Kopestonsky at St. Theodosius when he was priest there. Michele's Maid of Honor, Laura, was shorter than Michele. She held the crown suspended as required then, but switched hands quite often. We silently sympathized with her as her hands visibly acquired a bluish tint. For Laura, holding the crown was for sure a test of friendship.~

CHAPTER 22
MR. AND MRS. FRANCIS C. KURTZ

I did my Student Teaching at Robinson School in Akron the spring before I was married. Miss Ruth Price, the critic and supervising teacher to whom I was assigned, was the very experienced best. She had a wonderful, calm, caring, dignified manner that her fifth graders responded to. So did I. I wish I could have seen the beginning of the school year, and how she managed to set standards of behavior that none of the children seemed to want to test during the time I was with the class. She was truly a master teacher.

I had given some thought to my maiden name. It would be hard for most kids to say, and certainly to spell. I asked Miss Price if the class could call me Miss Olga. She agreed. Observing and testing my wings under Miss Price was an altogether valuable and pleasant experience. I knew then she was a good teacher, but after I had my own classes, I truly began to appreciate how exceptional her manner and methods really were.

Frank and I did manage a two week honeymoon fishing trip to a cabin in Canada. We returned on Saturday, and I started teaching my own fifth grade class on Monday. I don't remember anything that was even mildly disturbing – with the children, that is. From the stories I've heard from other first year teachers, mine seemed to go quite smoothly. Instead, in the very first days, I made a major social blunder with my co-workers.

There were no other beginning teachers that year at my school. The teachers I had most contact with were experienced and naturally older. At lunch, one of them asked me how I wanted to be called. Without thinking how this might sound, I blurted out, "Oh, call me Mrs. Kurtz. I like to hear it."

Weeks or maybe months later, it penetrated to me that everyone else called each other by their first names, while I, the youngest, was the only Mrs. When the dawn came at last, I asked the group about this. They answered, "Why, you told us to call you Mrs. Kurtz." Not till then did I realize my *faux pas.* I explained about my maiden name and recent marriage and apologized. From then on it was a much warmer atmosphere. They were generous with advice and materials and often were a sounding board. Every teacher needs this, but especially when starting out.

We made several major moves in our first years of marriage. To lighten the moves, we kept essentials and tried to eliminate other stuff. I kept no plan books or student names from the two years at Copley Elementary. I do have one picture with several of my students. I look so very young, and the kids were as tall as I was. I did have a large class, something close to forty. But more important, even though it was with that many kids, I loved teaching. Not just during the work day, but during weekends and evenings, my thoughts revolved so much around activities and plans to try to make learning more palatable. Of course, there were days when I doubted that I had accomplished anything, but I tried to learn from those and kept plugging away. I wanted to be a good teacher.

There were three things I didn't like. One of them was recess duty, when a teacher had to be on the playground with the kids. Another was the all important monthly Attendance Report that went to the state. Pupil attendance determined the amount of money the state sent to each school district. The numbers had to balance just like a checkbook. When they didn't (and that happened quite often) I resented the time it took to find the error. I don't like to balance my checkbook either.

Grading papers was just a never-ending chore. I know checking the work is important for judging progress and spotting weaknesses, but I wish I had made it easier on myself. Five arithmetic examples instead of twenty, or a paragraph or two instead of a long written paper can indicate quite a bit. Through my teaching years, I recruited Mary Anne, and anyone else who was around to help with papers, but I don't believe I ever caught up. There was always a stack waiting to be marked.

There was no doubt about it. Marriage made a huge difference in our lives. We were both very busy. I still couldn't drive, and besides, even if I could have, we had one car, so Frank's day started by driving me to work. He carried a full schedule of classes, and in the evening worked part-time at Cuyahoga Falls Receiving. It was a transient mental hospital which was good experience for a psych major. He studied at every chance and managed to maintain a high GPA.

I was trying to improve typing skills on my own with a manual, and teaching duties always seemed to extend to evenings and weekends. That part I didn't mind. The hardest for me were household chores like cleaning, laundry, and ironing. Doing laundry chores wasn't too bad because that came about once a week. On the other hand, there was always something to wipe or clean.

Since I like to eat, and eating out was a luxury, I was also learning to cook. One very practical wedding gift was *Betty Crocker's Cookbook*. It became my Bible. Nothing gourmet mind you, but a lot of basics, so that most of what I produced was plain, but edible.

During our courtship, Frank and I did a lot of talking about a lot of subjects. We rarely discussed anything that might come up to cause conflict in marriage like: division of household chores; who takes care of the money and the bills; when or if we would have children; how to divide holidays between the two families, and so many other stumbling blocks that can, and do, arise between couples. He and I had both been making our own decisions since we were teenagers. I, for one, assumed this would continue. I suspect Frank thought the same. All the touchy subjects did come up. It came as a shock to each of us that now there was another person to consider, and that those opinions and ideas were very often unexpectedly different. Resolving these issues made for a rocky couple of years, but we did come to agreement on most.

One of them was to travel, which meant a reliable car. By the first summer, we were able to buy (in payments) a new 1953 Ford Fairlane. Also our piggy bank had accumulated $300. We bought a two-burner Coleman camp stove, a pup tent, and set out on a 30 day cross country camping trip in state and national parks. We borrowed Mom's featherbed for sleeping, had no lantern, and the $300 was our total budget, including food and car gas. Costs for camping in parks was minimal, often only 25 or 50 cents a day and sometimes free. I realized then, and believe strongly now, that the park system in this country is one of its greatest treasures. When I hear now about opening the parks to private development, I want to scream loud enough for, in heaven's sake, someone to hear my protest! We took a northern route to get to the west coast and returned on a southern route. All the way we saw the beauty and marvelous variety of the land and people.

It's hard not to see a bear on brochures about Yellowstone National Park. We entered the Park on a side road. One of the first sights was our very own bear, and no other cars around. Both of us were thrilled. Frank stopped the car, got out with our Brownie camera, and told me try to get the bear's attention. I rolled down the window, but forgot the bag of groceries beside me next to the door. Bears of course, can smell. He was coming closer. I was delighted, and Frank was snapping away. The bear did not see the car door as a barrier. He simply used the chrome strip decoration as a step and was halfway in the window, grabbing a box of cereal that I was trying to rescue. Frank saw what was happening, jumped into the car, revved the motor, and luckily the bear dropped off. Some way down the road, it did occur to us that that probably wasn't the smartest thing we ever did. Later it crossed my mind: What if the bear had fallen into the car?

In Yosemite Park, we camped beside a lovely, serene lake. That night there was a full moon. The lake perfectly reflected a bald stone mountain. Such a beautiful scene! We woke up with frost on the inside of the pup tent, and a prairie dog on his hind legs beside his burrow, observing us as we watched him. The sequoia trees were immense. The trunk of one was big enough for a car to pass through it.

Through the years, we camped all over our country and Canada, first in tents and later in a small travel trailer. During the earlier years, one of our entertainments was to walk through the campground, chat with people who always seemed to be interesting, and also to make note of the ingenious ways they devised to make camping more convenient. It was a sociable atmosphere. Sometimes we were invited to share popcorn or marshmallows at a campfire. Once there were potatoes baked in the ashes of the fire and a sing-a-long. Both were wonderful, even with no butter for the potatoes.

I must briefly mention three people from that first trip. Toward the beginning, there was a couple, probably in their eighties, who had converted their Chevy sedan into sleeping quarters, including curtains for privacy. The wife kept their medicines in a chest beside her feet in the front. On the floor behind the driver's side, her husband had improvised a water tank. Just by turning a spout toward the ground, they had running water. He got a kick out of telling us about the time someone asked if he was a Buddhist. He was seen bending down several times. People thought he was praying, but he was washing his face. The sleeping arrangement was creative. He had removed the backrest of the back seat for space that opened into the trunk. The head of the bed was behind the front seat, while their feet went into the trunk. Behind the rider's side and under the bed was storage for whatever. We got the complete tour of that Chevy, and we never forgot them or the experience. Later there was a Gary Cooperish, lanky park ranger in Kansas who told us he loved Kansas because "I can see a ways." His words put a different perspective on that state that was miles of wheat with nothing much else to interfere with the view. I have such wonderful memories of people and places, but the last day, hour by hour, is seared in my memory.

I had kept a careful record of our expenses. Our good intentions lasted till Reno, Nevada. After that, we had to be extra frugal. On the last day of the trip, we had enough money left for a tank of gas and hamburgers. We were passing through Greencastle, Indiana. At a cross street, a man who was not in uniform, held up his hand and walked into the path of our car. Frank was not speeding, but the brakes screeched at the sudden stop. The man approached the car, said he was a constable, and wrote a ticket for speeding.

Looking back, I probably wouldn't have been too friendly to a couple like us either. Frank hadn't shaved for several days. His hair looked like it had been cut with an ax because I had "trimmed" it. As for me, style was not a priority. Neither was laundry on this trip. I suppose we looked like the first of the "hippie" generation that came in the sixties. Frank protested the ticket quietly, but with an edge to his attitude. The constable replied in a cold tone, "We'll let the judge settle this. Follow me."

When he mentioned judge, I imagined black robes, a paneled courtroom, and dignity. Instead, the constable led us up dusty wooden stairs. I noticed holes in the heels of his socks and that he had dirty feet that I could see through the holes. The "judge" was a justice of the peace with a none-too-clean sweater, in a small, disorderly room and a spittoon by the desk. I didn't make any of this up! Without any curiosity in us, he started typing basic information, and then asked, "Guilty or not guilty?"

We learned then that the absolutely wrong thing to say in a situation like that is, "Not Guilty." That however, was what Frank said. The next thing I realized in horror was that Frank was being hustled off to jail to await trial.

Suddenly, I was alone, in a strange town, not knowing a soul, with not enough money even to make long distance calls. I had to try to do something, but had no idea what. I don't know how long I stood at the top of those dusty stairs, my mind in a jumble and numb with fear. Eventually I noticed other doors, one of them with an attorney's name. It took nerve to go in, but I did. The lawyer was kind enough to listen to my story. He explained he would talk to the "judge," and that I should try to persuade Frank to change his plea to "guilty."

It didn't help one bit that a light rain was sprinkling as I walked the short distance to the jail. A woman answered my knock. When I asked to see my husband, she answered in a whiney voice, "It ain't visiting hours. I got the cooking and the laundry to do. Come back later." But after giving me a cold, hard look with a put-upon manner, she did let me in.

Frank agreed to change his plea. We did not have to wait for trial or return for it. We were fined $40.00 and had to telegraph Mom for the money. Four very, very long hours later, we were free at last.

Should anyone find themselves in a situation like that, my advice would be to respectfully sprinkle a generous number of yessirs, pleases, and thank yous to whoever is holding the ticket book. Obsequious comes to mind too, but that might be a bit much. Take it from me, being on the wrong side of the law, in a strange town, with no friendly connections or money, is not the smartest time to take a stand for justice

We returned to Akron for another school year and the same busy schedules. The following June Frank graduated. He was accepted into the clinical psychology department for graduate work at Colorado University in Boulder. We helped my brother buy a truck with the agreement that he would help us move to Boulder.

At CU the competition was intense. It was a bitter disappointment when the assistantship Frank had expected didn't come through. Even with the part-time GS3 (Government Service level 3) job purging personnel records I got at the Air Force Base in Denver, we couldn't afford to stay at CU. One of his classmates told him about an excellent psychology program at Highlands University in Las Vegas, New Mexico. He went for an interview and was accepted. We arrived in Las Vegas in time for the 1955 spring semester.

CHAPTER 23
THE OTHER LAS VEGAS

Everybody knows of Las Vegas, Nevada. Almost nobody outside of New Mexico including the two of us, knew about this Las Vegas till we heard about its university. We lived in Las Vegas, New Mexico, a small cattle town, for eighteen months and came to love the town, the people, the climate, the pace of living, and just about everything except the drought. Some highlights of our time there may give you an idea of why it came to mean so much.

We found a little house to rent from Laura Mae Naylor. She was a widow with a ten year old daughter, Anita. Her husband had been Brand Inspector for the state. He had to keep a record of all the different ranch brands, actually an important office in cow country. She was trying to continue maintaining their 4000 acre ranch, which was considered to be very small by the huge 100,000 acre (and quite a few larger) spreads owned by the cattle barons. Because of the ten year long drought in the Southwest, her ranch could not support 40 head of cattle. She had to buy feed for them.

Laura Mae and her daughter became dear friends. She told us her horses needed exercise and invited us to come and ride whenever we could. We did. Frank got to be quite good at riding horseback. I however, did a lot of hard bouncing. Maybe it was later that first Fall, there was one unforgettable time when the bouncing was worth it. It was a beautiful, starlit, full-moon night, almost a bright as day. The four of us were on horseback, ambling along and singing snatches of whatever cowboy or western songs we could remember. Then it came to me all of a sudden as if I saw myself on a movie screen. Was I really here? Could this be me? It was. What I felt then was pretty close to bliss.

In the upper right hand corner of the masthead of the local paper was listed the number of calendar days of the year thus far. Below that was listed the number of days of sunshine. By the end of August, there were 242 actual days with 200 or so days of sunshine. We saw more sunsets than we did sunrises, but both were spectacular, with every color in the spectrum. Las Vegas was 9000 feet high in the mountains northeast of Santa Fe. In summer it sometimes reached 90 degrees F., but we always slept with a blanket. When it snowed, the snow was usually gone by noon.

Las Vegas had two traffic lights and about 19,000 people. It was not exactly a busy metropolis. During one of our first days, we had to stop and wait for two pick-up truck drivers who were having a conversation under one of the lights. Of course we were impatient and annoyed at the delay. This just wouldn't be allowed in the East. That attitude did mellow in time, especially when Frank was teaching me to drive. It was the ideal place to learn. Frank gave me the basics and was quite patient while I tried to learn how to shift gears on a standard shift car without grinding the gears. It took a while, but I couldn't have had a better place to take a driver's test. Along the police station curb were about ten parking meters, all empty. My parking test was pulling up to any one of those meters. As you might guess, I passed the test. The first time I was able to drive to the store alone, it was such a feeling of freedom and independence.

Santa Fe, the capital, or Albuquerque were the places to go for shopping, culture, or night life. Santa Fe is about an hour's drive from Las Vegas. We visited there a number of times. It is one of the oldest cities in the country. For history and charm, you didn't have to go much farther than the town square. On one corner was the oldest church in America, built out of traditional adobe. Across the street, was the Government House. It had a covered portico where Native Americans displayed pottery, gorgeous, hand woven blankets, and jewelry in silver and turquoise. Santa Fe hadn't yet become the thriving cultural center that it is today, but artists were beginning to gather there and in Taos, a city northeast of Vegas.

There was a two lane highway from Santa Fe to Albuquerque. Most of this road was across open country with very little to interfere with the scenery, that is, except for Garcia's Gas Station and Diner. (I may have the name wrong.) The road conveniently curved around the business. The first time we passed this, our attitude was condescending. "Look at that. Garcia must have paid somebody off."

In later days when we passed, we had changed enough to understand. In wide open spaces like that, why force a business to move or to close? It just seemed more sensible for the road to skirt Garcia's.

Several times we went on to El Paso, Texas that was right across the border from Juarez, Mexico. Even though Juarez was a border city, to us it had all the flavor of what we thought was the real Mexico. We didn't have the opportunity to go deeper into the country, but we did see our first bull fight. I loved the pageantry of the whole arena scene. Many years later, I saw the difference in quality and skill when my daughter and I saw a bull fight in Mexico City. There we had the good fortune to sit behind an English speaking Mexican man. He heard us trying to understand what was going on and was kind enough to explain all of it step by step. If not for that nice man, we would never have had the thrill of knowing that that Sunday "we" saved the bull, and that it doesn't happen very often.

At the time we were there, San Miguel (our county) had the highest percentage of people on welfare in the country. The biggest employer in the county was the New Mexico State Mental Hospital. The psychology department at Highlands University had an internship arrangement with the hospital so that Frank was a part of the hospital staff.

Very soon I was also hired to help reorganize the medical records. Part of the job was picking up and delivering patient files to the professional staff. We often saw patients who were not confined. They ranged from shambling and uncommunicative, to just shy, to John. John was one of the most colorful characters I have ever met. He was a handsome, dignified, platinum-haired man, always dressed in immaculate white. Sometimes after he got to know me when we passed in the hall, we exchanged small talk. Other times he told hospital news. He always seemed to know what was going on with the patients and the hospital staff as well. It was very hard to understand why he had spent most of his life here as a patient. He appeared to be altogether normal.

One day as we passed, I made some offhand comment about the weather. That was the trigger. It's hard to judge time in a situation like that, but for the next fifteen minutes or maybe half hour, John expounded in great detail on his theories of conveying water from other planets to save Earth from an apocalyptic drought that was sure to bring about its extinction. Foolishly when I tried to interrupt with what I thought was reason, I was not heard. John was obviously well read. He would go off on some tangent about Roman aqueducts, or throw in scientific or engineering terms that made him sound downright reasonable. I've thought a lot about John. It would be fascinating to understand what trauma caused his intelligence to take such twists. I've also in my life, come across others like him who are not confined. Some views just get skewed too far for any moderation.

Most of the staff took meals in the hospital cafeteria. We all took seats anywhere they were available. It was a good way to get to know everyone.

The supervising psychiatrist was Dr. Ian Kerr, from Scotland. He became a mentor to Frank. He and his wife Margaret, were lovely, friendly, kind, people who became lifelong friends. I used to say of Ian that he was the only person I knew who didn't repeat his stories. My favorite image of him was standing at the fireplace with a Scotch in his hand and telling stories with his strong Scot's burr. One time at a party, he took us all by surprise when he started reciting the "Canterbury Tales" in Old English. I wish I had it on tape. It was beautiful! Both of us learned much from him, but for me, it was his wife who was the ultimate model in graciousness and good taste.

From the first time we first saw adobe architecture, we thought it was beautiful and unique. Dark wood beams protruding from the eaves, and all the exteriors in shades of adobe from cream to sepia. The buildings just seemed to nestle into the landscape.

One day in the car on a dirt road on the outskirts of Vegas, and quite by accident, we saw an adobe house that looked deserted. Just from curiosity, we stopped, got out, and walked around. From the back of the house was a view of a mesa that looked like it was placed there just for this house. We peeked through the windows and liked everything we could see. Later we made a few phone calls, got to see the interior and decided to rent the house. It wasn't easy to tell Laura

Mae we wanted to move, but she was very understanding. We wanted to be in it by Christmas.

The house had a large living room with a good sized dining table in one part and a wonderful stone fireplace in the opposite corner. There was also a kitchen whose window looked out on the mesa, two bedrooms, and a bath. We loved everything about it, but at first we didn't understand the significance of well water until we got muddy brown water trickling into the bathtub. We learned the hard way that when the water table drops steadily during a drought, well water is a very iffy proposition. Conserving water becomes a top priority. If we used too much water too fast, the well went dry. It's no fun at all to cart farmer's milk cans of water to our house and to ration the water from the cans. In no time, we learned to be very careful with water use. One of the very many rules for conservation we practiced was, "three pees and one flush." This rule was suggested to us by the locals. Still, we had many good times in our adobe house, including our first sukiyaki that got to be one of my favorite company dinners.

Frank served as an MP in the Occupation Forces in Japan at the end of WWII when he was twenty years old. It was his first exposure to another culture, as well as food he had never had before. He liked both. After we were married, he often mentioned skiyaki (sometimes called sukiyaki). At that time, there was only one Chinese restaurant in Akron, never mind anything Japanese. Cookbooks for every cuisine in the world are available now, but in the 1950s, it was pretty much Betty Crocker and Good Housekeeping recipes. There probably were international cookbooks, but certainly not very many.

Wouldn't you know it, of all places, there was a girl from Japan studying at Highlands U. Frank got acquainted with Yamiko and eventually asked her if she would be willing to show his wife how to cook skiyaki. (Heaven forbid that he should learn. In those days, cooking was the wife's job.)

Skiyaki is basically a stir fry. What made it unique to us is that it's cooked at the table on a charcoal burning hibachi. A hibachi was unknown to me, so we improvised with my electric skillet. Yamiko told us what ingredients to get. Nothing uncommon: carrots, green and yellow onions, mushrooms, bean sprouts, bamboo shoots or water chestnuts or both, lots of fresh spinach, oil, chicken broth, soy sauce, and a little sugar. Yamiko and I prepared, slivered and diced the veggies. The only tricky part was the beef that had to be sliced parchment thin. I had to explain to the butcher that it was to be steamed over the veggies.

Yamiko cooked the first batch that only took a few minutes, but long enough for the cooking odors to waft toward us. Then we passed our small bowls to her. She put in a tablespoon or so of already cooked rice in the bowl and then the skiyaki mixture and some juice on top. I loved the food, but especially that eating it was almost ceremonial: eat a little, drink a little, and talk much. Then cook more, and do it all over again as many times as tummies allow.

Skiyaki depends on who makes it and what ingredients they choose. I've served skiyaki to just about anybody I ever knew, but always the way Yamiko showed me. Eventually we tried to make it more authentic Japanese. We got rice bowls, tea cups, a sake set, chopsticks, and even a low coffee table and sat around on pillows on the floor. (That was in the days when it was easier to get up.) However, I did manage to avoid using an authentic hibachi. I had better temperature control with my skillet. Why ask for problems?

Jackrabbits in this part of the country were considered to be major pests. They were big, about as big as a medium sized dog. Sometimes there were local contests to see who could kill the most. Our adobe house was nine miles from town on a dirt road. We saw these animals all the time. Frank let it be known that a rifle was an absolute necessity. Santa was kind enough to bring him a brand new Winchester 22 rifle that he kept in the back seat of the car in case a varmint appeared or there was a chance for target practice. He made quite a stir at the hospital one evening when he came for a meeting and brought a string of five dead jackrabbits onto the elevator to the second floor meeting room.

Frank encouraged me to practice shooting, too. Once I was coming home from town after dark. There right in front of the headlights was a jackrabbit, still as a statue. I thought, "Why not try?" I stopped the car, got the rifle from the back seat, aimed and shot. The rabbit didn't budge. I fired a few more shots. The rabbit just sat on his haunches, front paws chest high, and staring. That's probably what saved his life. If he had moved at all, one of my wild shots might have done him in.

We had acquired two dogs, both mutts. One we called Sandy because appropriately he was the color of New Mexico dirt. He was content to stay around the house while we went to work. The other dog was black. He was named Fibber after a dog Frank had as a boy. He was more adventuresome. We thought he may have had a herder gene in his history. Across the road from us and down a ways was a small cattle ranch. We didn't know the people at all, but they must have been very tolerant. On occasion we would hear a sound like distant thunder. We looked out the front window to see if it was really threatening rain. It wasn't. The sun was shining, but there across the road were ten or so cows thundering across the field with Fibber in hot pursuit, yipping everywhere and keeping the cows pretty much in a bunch going in one direction. Our neighbors never complained. We always meant to talk to them about this, but sorry, we never did.

Fibber also must have tried herding porcupines and paid dearly for trying. It was a most pitiful sight when he came home with a snootful of porcupine quills. He wasn't whining, but it must have been really painful. Besides, the quills protruded from his head so that he couldn't get close enough to eat or lap water. Frank was told that the quills have barbs at the tips. The barbs will collapse to come out more easily if the outer end is snipped off. We found that's easier said than done. I tried to hold Fibber while Frank snipped. We got maybe three done. They still didn't come out easy. We took him to the vet who took care of it. I felt sorry for poor Fibber, but when he did the same thing a second time, I wasn't nearly as sympathetic.

Several times Frank and I happened to sit with the hospital accountant, Mr. Miller. This tall, dignified, handsome, older man was interesting to listen to. He had gone to college in Rochester, New York, so he had perspectives on both the East and the West. He was also the accountant for one of the big ranches. We must have let him know of our curiosity about this part of the country, because tentatively he asked if we would want to be a part of a "roundup." We didn't know him very well. Was he serious? Did he really mean it? If he did, what a wonderful opportunity, even if all we knew about roundups was from the movies. He went on to tell us If we wanted to go, we should be ready at 4:00 in the morning on Saturday and come prepared to spend the night. That's what he usually did since it was a distance to the ranch. He would pick us up and bring us back Sunday evening. We had no doubts at all. Saturday couldn't come soon enough.

As if it was putting on a show especially for us, that Saturday sunrise was more spectacular than many spectacular sunsets. Shades went from pastel to intense in every color. Every change by the minute was a breathtaking panorama of beauty.

We arrived in time for a ranch hand breakfast that was heartier than any breakfast I had seen. There were about ten other people, mostly Spanish, including the Foreman and his wife. She and another woman kept bringing platters of ham, sausage, biscuits, beans, tortillas and pitchers of coffee and milk. There was some conversation in English and Spanish. Frank and I were asked a few questions, but food was the center of interest.

On the drive to the ranch, Mr. Miller had explained what was done at a roundup. If we wanted to, Frank and I could go on horseback with the other men to drive the cattle from the open range into the corral. That was just a small part of what had to be done. Frank did go, but I wasn't up to that much hard riding.

After the cattle were rounded up into the corral, they were prodded into a fenced chute that brought them one at a time to a steel frame. A cowhand worked the frame that grasped the cow from both sides. The confined cow was tilted on its side so that what needed to be done could be. Different people did different jobs. Branding, putting salve on the cow's eyes (to prevent pink eye, I think), and some kind of vaccination were the easier parts. I took turns doing all three of these jobs. Dehorning, actually scooping out the roots of beginning horns with a special tool, took physical strength that I couldn't do. The last part was castrating the bulls. I didn't know till then that that's what made steers. I figured I could do without that experience. The men were probably relieved that I didn't show any interest. The whole procedure on each animal was done in about ten minutes.

Very soon after we arrived in Vegas, Frank and I both got straw, Stetson-like cowboy hats. The sun could get intense. We never appreciated those hats more than we did during that roundup. We started work about 7:30 a.m. and worked right through the heat of the morning until 11:30. No one was obvious or rude, but I knew very well that we were being observed as to whether or not we could take it. There was a rhythm to what was done with the cow in the frame. Walking away for a drink or just to rest, interrupted the rhythm. Instead, someone came around with a water bag with a long swig of the best water I ever tasted. I worked right with the rest of them until the dinner bell sounded. It was a wonderful sound. Not only was I tired, I was starving.

We walked to the ranch house where pans of water and towels were waiting on the wraparound porch. I can almost this minute feel that most welcome, cool water on hot, dusty, face and hands. It was noon. I don't remember what we had to eat, but it certainly wasn't lunch--more like a feast. There were mountains of food, all welcome and tasty, too.

I could very well understand how a siesta could become an easy habit. I probably could have found a corner somewhere and disappeared. After lunch it was back to what we had been doing in the morning. The pace seemed a little slower because there were fewer cattle to roundup and send toward the chute. As far as I was concerned, we were kept busy enough.

It seemed to be much longer this time till the dinner bell sounded. On the walk to the ranch house, there were some smiles and nods in my direction. I was tired, but proud of myself. I had stayed with it and had done my part. I like to think I earned the smiles.

Dinner was the usual huge platters of varieties of food that smelled delicious and tasted better. After the dishes were cleared away, everyone lounged wherever they could find a place to sit. Above us the stars were appearing. Around us the men were rolling cigarettes, lighting them, and then the lit end would flicker like a firefly. There were some murmurs of conversation, but not much. Someone started to quietly strum a guitar in just the right notes and mood that added to the peace of the setting.

Mr. Miller didn't stay around for long. The men and the guitar player began drifting away, too. It was probably only about nine o'clock, but tomorrow was another early day of work. Two cots made up for Frank and me had been set up at one end of the porch. The last thing I remember was from under the blanket of my cot. I was looking at billions and billions of brilliant stars that seemed close enough and big enough to touch.

Frank got his Master's degree from Highlands University in 1956. Dr. Kerr had already taken a job as director of the Child Guidance Clinic in Niagara Falls, New York. He was kind enough to offer Frank a job as child psychologist at the clinic. That summer we moved to Niagara Falls.

The day we were leaving, with the U-Haul trailer with all our worldly possessions hooked to our car, we saw a couple we hadn't seen for some time. Both cars stopped as we talked for some minutes. When we drove on, I started laughing. It was the very same light where we had been annoyed, not so long ago, at the two pick-up trucks that had kept us, then as impatient Easterners, waiting.

CHAPTER 24
THE RED HOUSE ON THE HILL

Frank was well on his way in his profession. I had taken a few classes at Highlands University. We decided it was time I completed my degree.

Our one car determined where we would live. In Niagara Falls, we found an apartment on Main Street that was close enough that Frank could walk to work while I drove into the city to the Buffalo State Teachers' College. Within a year, Frank interviewed for a school psychologist position where his time was divided between Hamburg and West Seneca Schools, both suburbs of Buffalo. We moved to an apartment in Buffalo on Allen Street. I could take a bus straight up Elmwood Ave to the College, and Frank could have the car for work.

Niagara Falls on the American side back then was not nearly as attractive as the Canadian side. Buffalo's Lake Erie shore was a hodge-podge of unattractive industrial buildings. Nothing had been done around the Falls or the surrounding area to preserve any natural beauty or to improve on it. The contrast between the two sides of the Falls was a disappointment, to say the least. Still, Niagara Falls itself was a big attraction. We had lots of visitors and always went to the Canadian side. At that time, all you needed to do to cross the border, was to state your American citizenship. No passport was necessary.

I got my B.S. degree in June of 1958 and was hired to teach sixth grade at Ebenezer School in West Seneca. It did take me eleven years instead of ten, but we both did reach our goals. For the first time, it wasn't work and classes and readings and papers to write and to type. It was household chores and whatever needed to be done for work. There was free time.

Partly as entertainment, we started looking at houses. This went on for several months before we got serious and contacted a realtor. Then one day in North Boston, a place no bigger than a crossroad, we saw it. There was a red building nestled on the side of a hill and surrounded by trees. I knew it was something special when we went up a curving walk of 72 irregular stone steps (counted later) leading up to the building. It was summer. As we climbed, we saw a cement patio with a stone fireplace surrounding by blooming red salvia. Better and better.

From the patio, we entered into a small kitchen next to a small dining area that opened into a large living room with another fireplace. This one was huge and made of natural stone. There were also three small bedrooms. Except for the bathroom, the interior was pine paneled. To top it off, behind the house was a tiny red house that had two bunk beds and a crude cupboard. That was the clincher for me. We made it grand by calling it a "guest house" Any kids who came to visit, loved staying in it. After the tour of the property, I fell in love with the place so badly that I was trembling as we walked down the hill.

We were told that the house was originally built as a hunting cabin. The property included three acres of wooded land. The only negative we saw was that the house had well water, but we were assured quantity would not be a problem. We wanted to believe, made an offer, moved in by the fall of 1960, and lived there for fifteen years.

For ten of those years, we really did achieve what we had worked for. Periodically, there were disturbances between Frank and me. But there were so many happy, fun, pleasant times that it was easy to ignore the disturbances until they couldn't be ignored. In the meantime:

Both of us loved our jobs and loved the Red House as well as most of our life in it. We developed good friends. Also, since we lived away from our families, there were visits from them to us or us to them for long weekends or sometimes for a week either to Akron or to York, Pennsylvania. Frank's father Harry, and his wife, Maggie lived in York. We usually spent wonderful Thanksgivings with them when Maggie put the turkey in the oven at dawn, and we woke to roasting turkey aroma wafting through the house.

<u>About Ted and Mary:</u>
I need to tell you about the rest of the in-laws. I lucked out all the way around; not just with the in-laws my kids have brought into the family, but with my own. I was fortunate to acquire Theodore and Mary Smith, Frank's sister and her husband. Frank's mother, Ethel Kurtz, was living with them at the time. Mary and Ted had three children, Patty, Don, and Joyce that I saw develop into adults that made all of us proud. Later they had their own families that are just as nice.

During the years Frank and I were married, we (including my side) had many happy times with the Smiths as well as Dad and Maggie. We visited back and forth, camped and fished together, shared Christmas Day or other holidays, and on occasion one of the kids would stay with us for a week or so. I'm happy to say the relationship has continued.

Mary and Ted are remarkable people, and probably more modest than anyone I've known. They are both in their nineties now and celebrated their 70th wedding anniversary on Thanksgiving, November 27, 2011. They were married in 1941 just before America entered WWII. Very soon, Ted was drafted into the 2nd Armored Division under Gen. George S. Patton. I can testify to their modesty because sixty years later, I have just recently learned about some of their accomplishments that deserve to be mentioned.

Ted was in the campaigns in France and Germany as part of the D-Day invasion and also served in Africa and Sicily. During the more than three years Ted was overseas, Mary worked at the Firestone Tire and Rubber Co. in the office. After he came home, Ted didn't talk about his experiences because he said, "You wouldn't believe me if I told you what I've seen." He had earned seven medals, but in the rush to return to civilian life, he never received them. When his children and grandchildren started asking questions about his service in WWII, Ted asked Ohio's Senator, Sherrod Brown, to intervene. Ted did get his medals in a special ceremony honoring him and six other Summit County veterans at a game at the Aeros Stadium in Akron on August 28, 2011. Ted and Mary's children, Patricia Troxell, Don and Sylvia Smith, Joyce Butler, and sixteen other family members attended the ceremony.

Mary and Ted always had a huge garden. Even after Mary returned to work at Firestone when the kids were in school, vegetables from the garden were frozen or canned to enjoy all year. They attended church regularly. For more than twenty years, both have been involved with disaster relief all over the eastern part of the U.S. They went wherever there was a need and often under primitive accommodations. They didn't receive medals for this work. Instead, in their usual quiet way, this good and honorable couple didn't talk about this contribution, either.

An aside:

Sometimes Dad Kurtz would get started telling stories about his life. That's how we learned that Dad knew Dwight and Mamie Eisenhower long before Dwight became a general and later became president. Dad was in the Infantry between WWI and WWII, stationed in Texas. He was manager of the unit's baseball team. The team played in a field close to officer housing. Dad mentioned that he used to chat with Mamie when he saw her in her back yard. I think he even said it was when she was hanging laundry on the clothesline like an ordinary person. I got such a kick from his story because Dad was so casual about telling it as if it was commonplace.~

Summers always included a succession of visitors. One summer I counted the stay-over visitors and the two extra meals a day (usually there were only snacks for lunch) and the numbers surprised me. I remember something like a1000 meals, but that's hard even for me to believe. I didn't write the number down anywhere unfortunately. I do believe that was the same summer that Chris started calling his Dad "Uncle Frank," probably because he heard others call him that. No doubt that our house had its attractions: hikes in the woods, sled riding down the hill, hunting with guns and for mushrooms, and THE GULLY SWING.

On each side of the house there were eroded gullies with huge over-hanging tree branches. Frank and his brother, George, conferred and decided the setting called for a jungle swing. They selected an appropriate tree. Somehow, George climbed to a sturdy lower branch, looped a heavy rope over the branch and lo! We had a swing that could rival any Tarzan vine. On the side of the gully, they built a launching/landing site, and fixed a tire on the end of the rope. The ride was spectacular! The swing made an arc of about 150 feet. At the highest point of the arc, you were about 75 feet off the ground and sometimes could touch high tree leaves with your toes. The first time on the swing was a stomach-churning ride that called for more. Everybody who visited remembers that swing.

We moved to New York because that's where the job was offered. It didn't occur to either of us to consider the climate. Even if we had, we probably would have made the same decision. Now thanks to TV weather channels, everyone knows about the Lake Effect snows in the Buffalo area. The first exposure to winter there can be a shock that takes serious adjustment. Frank decided to take advantage of what was here. He took up skiing and encouraged me to do the same. We got skis, boots, and outfits. I pretty much gave up on skiing when, after weeks of practice on beginner slopes, I couldn't make it up a small mogul (ski term for a bump in the path) without taking off my skis. The other option was to observe the skiing scene — such fresh faces and strong bodies and smart outfits. And I could observe all of this inside by the huge fireplace with hot chocolate or some other warming substance in my hands. I learned that the term for someone like me was "snow bunny." She dresses like a skier, but rarely goes out. We also took up bowling in a teachers' team. I did much better at that. It started in a warm place to begin with.

We finally did get a second car for me. It allowed me so much more independence. Frank tended to run late. I didn't have to rely on him or anyone else to get me to and from work. It was wonderful, except winter was a drawback. Not only were winters generally severe, but the Red House was also in the real "snow belt" south of the city. I might leave Ebenezer School after work with a pretty soft snow coming down. A half mile farther south, I crossed Route 20. I called it "the wall." Suddenly the snow would become blinding. The rest of the five miles to home was a white knuckle, scary trip. There was no relief until I skidded into our driveway, hiked up the hill, and sat. Maybe if the next day was Saturday, I could look out our sliding kitchen door and appreciate the beauty of the pristine new snow.

If the next day was a workday, I wished for snow days even more than the kids did. But the Buffalo area was well prepared. Since it often has more snow than parts of Alaska, it had then, and probably still has the most snow removal equipment of any county. School buses came around as usual. Akron schools probably get more snow days than we got in the Buffalo snow belt.

CHAPTER 25
OUR HOME AWAY FROM HOME

There was one obvious advantage with both of us working for the schools. Neither of us worked during July and August. This was also a major disadvantage since neither of us got a paycheck. Still, most summers we managed to fit in about a month of travel. We were able to do this by camping in state and national parks. Tent sites during our first trip with the pup tent were often free or 25 or 50 cents a day. Costs gradually went up during our camping years. By the time we got our very small 16 foot trailer, costs had gone up considerably, but probably $5.00 or under.

Compared to how we started, our trailer was almost luxurious. It had a lamp and three burner stove both using propane gas, an ice box, a sink with running water (if we got a hookup), an eating booth for four that opened into a bed, and on the other side, a double bed. That left an open space in the middle of about a square yard.

Except for laundry, my duties while camping were very much like those at home. They were simpler, but conditions were also much more primitive. Still, I loved the opportunity of seeing the country. For me it was an acceptable trade.

One of our trips was to Key West, Florida by way of the Outer Banks of North Carolina. Cars can cross between larger islands in the Outer Banks by ferry. There are miles of wonderful beaches, and we got glorious tans. Frank was fair-skinned and got a golden tan. I usually got quite dark. As we traveled the coast farther south, sometimes we got hostile looks. At first we didn't understand why. Then we realized the beaches were segregated. Some people probably assumed we were a mixed race couple. In some southern states, interracial mixing of any kind was illegal.

Someone advised that we should try clam digging, a new experience. We did. You carry a bucket and walk along the shore in knee-to-thigh high water until your bare feet feel a hard lump. That's the clam shell. Stoop down, pick it up, and put it in the bucket. Some experienced clammers could bring up the clam with their toes so they didn't need to stoop. A neighbor at the campground told me how to make a clear broth clam chowder that was excellent.

We also tried deep sea fishing in Key West. Neither of us caught anything at all, but an Old Salt told us some entertaining stories. After that, we came north where we camped in the Everglades. That was a bad mistake that spoiled summer vacations in Florida forever. The temperature was a steamy heat that drained us of all energy, and we had no air conditioning. The only relief was hosing ourselves with water from the camp spigot. We left without spending the night, but not before we were attacked by no-seeums that left itchy bites that lasted for days and ruined our tans.

Another summer we took my sister Vicky who was sixteen years old. That trip was a northern swing through New England and mid-east Canada. We camped in Acadia National Park in Maine. The coast here had huge boulders where the ocean thundered, sprayed, and foamed against the rocks. We found a small picturesque cove where we went to swim until we recognized the black things floating in the water were not twigs, but leeches.

In those days right alongside the road, were large oil drums with a fire in the bottom. These were manned by vendors with fresh lobsters in tubs of water. You selected a lobster. It was dropped into the boiling water in the drum. A few minutes later you had a to-go dinner before fast foods were common. That's how we had our first lobster. It was smart that we took it back to the privacy of our trailer. We had no proper nutcracker, so for the claws, we improvised with pliers and a hammer. It was a messy process, but fun and delicious.

Vicky was a good traveler and was helpful in many ways including helping Frank hitch the trailer. One of my jobs was to help guide Frank in the car as he backed into the trailer hitch. This was tricky. The back of the car had the part of the hitch that was a metal cap that fit over a smaller-than-baseball size ball on the trailer part of the hitch. For me it was like threading a needle. I was always off a few inches which meant three, four, or more tries for Frank. That didn't improve his temper at all. Vicky took over and was mostly able to guide him on the first try. Good for her!

When you cross the border into Mexico, you know you're in another country. It's an entirely different atmosphere. In this respect, from the beginning, Canada was a disappointment; not much different from the U.S. That is until we came to Quebec. Quebec is much more colorful. Their language is French. One shopkeeper wasn't very sympathetic to English speaking Americans. I went into a small grocery store and tried to explain what I needed. I got no help. The man practically sneered at me, and I walked out without buying anything. We learned his attitude was not uncommon. There were compensations with the history in Quebec City and Montreal. It was interesting to get the Canadian versions of battles between the French and English during colonial times.

A few times during a trip we would treat ourselves to restaurant food. What better place than Quebec City to have our first, not just French food, but French cuisine. We took the recommendation of a cab driver and lucked out. It wasn't a fancy place, but the food was superb. I'm sorry that I don't remember the name of the restaurant or what Frank and Vicky had. I followed the waiter's suggestion and ordered both escargot and frog legs (first time for each) and loved them. The snails were small and especially intriguing when I was given a straight pin as the utensil to coax the snail from its shell. Vicky felt very grownup when, without question, she was served wine too, as is the custom in France.

We also continued traveling after we adopted the children. Both of them were camping before they were a year old. Now, I won't go into details, but this was in the days before disposable diapers. I'm giving myself some well-deserved credit.

Both kids before they could walk loved the Jolly Jumper. It was a kind of harness around the child's body on a rope that could be hung from some kind of projection. The feet touch the ground so the baby can bounce and twirl. It's freedom for the child. Chris was already walking his first summer. Missy was just six months old. I would put her in the Jolly Jumper and hang her from a tree branch. Every child or adult who went by would stop and talk to her while she charmed them with huge toothless smiles and lots of happy bouncing. That picture in my mind still gives me pleasure.

While the Red House was isolated from the neighbor kids so that I had to arrange play dates for ours, there were always other kids at the campgrounds. Chris' birthday was in August. There were several years when he had two birthdays; one at home and one with bought cake and ice cream with campground kids.

The hardest part of traveling with the children besides the diapers, was all the paraphernalia: the favorite toy, the binkys, the indispensable blanket, and on and on. Heaven forbid that anything should be forgotten.

When Frank was working on his doctorate, for two summers, we rented space at Rainbow Lake, about a 40 minute drive from the house. We tried to go there most weekends. The worst part was getting all the necessaries to the trailer that was by the garage at the foot of the hill. I would load Chris' little red wagon, and he and I would guide the wagon several times up and down the hill. Forgetting something is almost inevitable in spite of lists. One of the first weekends, I overlooked Missy's security blanket. That was a catastrophe that I vowed would never happen again. I tried to keep these traumas at a minimum by keeping duplicates in the trailer, but as with the blanket, that wasn't always possible.

Those security blankets are very personal, as it was one summer. There was a little boy the same age as Missy one trailer over from ours. What do you suppose the chances would be that his ever present blanket would be identical in color and texture to Missy's ever present blanket? Yet, there they were, dropped whenever attention was distracted. Inevitably, he or Missy would claim the wrong blanket not remembering where theirs was dropped. There was angry tugging and anguish and tears, until ownership was established. Mothers learn to be problem solvers by resolving dilemmas like that.

After a few weekends one summer, as we drove into the grounds of Rainbow Lake, Missy was sitting on my lap (no car seat laws then). She had been attempting to try words. She started bouncing and calling "Neeng! Neeng!" She recognized that we were coming near the swings that she loved.

Confinement in the small space of the trailer when it rains, isn't pleasant for adults or children. Adults can read or find some job to do. It's harder with children. Even though I tried to keep surprise indoor activities to magically produce for those rainy occasions, I did hope the rain didn't last very long. If it did, the novelty of the surprises wore off fast. Then either Frank or I had to create diversions. Still, I do believe both children thrived with camping.

The World's Fair was in New York City in 1964. We decided to go and found a campground not too far from the city, in Peekskill, New York. We invited my sister, Mary Anne, and our niece, Joyce, to come along. However, the decision to go or not to go got to be very iffy. Frank, who did all the driving with the trailer, was almost recovered from an appendectomy. Each day was an improvement, but there were doubts until the doctor gave the okay.

Chris was ten months old. This was our first trip with him. We started off at night, thinking he would fall asleep immediately. Oh no! Babies sense the unusual. Chris, between Frank and me on the front seat (no baby seats then) proceeded to be charming by smiling and chatting to himself, and with one leg hitting the seat regularly like a metronome. After several hours we handed him to Mary Anne and Joyce in the back seat where he happily continued the same. We couldn't believe his stamina, and of course, none of us were able to doze. My appreciation for my son's good cheer decreased as the night passed. I dreaded the coming day thinking Chris would be cranky and impossible. We arrived at Peekskill in the morning. To my relief, my little boy was as cheerful as he could be, though he did take an early nap. The adults were none the worse, either.

Frank stayed with Chris while the three women went to the Expo. Frank's brother, George was a social worker in the City at the time. He gave us directions for bus and subway to the World's Fair. After about twenty minutes or so on the subway, all the other people got off. It was right at that moment that one of my mental quirks chose to kick in. Whether it was because we had just passed a sign for Shea Stadium, or whether I expected to see a big sign for the Fair exit, I casually observed to Joyce and Mary Anne, "There must be a game at Shea Stadium. Everybody's getting off." The two of them accepted my words without question. After all, I was the mature, experienced traveler. We continued to sit.

It wasn't until the train stopped and no doors opened that serious doubts started. "Oh my gosh, we're nowhere!" and "We must have missed our stop!" and "There's no one around!" and "What should we do?"

Like a hero come to our rescue, a conductor entered the car. At sight of the three of us who must have had the blank look of lost sheep, he stopped dead, but recovered quickly, "Let me guess. You missed your stop, right?" We nodded and explained, also sheepishly.

That kind man told us this was the end of the line, and where the train turned around. We could stay on till the Shea Stadium stop. That was the stop for the World's Fair, and also why everyone else got off. There was no game.

I've heard people say they hate New York City; that the people are so rude. I strongly disagree. I love visiting there. There's so very much to see and do. As for the people, that conductor was an example of New Yorkers that I've had the good fortune to cross my path.

At the Fair practically every country had an exhibition. The Vatican exhibition alone was worth the trip. Visitors were on a moving walkway that circled a bullet-proof, glass case protecting Michaelangelo's "Pieta." The sculpture was of a translucent pinkish marble. The genius of the artist was that in cold stone, he managed to portray the anguish of Mary as she held the lifeless body of Jesus after the Crucifixion.

During our camping days, there were so many memorable experiences: In Florida during sweltering August heat, dipping into the icy water of Silver Springs. In the Great Salt Lake, keeping afloat because of the salt in the water. Fishing and catching a two pound walleye in a remote lake in Quebec, or a one pound catfish closer to home in Lake Erie. I've also had the privilege of seeing so much beauty: the grandeur of the Grand Canyon; the majesty of sequoia trees or of the Teton Mountains; and the breathtaking sunrises and sunsets of New Mexico. I must say though that this many years later, the manmade "Pieta" is still one of the most beautiful sights I have ever seen.

No doubt that camping is basic and crude. Of course I would prefer a hotel, with a hot tub, pool, and room service. On occasion we were able to take a weekend and do just that. But we could never have afforded three or four weeks of that kind of indulgence. I don't think I would have enjoyed it for that long, either. By camping, we were able to see the wonderful beauty and variety of our country, and sometimes to share it with others, too.

Chapter 26
TEACHING

When I was about nineteen years old, a friend of mine who had gone through a bad time in her life, came into the Garden Grille to tell me she had just become engaged and was very happy. I was happy for her. Since her husband was chef, Pauly Anthe came into the restaurant often. With that youthful optimism, I gushed to Pauly, "Isn't it wonderful how everything works out for the best!" Pauly took a long, serious look at me and stopped me in my tracks with a severe, "Oh no it doesn't. It's what you do with what happens to you that counts." I've never forgotten Pauly's words. They've sort of become my guide, and proved to be true many times, which brings me to one of my regrets.

I happily gave up teaching to be a stay-at-home-mom. The common assumption then was that you can always return to teaching. This certainly wasn't true ten years later in 1974 when I tried to do just that. I did what I had to do, but had no idea that the choices I made then would altogether lead me away from the schoolroom.

I did return to formal teaching much later with a ten week course in "Business Plan Training" for women who were considering going into business. The course was offered two or three times a year. I taught those classes for five years and enjoyed the experience very much. It made me realize how much I missed teaching. Truthfully though, I don't believe I could adapt to conditions and standards as they are in public schools today.

I loved teaching. Not every part of the job, but by far, most of it. I loved my sixth graders. They came to me as eleven year old children, and left as cocky upperclassmen going into junior high school. During the ten months with me, many of them got a major growth spurt, sometimes as much as four inches with clumsier arms and legs and voice changes. Yet, they were the same children and somehow more endearing.

<u>An aside:</u>
I have an opinion that contradicts the entire education establishment. I think segregating this age group into junior high schools was a serious mistake. It seems to me that K-8 is more sensible for this reason: junior high schools are usually for 12, 13, and 14 year olds, who are often at the most difficult and rebellious age. Yet, the 14 year olds are upperclassman in junior high, the least qualified to set examples. In contrast, with the K-8 system, when the 14 year old enters high school, his is a lowly status. The ones who do have status are the more mature seniors on the verge of adulthood. ~

The basic sixth grade subjects were reading, arithmetic, social studies (including Europe and Asia), English, spelling, and health (two days) and science (three days). It was a continual challenge to present the subjects so they would be interesting to the students. This part was all-absorbing for me. I was constantly in search of ideas or projects and experimenting with them. Some worked and were incorporated. The failures were so obvious that I myself couldn't get rid of them fast enough.

One of the first things I learned as a teacher was to keep the kids busy. Idleness invites mischief. However, the worst teaching experience I ever had was one afternoon as a substitute teacher. The regular teacher left very thorough plans. The trouble was, they were all written on the board for the children to complete at will. This left me with no control. In what seemed like a mere half hour, the children completed all the assignments. At this point, an experienced teacher, which I was at that time, would have come up with any number of all-purpose projects that put the class back to work. Instead, for no reason that I can explain, I went brain dead. Not one idea from my bag of tricks came to my rescue. In minutes the class was in total disorder. I did get through that afternoon, but I'm not sure how, and it was with a complete sense of failure. This was not a good feeling at all, especially since I knew this could have been avoided. I can imagine how devastating this could be for a beginning teacher. It could take great strength of will to recover and assert oneself enough to be effective again.

Many teachers will say that their first teaching day, when the door is closed and the teacher is left alone with 20 to 30 or more kids, was the most frightening. That wasn't what was frightening for me. I found that at the beginning of the school year, there was what I called a "honeymoon period." Generally the kids, in spite of their complaints, are glad to be back at school. All the fun of summer has become stale. They look forward to seeing friends again, and some may have curiosity about this next grade and their new teacher.

My approach those first few days probably caught the children off guard. Rather than behavior rules coming only from the teacher, the class and I made up the rules together. What happened during the process was that what they wanted and what I wanted wasn't much different. Mostly behavior rules require respect for other people. The one rule we disagreed about was gum chewing in class. The kids saw nothing wrong with it. When I demonstrated how distracting gum chomping or gum cracking could be, they laughed, but got the message, and that rule was added, too.

There usually followed a week or two of democratic bliss, the "honeymoon." Then as every teacher knows, a shoe is bound to fall. Someone will, in one way or another, serious or minor, test the rules and the teacher. To me, that was the scary part. The test is usually when least expected, but the teacher must be prepared. How the teacher handles that first confrontation will determine much of what happens in the classroom from then on. Whatever action she/he takes, the end result must be justice. A teacher does not ever, ever want to be labeled as "unfair." Unfairness breeds hostility.

My teaching style tended to be eclectic. Depending on the situation, whether pearls of wisdom from me or reports and comments from students, order and at least courteous attention were required. Other activities were more informal. Desks could be moved, and students could talk to each other and move around. There is a difference in sound between work that is busy, and disorder. As an example, part of the English curriculum was making an outline, an important tool in organizing writing, but hardly exciting either to teach or to learn.

Somewhere I heard of student art called "Whatizzits." These were grotesque, sci-fi figures with cut spiral eyes, dragon tails, antenna, claws, and any other weird appendage the imagination could concoct. All of the characters were made with colored construction paper, scissors, and glue. My class did the art first. Throughout the construction, there was busy conversation, consultation about ideas or sharing paper and glue. That kind of purposeful buzz can be very satisfying.

Next the kids had to decide what they wanted to tell about their Whatizzits: history, origins, characteristics, or other qualities. These were the Roman numeral main topics. Under each main topic were at least three sub-topics (A,B,C) to support the main topics. Some of the students caught on and got into sub-sub-topics (under A, 1, 2, 3, etc.). Voila! Effective, painless, outlining. I used that idea every year after.

I would feel sorry for a teacher whose sense of humor was limited. So many things that happen in a classroom are unexpected. Humor adds perspective, resolves minor matters, and adds fun as well. A sense of humor is essential and invaluable.

I do believe it helps for a teacher to be a bit of a ham actor. There are times when dramatic, exaggerated voice and actions are useful attention getters, or help to get a point across, as in gum chewing. This might be a bias in my favor since it's part of my style. On the other hand, I do remember Ruth Price, my supervising teacher during student teaching. Her manner at all times was serene and undramatic, yet her quiet teaching methods were effective and respected.

Probably one of the most unusual things one of my classes did was what we called "Russian School." This was done as a supplement to information in our textbooks. One thing just sort of led to another. It started when the class was divided into committees for subjects important to the USSR. (In the 1960s it was called Union of Socialist Soviet Republics.) Some of the topics were manufacturing, farming, natural resources, religion, education, etc. At that time it was difficult to get current and accurate information about the USSR because the country was such a closed society. However I was subscribing to "The Christian Science Monitor," a respected international daily, still publishing. The paper had just carried a serious of articles with recent, authoritative information about the USSR, which I saved. The committees were to do research on their various subjects using available sources, including my CSM articles, and then give oral reports to the class.

I don't remember what specifically sparked the interest, but when the education committee gave its report, there were all kinds of questions from the class. The best part was that the committee members had most of the answers. Maybe it was intuition, but I picked up on the interest and asked if the class would like to try doing school the Russian way. By vote, the majority wanted to give it a try. We set the basic guidelines as we understood them, although I may not have remembered all of them.

- We would do Russian School for three days starting the following Monday.
- Two students usually shared a desk or a table. Our class moved two desks together.
- We would not have uniforms, but a white shirt or blouse and dark trousers or skirts were required, if possible.
- Everyone was to wear a red scarf or tie signifying they were Pioneers (something like a national after school program).
- The class would stand in respect when the teacher entered the room.
- Teachers were caring, but dignified and serious.
- Hands raised for questions or answers were not to be waved. The elbow was to stay on the desk.

On Monday morning, there they were with shining faces, white tops and red ties. There was not the usual morning hubbub. When I stood before them to begin class and said, "Good morning, children," the class stood up and respectfully answered, "Good morning, Mrs. Kurtz," and then sat down. The atmosphere in my classroom had changed entirely. It was as if each of them had assumed a role in a movie. Furthermore, most of them maintained that role for the three days. We did cover the required subject matter, but in a much more formal and more serious way. There was no hand waving or speaking out of turn. Students stood up when they spoke in class. There were a few slips in behavior, including several by me, but the almost tangible attitude of the class to those who slipped up was a not- so-pleasant-look that said, "Get with it!"

On the Thursday morning after our three days of Russian School, we spent about an hour talking about the experience. I wish I had kept a written account of some of the opinions, but I didn't. Two have stayed with me. One was that the kids told me their mothers weren't too happy about the white tops for each day. For the mothers, it was a legitimate nuisance that I hadn't considered. The other conclusion was absolutely unexpected and took me aback.

Not at first, but as the discussion continued, what seemed to become more obvious was that some kids liked the formality. I tried not to show my surprise because I didn't want to influence what I thought they were saying. As casually as I could, I asked for a show of hands for those who liked the way we thought it was done in Russian schools. A majority of hands were raised. I tried to get more specifics through questions. Those who offered opinions, liked the order and the seriousness.

I know this is one experiment with one teacher with one class. It is not a formal study, but it surely did raise some questions in my mind. Was Ruth Price's dignified manner what had earned respect from her students? In spite of obvious objections, did children secretly crave discipline and order? Were my opinions on haminess and drama all wet?

I'm assuming that "Russian School" was done in my last year of teaching sixth grade. If it was done earlier, I have no idea why it was done only one year.

CHAPTER 27
UPHEAVALS

There have been, and no doubt will continue to be, hundreds of books written about the social upheaval in America during the 1960s. All kinds of explanations and theories have been offered as to why three major issues of our society, the Vietnam War, Civil Rights, and the Women's Movement came under attack during the same period, roughly between 1950 and 1980.

I'm inclined to think that protests against the War ignited the other two. In the first place, there seemed to be no end in sight as to our involvement. Not only were billions of dollars being spent, but precious lives were being lost. Yet the country continued to get in deeper and deeper. The question being asked by more people more frequently was "why?" Worse, dribs and drabs of information coming from our trusted leaders was being revealed as questionable at best. It was shocking for most citizens to believe that our leaders could be misleading and downright deceitful. Once the mind was willing to accept such an unwelcome thought, it was much easier to doubt other customs and rules that had been in place for a long time without question. Maybe everything done by our country and in our country wasn't so right after all.

But there was no doubt that opinions in the whole country were deeply divided. There were those who felt everything was pretty much as it should be. We lived in the greatest country in the world. We should be thankful for our blessings and support our leaders and their decisions.

There were others who continued to question our involvement in Vietnam. These people were growing in numbers and becoming more forceful with organizing demonstrations at home and in Washington against the War. There were such strong feelings between the two groups, that on many occasions, it led to violence.

As for me, the best I can say is that I did try to keep informed. However, it took me much longer to take a stand against the War, and there were many like me. What follows next is my limited, but memorable participation in an anti-war protest, and my memories of the other historical movements. I've included Watergate since it contributed greatly to the upheaval during this period.

CHAPTER 28
VIETNAM DAZE

I don't hear it very often these days, but if I should happen to hear Simon and Garfunkul's "Bridge Over Troubled Waters," visual memories sweep over me as if I were living through them again. At that time, my suburban housewife role of children, housework and errands seemed to be apart from the rest of the real world. Yet for one weekend, I got a glimpse into that other world. I was able to participate in an anti-Vietnam War demonstration in Washington D.C. That music was part of an experience in my life that has been unforgettable. I have to set the scene so that you can understand the contrast.

I, and people of my generation, were products of World War II. We believed in just wars. Americans were good people who went to war only to defeat evils. Hadn't we defeated the Fascists, Nazis, and Japs? As a result, many of us came to believe that right was on our side. The Communists however, were another menace infiltrating other countries and now Viet Nam. Communist influence must be stopped. Most of us supported what our government was reporting. We didn't know for years about government deceptions.

At First America became involved in Vietnam in small ways. That was in the early 1960s during the presidency of John F. Kennedy before he was assassinated. His successor, Lyndon Johnson involved us deeper and deeper. Young men were being drafted. Worse, the body count was growing by the month, with very little to show for our efforts, expenditures, and anguish. The first national anti-war protest came in 1965. Most of us assumed these doubters were unpatriotic rabble rousers. Or maybe even young men who, unlike the heroes of WWII, wanted to avoid military service altogether. Early on a friend of ours had two sons eligible for the draft. She was one of the very first who said if either of her boys were called, she would encourage him to defect to Canada. What's more, she would go with him. At the time, such a thought was incomprehensible to me and to most of the country.

There were a very few observers who noted that those with connections that come with wealth and power, were much less likely to be drafted. If they were drafted, they were often assigned to duties that were out of harm's way. At the time, those opinions were either scoffed at or ignored. It did eventually come about that men who became prominent like Presidents George W. Bush and Bill Clinton, Vice-president Dick Cheney, and others had a hard time explaining their various Viet Nam military service evasions.

The problem continued to worsen. Trouble makers were increasing in numbers, being more aggressive, and getting more attention. Besides, well known personalities were joining the cause. Martin Luther King, Jr., leader of the Civil Rights movement, and Robert Kennedy, President Kennedy's brother and running for president himself, were speaking out against the war. Other prominent personalities were demanding answers to questions most of the rest of us had never considered asking: Should we be fighting in Vietnam at all? On that question the country was seriously divided — to the point of violence. Within three months of each other in late spring of 1968, both Martin Luther King and Robert Kennedy were assassinated.

A year later in '69, the people had a hard time comprehending the ugliness of My Lai. A platoon of our American soldiers led by Lt. Calley (and most likely with the knowledge of their superiors) attacked an enemy village of civilians. Our soldiers massacred 500 women, children, and old people. Other loathsome acts were committed including small children being tossed into the air for target practice. How could this happen? Our upstanding young men didn't commit atrocities. They were the good guys. That year in November, 600,000 people came to protest in D.C., the largest number before or since. Lt. Calley was brought to trial and convicted. In spite of the horror of what had been done, no other officers were charged. Lt. Calley served four months.

Maybe My Lai was a symptom of something else equally as hard to comprehend. Reports began to appear about the increasing drug use among the troops. Vietnam veterans were returning with serious problems. There was no knowledge then, and certainly no tolerance for PTSD (Post Traumatic Stress Disorder) either by the public or the military. It just seemed that so many veterans looked scruffy and didn't behave as they were expected to. Instead of being respected for military service that was forced on them, in general they were ignored, or much worse, because of My Lai, labeled as "baby killers."

Carole Brocious and I got to know each other through the Unitarian Church in Hamburg. We had much in common. She had two boys about the same age as Chris and Missy. Her husband, Don, and my husband Frank, were both in psychology with the schools. Frank had started his doctorate work at the University of Buffalo. He often came home with stories about anti-Viet Nam War protests on campus. We were all trying to make sense of the conflicting views about the war. Carole and I tried to keep informed, though she had done more studying than I had. However, we were stay-at-home moms. Our conventional, suburban lives were totally separate from the upheaval we were reading and hearing about. Then it was brought close to home.

At Kent State University in Kent, Ohio, about ten miles from where I grew up in Akron, and where my sister, Mary Anne, went to school, state troops were ordered to suppress an anti-war demonstration. The Ohio National Guard killed four students who were taking part. That our government, *our government* of the Bill of Rights and the Freedom to Assemble, would kill its own protesting students was too much. A major protest was being planned for that weekend in Washington, D.C. I called Carole just to sound off about what happened at Kent, but the more we talked, the more everything we knew about Vietnam caught up with us. We felt compelled to do something, somehow, if only to be bodies at the protest. It was Friday. Carole called Don who also wanted to go, and the improbable was put together in a matter of hours.

Don's colleague at work was Jim who had attended Catholic University in D.C. Not only was he interested, he still had connections and friends at CU. We could have a place to stay. Carole had to arrange for a reliable baby sitter. My son had the mumps. If I went I would be deserting my child when he was sick. To make it worse, Sunday was Mother's Day. Mothers could not disappoint their children on that particular day. It was their duty to be home with them. Still, it all came together as if it were meant to be. Carole's friend agreed to babysit, and Frank agreed to stay with ours so that I could go. By 9:00 Friday night, Carole, Don, Jim, and I were on our way. We took turns driving all night so that each of us could get some sleep. We arrived Saturday morning into an alien world.

Catholic University, as well as other universities and organizations, were well prepared for demonstrations. They had accommodated several others. There were lists of people who opened their homes, apartments, and dorms to students from other schools. Jim dropped us off at an apartment of his friend. Our hostess was expecting us, quickly told us what was necessary, gave us a little time to freshen up, and then directed us to the auditorium where hundreds had already gathered. Very welcome coffee and doughnuts were offered while we waited for buses to arrive.

A young man who was leader on our bus, explained what we could expect from both police and other protesters. He spoke well of the D.C. police and advised us to cooperate with them. They're well trained and mostly don't want confrontations that can overload jails. His directions, both on paper and verbal, brought home the reality of what could happen. Two previous protests had become violent. He gave us other directions also, but the following are the ones I remembered.

- Should we need any legal help, look for volunteers with arm bands that say "LAW."
- There are First Aid tents set up. Look for Red Cross arm bands if you need help.
- Stay away from anyone you see jumping up and down. He said these people were trouble.
- Long sleeves and long trousers are the best protection against pepper gas spray. At that Carole and I looked at each other, concerned. It was warm. We had on skirts, panty hose, and short sleeve blouses.

The center of activity was at a wide open area called the Ellipse between the White House and the Washington Monument. The bus dropped us off on a grassy knoll close by. Groups of people either sitting or standing were already clustered. We found a place to sit and just observed. It was quiet, but there was a friendly atmosphere, people chatting as if at a picnic. We talked with an older couple who had driven in from Boston and had nephews in the service. The rowdy, disheveled protesters we saw in the papers and on TV, was not what we were seeing here.

Busload after busload stopped on the incline to let people off the bus. There was every variety of ages, skin colors, and shapes of people. Contrary to what I had expected, most of them appeared to be quite ordinary. Since we were seated a little lower than where the buses stopped, the image that has stayed with me is the endless stream of steady, unhurried feet, mostly in sneakers or comfortable shoes walking, walking, walking, down the sidewalk toward the Ellipse. After a while, Don, Carole, and I did the same.

First we noticed the obvious. Among the young people there was almost a uniform: well-worn jeans, sneakers, and mostly a blue, cotton, long sleeved shirt like workmen wear. Sometimes a girl would have a gauzy white blouse. This morning at the apartment, a young man knocked. When he came in with his duffel bag, he wore chino pants, a neat shirt, and white buck shoes. (He was from Harvard.) A few minutes later he was wearing jeans and the blue work shirt. I wondered why he had changed. Now I understood.

We did see LAW and Red Cross arm bands and several tents set up to accommodate them. Every now and then we also got a whiff of an odd small that I was told was marijuana. Around the First Aid tent, several bodies were lying on the ground. They appeared to be unharmed, probably just sleeping off what they had too much of. Farther away from where we were, there was a speaker's platform with a sound system, but I don't remember hearing speeches. We were either too far away or too occupied with taking in everything else.

In spite of all the people on the Ellipse, the general atmosphere was purposeful, but subdued. That is until we heard boisterous sounds from one direction. We worked our way closer to a ring of people bunched three and four deep around a center that we couldn't see. They were singing and cheering. Every now and then, something that looked like clothing would be tossed into the air and got louder cheers. My curiosity got the better of me. I squeezed my way to where I could get a look at the inner space. Here was a group just having fun.

The center was a small wading pool where eight or ten young male and female bodies, arms linked, were frolicking in a disorderly chorus line. Not only were they "dancing" in the pool, they were completely nude. I couldn't help myself. I watched. Then several of the dancers taunted and splashed water at those who were gawking. I was standing in front of an immovable picnic bench when there was a backward surge of people that for an instant seemed they would stampede over me.

That did it. I got away from that group fast. What was I thinking? What if I had been hurt? Guilt swept over me as I imagined an article in the local paper: "Mother who deserts sick child to protest war in D.C. is trampled as she watches nude dancers."

For the rest of the afternoon, the three of us wandered, observed, listened, and absorbed. At home we were isolated and reluctant to speak. Here we were a part of thousands whose physical presence demonstrated how we felt. Maybe we could make a difference.

Later on our way back to CU campus, we saw for ourselves what the leader on our bus told us about D.C. police. We were walking a short distance behind three young people. One of them just finished drinking from a Coke bottle. Beside us on the road a cop on a motorcycle, in an immaculate gray uniform and helmet, was cruising slowly. Then for no reason except mischief, the bottle was dropped from shoulder height and shattered on the sidewalk. I was appalled at this deliberate defiance. The policeman, rather than make an issue of a childish action that could become volatile, let it pass. In normal circumstances, a person could question whether his inaction was or was not neglect. In this case, I'm inclined to agree with the cop. He kept a minor infraction from becoming a confrontation.

On campus, signs directed us to the college gym. Volunteers offered coffee and tea and cheese or bologna sandwiches (with nothing else) on white bread. Nobody paid attention to a sleeping body curled up on the floor near the door.

Back at the apartment, in our honor as "older" visitors, three cots were set up in the living room. Otherwise, there were more knocks at the door by visitors with their own sleeping bags looking for a place to sleep. I'm not sure how many stayed in the apartment that night, but none were turned away. Young men and women plopped down their bags in living room or bedroom wherever there was space.

In my cot, sleep didn't come immediately. There were so many images to relive and so many perspectives to mull over, like the sleeping arrangements here. Mind you, this was in the days before coed dorms, and when girls (not boys) in college housing had curfews. Yet in this apartment, males and females including us, were all mixed together. In spite of the older generation's fears of loose morals, I had to reconsider. This mix seemed to have a lot more to do with convenience rather than hanky-panky.

Someone put on a record. I had not heard "Bridge Over Troubled Water" and certainly didn't know who Simon and Garfunkel were, but the music was beautiful and plaintive, and the words were hopeful. Both were perfect for this day:

When you're weary, feeling small, when tears are in your eyes, I will dry them all.

I'm in your side when times get rough, and friends just can't be found,

Like a bridge over troubled water, I will lay me down,

Like a bridge over troubled water, I will lay me down.

Sunday morning it was reported everywhere that President Richard Nixon, who had not appeared at any previous anti-war protests, did speak to a few students at the Reflecting Pool by the Washington Monument. What he had to say were just words that seemed entirely irrelevant. The official numbers for our demonstration were greatly underestimated. We also learned that across the country some 450 colleges and universities were closed because of protests in sympathy with Kent State. It didn't matter. Nixon and the powers propelling this war just didn't get the message. The war went on for another two-and-a-half years until a cease fire was signed in January 1973.

Besides friendship, Carole and I have this bond. In the forty years or so since our shared experience, whenever she and I talk, that weekend is almost always included in our conversation. What we saw and heard then, may not seem very dramatic to others, but to us, taking part in an anti-war demonstration certainly was not a part of our everyday suburban lives. It had a profound effect on me.

Chapter 29
NATIONAL NIGHTMARE

From the first time Richard M. Nixon appeared on the national scene, I was not willing to accept any positive qualities in him. The man who eventually became president, had already acquired the label of "Tricky Dick" through his support and defense of Senator McCarthy and his Communist hunt. When Republican Dwight Eisenhower selected Nixon as his Vice-Presidential running mate in 1952, there were also suspicions of him accepting gifts in return for political favors. He redeemed himself through the famous "Checkers" speech where he stated Checkers, a dog that was also a gift to his two daughters, and was the dog under suspicion also? I intended to vote for Adlai Stevenson, the Democratic candidate. I had also just been married and neglected to re-register with my married name. It was a real disappointment to be turned away at the voting booth. Nixon won the election. Nothing that I learned about him through the years was favorable enough to change those first impressions. There are those who even now maintain that Nixon was brilliant. Maybe he was, but investigations of the shady, illegal practices of his administration that became known as Watergate tore the country apart for several years. The secret Pentagon Papers from the Vietnam War helped to lay the foundation for suspicion of our leaders.

Daniel Ellsberg, an army analyst, revealed the Pentagon Papers to *The New York Times* which published them in 1971. These were secret government reports that showed that John Kennedy and Lyndon Johnson, who were presidents before Nixon, misled the American public about the Vietnam War. This added much fuel to the anti-war forces. The country was being forced to face the reality that leaders that we trusted were deceiving us with lies, and worse, with actions that were downright illegal. This was a fertile foundation for Watergate.

The basics of what triggered the Watergate Scandal seem almost inconsequential. Burglars broke into the National Democratic

Headquarters in the Watergate Hotel. This was in June during the 1972 campaign for president when Republican Richard Nixon was running against Democrat George McGovern. The incident was suspicious enough that several investigations lasted through the election. They produced nothing conclusive, and Richard Nixon was re-elected in a landslide victory.

Then there was a surprising break. One of the burglars had a connection to Nixon's White House through the Committee to Re-elect the President (for short, appropriately known as CREEP). Investigations continued and revealed there was a secret taping system in the Oval Office of the President.

Archibald Cox was the prosecutor who requested the tapes. Using "executive privilege," Nixon refused to release the tapes and fired Mr. Cox. That action became known as "the Saturday massacre" and brought sympathy for Mr. Cox. In defense of principle, Cox stated that "either this was a nation of laws or a nation of men." The case was taken to the Supreme Court whose decision was that the tapes must be released.

There was no cable TV at the time. The investigation was played out daily on one or another of the three major TV channels. For millions of us, what was happening in real life was more compelling than any soap opera. The tapes revealed wire tapping of journalists and other citizens, all kinds of political espionage, and other illegal acts originating from the highest levels of the Nixon Administration. I especially remember the testimony of John Dean who was counsel to the President. He seemed to have almost a photographic memory as he answered questions that contradicted Nixon's denials. Calmly, over and over, he stated occasions when he had discussed the break-in and cover-up with the President. Nixon continued to cover-up and deny.

An aside:

The Senate hearings to me were better than soap operas. Once that comparison got into my head, I started playing around with it. And so, using titles of TV programs and soaps, I tried to fit the personalities of committee Senators to TV titles. It wasn't exactly great poetry, but hey… (Note: the italicized words were titles of programs at that time.)

Gunsmoke from the *Wild Kingdom*

An addict, I watch TV. Whatever is on is fine with me.
Now that my daily fare is switched,
I find that I am still *Bewitched*
By programming that is not fake
But real, and still keeps me awake.
I feel compelled to make some comments
On *Today*'s show's historic moments
With a quote or so from literature,
But sorry, I'm a TV viewer.
Since I've been reading from the screen,
My imagery comes from what I've seen:
The Senators who probe and quest
Put *As Our World Turns* to the test.
(There follow twelve lines about six Senators whose names now are insignificant, and therefore omitted. Sam Ervin however, was the honorable chairman of the Committee.)
As *Let's Make A Deal* plots unravel,
Old Sam Ervin wields his gavel
Like prophet and *Guiding Light*,
He leads us through *The Edge of Night;*
Of Henchmen recalling the *Mod*less *Squad.*
Their testaments sure do seem odd.
(After the Supreme Court ordered that Nixon's secret taping of
conversations in the Oval Office had to be released, fifteen minutes of
those tapes were "erased by accident" supposedly by Nixon's secretary.
I'm especially proud of the last two lines. They were written before the
erased tapes became known. Honest!)
Not *Mission Impossible* if the Senators lucked,
And got those tapes pre-self-destruct.~

Adding to the evidence against President Nixon and his administration were a series of reports by two young, investigative reporters, Bob Woodward and Carl Bernstein from *The Washington Post.* (They jointly received the Pulitzer Prize for Public Service in 1973.) The reporters had a secret source known as "Deep Throat," who fed them leads that eventually helped to untangle the intricacies of the scandal. This series of articles by the two reporters eventually led to a bestselling book titled, *All the President's Men,* that was also made into an excellent movie by the same name. The question repeated over and over throughout the country was, "What did the President know, and when did he know it?"

An aside:
Right about the time that people were asking "What did the President know…etc." Frank and I and the children were visiting our nephew, Don Smith and his wife, Sylvia, who were living in D.C. We were typical tourists walking around the Washington Monument when I was approached by a local TV reporter. His question to me was, "Do you think President Nixon knew about the Watergate break in?"

We rushed back to Donnie's apartment to make sure we saw me on TV being interviewed on the 6:00 evening news. We did get there in time. If I do say so myself, I sounded quite authoritative as I answered the reporter's question with no hesitation, "Oh, I'm sure he had to know. That was his nature."

I was so confident in my answer because of William Manchester's, *The Making of the President 1960.* After the 1960 election in which charismatic John F. Kennedy defeated Richard Nixon for president, I read the book. It was an excellent, detailed account of the entire campaign, but it was especially thorough in describing the differences in the character and nature of the two men. Kennedy and his campaign staff were open and accommodating to anyone interested, especially reporters. Nixon tended to be secretive and controlling even with those closest to him. (Years later we also learned about Kennedy's deceptions.)~

Although Spiro Agnew was not directly connected to Watergate, he was the Vice-President. In that role his problems contributed to the complications. He had been assigned several positions in different departments. Mostly he aggravated rather than accomplished. He got much media attention by the use of colorful expressions like, "If you've seen one slum, you've seen them all," or America has too many "nattering nabobs of negativism." Evidence was accumulating against Nixon. There were those who were willing to bring impeachment charges against him. However, if Nixon were found guilty, Spiro Agnew would become president. Very few considered this to be an acceptable alternative. This complication was resolved when Agnew was charged with accepting bribes and filing false tax returns for many years and also during the time he was vice-president. He resigned from office on October 10, 1973.

The United States had no vice-president. This wasn't so unusual. Previously there had been seven other times when the VP had died or resigned, with a total of 37 years when the country operated without a VP. Fortunately the 25th Amendment to the Constitution was passed in 1947. This was the Presidential Succession Law. It directed that in case of a VP vacancy, the President could nominate a person who then had to be confirmed by a majority of both houses of Congress. President Nixon named Gerald Ford who was confirmed as VP on December 6, 1973.

A month later Nixon subjected the country to his "I am not a crook!" speech. I could hardly bear to watch. As much as I disliked him, still it was sad to hear the President of the United States use such demeaning words to refer to himself. Yet for another year, investigations, accusations, denials, and trials continued to agitate the country. Millions of citizens had begun to doubt whether or not the country could survive the turmoil. However as slowly as the wheels of government seemed to move, they were moving. Impeachment charges against Nixon were being prepared. When Nixon was presented with the certainty of Impeachment proceedings by members of Congress, he agreed to resign on August 1, 1974. He was the first president to do so. Gerald Ford became president. He pardoned Nixon a month later beginning with the words, "Our long, national, nightmare is over." It certainly had been that.

Epilogue to Watergate:
Charges were brought against some forty members of the Nixon administration. Only seven of them actually served jail time; three of them were men closest to Nixon.

John Mitchell was Nixon's law partner and loyal friend and supporter who became the President's "law and order" Attorney General. As such he was the most powerful member of the Cabinet. He resigned that post to become director of the Committee to re-elect the President (CREEP). His was the guiding hand in the shady, illegal practices that produced Watergate. He is the only Attorney General of the U.S. to ever serve jail time.

Bob Haldeman was Chief of Staff and John Ehrlickman was Chief Domestic Advisor. Their names are usually linked as part of the team of closest advisors to Nixon. They promoted some of the practices as well as the cover-up of CREEP, and heaven knows what other nefarious deeds.

G. Gordon Liddy and Howard Hunt were not a part of the inner circle, but they were part of the Special Investigations Group commonly known as "the Plumbers." Their assignment was to stop leaks from the Nixon administration. They worked to accomplish that by illegal phone taps and stealing documents. In an effort to discredit Daniel Ellsberg (Pentagon Papers), both of the men planned the burglary of the office of Ellsberg's psychiatrist.

Four of these men have died. G. Gordon Liddy is currently a radio talk show host who can be heard on some 200 stations. He is one of the other three men who served time but have redeemed themselves in one way or another.

Charles Colson's prison time did have an effect for the better. He had been special counsel to Nixon and was considered by some to be the "evil genius" who was working behind the scenes. Among many other nefarious acts, he hired thugs to beat up peaceful anti-war demonstrators and schemed to discredit the credibility of Daniel Ellsberg. Colson had been an evangelical even then, but seven months in prison changed his perspectives. He started a prison ministry that he called Inner Change. He preached and taught "restorative justice;" that non-violent criminals should be permitted to remain in their communities so that they can work toward restitution to the victim and to the community. President George W. Bush gave Colson's ideas major recognition by accepting his methods into the President's "faith based initiatives." Colson's program has been incorporated in many states, although there are criticisms that restorative justice and restitution are not as important to the results as evangelical converts.

While I was absorbed in hearing John Dean's testimony during the investigation, I knew very little about him. Recently when I was checking accuracy of this material, I was surprised to learn that John Dean was born in Akron and that he went to the College of Wooster in Ohio. Even though he testified against Nixon, he was found guilty of obstructing justice and served four months in a witness protection program. Since then he has distinguished himself by writing numerous books on political subjects. Among them was *Blind Ambition* about the Watergate Scandal, and *Worse than Watergate: the Secret Presidency of George W. Bush.*

Bob Woodward and Carl Bernstein seem to be the biggest beneficiaries of Watergate. Their investigative journalism is a model for aspiring news people. Both men are respected in the field. Woodward is now a managing editor of *The Washington Post* while Carl Bernstein has worked for a variety of publications. Both men are authors of well-received books. Neither man ever revealed the identity of Deep Throat in spite of years of speculation. Finally in 2005, W. Mark Felt admitted that he was their secret source. He had been the Deputy Director of the F.B.I.

Should you see them on TV, or hear on the radio the names of James Dean, or Bob Woodward, or Carl Bernstein or G. Gordon Liddy, on any given day they may appear as political commentators. These are the very same men who played such important roles in the Watergate saga and who have managed to overcome the experience and are still around to tell about it.

CHAPTER 30
SEPARATE AND UNEQUAL

During my two week training period at the Garden Grille after high School, Blanche who was our supervisor, explained the restaurant's policy about serving Negroes. (At that time, Negro, colored person, and black were the accepted terms.) In general they were not encouraged as customers. However, one Negro attorney did come in periodically for lunch. We were to serve him like anyone else, but the hostess would seat him in a room by himself.

One day it was my turn. Even though the dining room with its white cloth tables was half empty, this well-dressed, tall, slim, nice-looking young man was seated in another empty room. I went in to take his order. He was polite and pleasant, ate his lunch, tipped appropriately, and left. At the time, I accepted this practice without question. My world was the white world. I knew nothing about the lives of colored people.

It wasn't until after the racial protests of the 50s and 60s, that I began to understand how offended, and yes, angry, too, that well-educated, smart, well-dressed, young black attorney must have felt to be treated in such a demeaning way. The protests forced people, including me, to confront the basic injustices of segregation. But the understanding did not come easily. It was slow, painful, costly, and disruptive throughout the country.

Segregation was always a part of American life, worse in some places than others. After the Civil War, state by state (with the Southern states being more severe than those in the North) enacted segregation legally with what became known as Jim Crow Laws. Everything about these laws was intended to dehumanize Negroes and to maintain that whites were superior in every way: intelligence, morality, and civil and sexual behavior. These laws kept blacks "in their place" for one hundred years. That place was always as an inferior or worse.

• Famous Negro entertainers or speakers did perform at White hotels and restaurants. The insult came when they had to find a place to eat or sleep that was for "COLOREDS ONLY."

- Marian Anderson, a world renowned Negro contralto who was received by kings, was barred from singing at Constitution Hall by the Daughters of the American Revolution. Eleanor Roosevelt, the President's wife, intervened and got permission for Ms. Anderson to sing on the steps of the Lincoln Memorial. Thousands came to hear her as she sang a beautiful "Ave Maria." (If you Google her name, you can hear her sing it.)
- There were countless rules of behavior that colored people dared not break like: not extending a hand to shake to a white person first; never, even by accident, should a Negro man or boy touch a white female, and on and on.
- Negro maids, cooks, nannies, and other servants who performed intimate duties for their white masters, had to use separate privies.
- On trains Negroes sat in separate cars. On buses they sat in the rear. What made the bus ride worse was that the bus driver could change the dividing line. If more whites got on the bus, Negroes had to move farther back and stand if necessary so that whites could sit. If the bus got too full, blacks who had paid their fare, could be put off the bus.

The Jim Crow Laws were named after a song made popular by a white actor who worked in Blackface. His character was a lazy, stupid, shambling, Negro look-alike named Jim Crow. That image was perpetuated for decades by minstrel shows, movies and radio. In some old movies, that same character is an embarrassment to watch since he bears no resemblance to any human then or now, and yet he became a common stereotype for black people.

From earliest times, there were instances when blacks protested and fought against conditions like these. When any did, one way or another, they paid dearly. The system worked against them. Sheriffs, judges, politicians, and employers were all white. Besides, there were organizations like the KKK (Ku Klux Klan) many of whom were thugs filled with hatred, who resorted to intimidation, beating, lynching, and castration to punish any "uppity" blacks who dared to step out of line.

In December of 1955, one small, middle-aged woman had been pushed around once too often. Rosa Parks was a seamstress taking the bus home from work in Montgomery, Alabama. More whites got on the bus. The bus driver ordered her to give up her seat and stand at the back of the bus. She refused. The driver threatened jail. Ms. Parks had had it. She would go to jail if she had to. What seemed like an insignificant stand by one woman, was the spark that set off the Civil Rights movement.

Dr. Martin Luther King, Jr. was a dynamic, charismatic young minister who was preaching something about his dream of all people being equal. He knew such an idea would be a difficult battle. What made his message extra powerful was that the battle was to be taken up using non-violent methods. What Rosa Parks had done was an example. Negroes in the North and in the South, as well as fair-minded whites, began to respond.

When Rosa Parks' case was brought to trial, Negroes who depended on bus transportation, started a boycott of buses in Montgomery. Those who could not get a ride to work, walked, some of them as much as twenty miles. Yet the boycott lasted for over a year until the law was changed.

There were organizations who had continually worked for equality. The two that were the best known were the ACLU (American Civil Liberties Union) who worked to preserve the ideals of the Constitution for all people. The other was commonly called N Double A C P (National Association for the Advancement of Colored People). Many people did not consider that either organization was working for the general good. Rather they thought those groups were just stirring up trouble. Whites just did not understand the indignities that confronted blacks daily. Each of them lived in a world separated from the other.

Another great source of irritation were the lunch counters that were common in drug stores and in Five and Ten Cent stores like Woolworths. Negroes were welcome to spend their money in these places, but they could not eat at the counters with whites. Teams of usually four, well-dressed, polite, young Negroes were sent out by those and other organizations to challenge the laws. There were sit-ins at counters all over cities in the South. Observers reported that it was quite a contrast between the mannerly, colored protesters seated at the counters, compared to the raucous, poorly-dressed white citizens who showed up to protest their presence.

Probably the grievance that was most disturbing to colored people, was the education system. The whole country was operating under a law that was passed over fifty years ago in 1896 (Plessy vs Ferguson). Schools could be segregated as long as the facilities were equal. States made their own laws. In the North, segregation occurred more by neighborhoods that were clearly either white or Negro. The school reflected the neighborhood.

In 1953 during my second year of teaching at Copley School in Ohio, a Negro boy was placed in my all white fifth grade class. I was given no information about him. Coincidentally from other pupils in my class, I was getting reports of thefts. Whether or not the boy was responsible, I was totally unprepared as to how to handle the situation. Was he the thief, or was it a set-up? (During those times, it could very well have been a set-up.) He came into my class toward the end of the school year. I don't know what happened to him after that, but I certainly didn't help the situation at all, and I don't believe anyone else did either.

People who visited the South back then could see that schools were definitely segregated. The stark truth of actual conditions inside the classroom was not as obvious. The buildings were the barest shells with minimal equipment and facilities. School sports and other activities were pretty much nonexistent. Textbooks were hand-me-downs from white schools, outdated, mistreated, with torn or missing pages. Schools for Negros were anything but equal.

After countless efforts at overturning "separate but equal," the ACLU adopted a very simple principle. Separate cannot be equal. This principle was argued before the Supreme Court by Thurgood Marshall, who later was the first black judge appointed to the U.S. Supreme Court. In 1954, almost sixty years after the "separate but equal" ruling, the Court agreed that separate cannot be equal. The case of Brown vs the Board of Education ordered public schools to be desegregated "with all deliberate speed."

In one way or another, desegregation affected almost every community in the country. In the South where segregation was a part of Jim Crow laws, to obey the Supreme Court decision meant destroying an entrenched way of life. These communities used every resource including police and the National Guard to prevent black students from entering white schools.

In cities where schools were segregated because of housing, like Akron, Ohio or Hamburg, New York, busing became an issue. Hamburg was an all white community. Either white children from Hamburg, or black children from inner city Buffalo, would have to take buses that could add as much as two hours to their days. Some members of the Unitarian/Universalist Church that we attended in Hamburg, volunteered their children to ride buses to achieve integration. Akron was faced with busing children out of their own neighborhoods to go to unfamiliar schools. There followed many years of additional turmoil. President Eisenhower, to help uphold the Supreme Court decision, sent Federal troops wherever necessary to enforce the law. Some encounters were shocking to watch on TV as local law enforcement used dogs and clubs against its own black citizens trying to follow the new law.

It was not uncommon that black churches and businesses were bombed, or that the leaders and their families were threatened, or kidnapped and beaten, or worse. During this period of obvious racial strife, there had been 21 bombings of black churches in Birmingham, Alabama alone. Then on a Sunday in September 1963, a Negro Baptist church was celebrating "Young Day." There were some 80 children and 400 adults in attendance. A bomb thrown from a passing car caused great destruction to the church and injured twenty people seriously enough to be hospitalized. Worst of all, four innocent girls, ages ten to fourteen, in their pretty Sunday dresses, were killed. Negroes, as well as other people, were incensed at the horror that children, or any persons, could be murdered while in church. Riots and demonstrations erupted almost everywhere in the States so that mayors and governors requested Federal troops to try to maintain order.

<u>An aside:</u> After his election as president in 2000, George W. Bush, named Condoleezza Rice, an African-American woman, as his National Security Advisor, and later as Secretary of State. Ms. Rice speaks Russian and French fluently, was an accomplished figure skater, as well as an exceptional pianist. She had lived in Birmingham at the time the four girls were killed and knew two of them.

My son-in-law Hank Jones, is with the security services in the State Department. He was part of the team that accompanied Ms. Rice on one of her Africa trips. He said more than once Ms. Rice was one of the nicest people he ever met.

The four girls who were killed never had a chance to accomplish anything. ~

Young, handsome, inspiring, John F. Kennedy was President. Part of his agenda (as well as presidents before him) was to pass Civil Rights legislation. Just two months after the church bombing, on November 23, President Kennedy was assassinated. The country went into deep mourning, glued to television sets for every detail of this tragedy. None of us can forget the picture of John-John, the President's three-year- old son, saluting his father's casket or the prancing, riderless stallion following the flag-draped coffin in the funeral cortege.

Lyndon Johnson assumed the presidency. He had been a powerful Senator before he was Vice-President and had other assets that worked in his favor. He was very persuasive and not above using arm-twisting tactics to gain advantage. It was also a help that he was from Texas that was considered to be more sympathetic to the Southern viewpoint. Besides, he was shrewd enough to capitalize on the country's sympathy for Kennedy's death. The time was right. Using all of his persuasive powers, Johnson was able to accomplish what other presidents weren't able to do. Now at last after years of divisive conflict, The Civil Rights Act of 1964 was passed by Congress. It meant that the ideals of the Constitution would be upheld for all citizens of the United States. Passing this very important legislation alone could have earned President Johnson a place among the great presidents. Unfortunately to his detriment, he became more deeply involved in the Vietnam War.

Firestone Park where I live in Akron, used to be an all white neighborhood. Before and after the Civil Rights laws were passed, all kinds of dire predictions were being made: desegregation would bring down property values; the crime rate would rise, white girls wouldn't be safe, etc., etc. The area has changed considerably. Of course, it's an older neighborhood, too. My house is almost one hundred years old, but the houses are well-maintained. Property values have not declined. One of the properties that looks almost immaculate, is owned by an African-American family. (African-American became the accepted term for Negroes after The Civil Rights movement.) Another one has a wonderful display of flowers that bloom for different seasons because gardening is the hobby of the African-American lady of the house.

Garfield High School now has a mix of more than half Latinos, Asians, and African-Americans. There are four Asian markets with all kinds of interesting produce as well as teas, and different kinds of rice. It's fun to go in and sample something new to me. A peaceful picture that has stayed with me was when I drove past an African-American and his white neighbor both raking their lawns. They leaned on their rakes and were talking. It crossed my mind that that's as it should be, neighbors being neighborly. Next door to me is a mixed race couple. They and their two children are wonderful, thoughtful people. I couldn't ask for better neighbors.

The major unwelcome difference that I've noticed is the frequency of foul language including the "f" word. But then I realize, it isn't just my neighborhood. It's TV, radio, movies, and everywhere else.

Too bad.

Chapter 31
"THE LITTLE WOMAN"

This is the way we wash our clothes, wash our clothes, wash our clothes,
This is the way we wash our clothes, so early Monday morning.

This is the way we iron our clothes, iron our clothes, iron our clothes,
This is the way we iron our clothes, so early Tuesday morning.

This is the way we sweep the floor, so early Wednesday morning.
This is the way we mend our clothes, so early Thursday morning.
This is the way we clean the house, so early Friday morning.
This is the way we bake the bread, so early Saturday morning.
This is the way we get dressed up, so early Sunday morning.

When I was growing up, this little ditty was sung with appropriate hand motions, by every little girl from her earliest days. All the verses were sung repetitiously like Monday and Tuesday. (Sunday has apparently been politically corrected. I learned it as *This is the way we go to church).*

There was nothing similar for little boys to sing. Boys grew up to be men who went out to work wherever their interests took them. Little girls grew up to be women whose work was clearly defined. Women stayed home and did the household work very much as described in the verses, quite often on the very same days.

The man's role in the family was by far the most important. After all, he got paid for his work. The money was his. He could do with it whatever he wanted.

The wife also worked, but at home. She did not get paid. If she was lucky and her husband appreciated, or even acknowledged her contribution, they were a team and the family benefitted. If he considered his wife and children a hindrance or a burden (and many men did), he did as he pleased. The family had to resort to pleading, or tried to manage on his leftovers, if there were any.

There was what was known as "feminine wiles" that some women were known to use to gain a little advantage, but it took skill and tact. If she was too obvious, she was labeled a "nag." If her husband did mostly as she asked, he was considered to be "henpecked."

Both sexes are blessed with a brain
Which in youth they're encouraged to train,
But girls are mislead.
When they are wed,
In the main, they must rein in the brain.

WWII came along and forced changes in the traditional roles between men and women. As men left for the military, women who had never worked outside the home, learned to do the work that only men had done before. Two recruiting posters were seen everywhere. One was of Uncle Sam, in his top hat and flag outfit, seriously pointing his finger with the message, "Uncle Sam needs you!" Men did voluntarily enlist. So did women. The first women joined the army as WAACS (Women's Auxiliary Army Corps). They were mostly given clerical or nursing duties that would relieve men for battle. Later the Auxiliary was dropped from the name as women proved their usefulness. By the end of the war, they were serving as truck drivers and airplane mechanics. Women served in every branch of the service as WAVES, WASPS, and SPARS. By law there were restrictions: a cap was put on the highest rank that a service woman could reach and, if she had dependents, they didn't get the benefits given to those of the men. Regardless of the limitations, 250,000 women served in the armed forces during WWII. Sixteen women were awarded Purple Hearts for injuries during enemy action.

The other recruitment poster was of a pretty, curly-headed woman holding a tool like a welding torch. She was "Rosie the Riveter." Women were needed to do factory work normally done by men, and they were hired in factories all over the country. Many years later, my neighbor, whose name really was Rose, showed a group of us her factory I.D. card during the war. Her job was stripping a compound between joints on planes to seal the joints. With no hidden intent, the card simply stated, "Rose Mobley, Stripper."

For a brief four to six years during the war, women had the opportunity to do more than household chores. They proved their abilities in countless ways. They managed work and home and children and shortages, as well as the emotional stress of worry for their absent men, their wounds or their death.

And then the war was over. As quickly and willingly as women had assumed responsibilities outside the home during the war, when the men returned, the women just as quickly and just as willingly (for the most part), reverted to their previous roles. To speed the transition, there were subtle and not-so-subtle influences for "all of us" (meaning "us" to be the women) to "make room for our brave men to take their rightful places again." Probably more important during the transition however, was the attitude of the women themselves. They were so happy and grateful when the men came home, that their jobs (not "careers") didn't matter at all. It was easy to revert to the old familiar patterns of division of labor. Men went to work, and women stayed home.

Television was fairly new. "Leave It to Beaver" was a delightful weekly TV program during the early fifties. It portrayed an American family of four: Father Ward, Mother June, and two boys, Wally and Beaver. Ward went to work in a suit. June did housework in heels, beautifully coiffed hair, and a frilly apron. When Father came home, the family had dinner together in the dining room while Mother brought in steaming casseroles to place on the white tablecloth. Ward and the boys were ever respectful of June, but all problems were referred to Ward who made the decisions. Those who are nostalgic about the "good old days," think they remember an idealized picture like that. It may have existed for a very few, but for the majority of families, it was an entirely different story.

His world and her world were sharply divided. Since men rarely experienced a week or even a day of the woman's typical work at home, it was easy for him to assume that while he was working hard to support his family, she was "free" to listen to soap operas or to shop. Only the most perceptive or sensitive men really understood or appreciated the efforts that went into homemaking: shopping for and preparing meals, the hours spent in washing and ironing clothes, and the drudgery of the ever-present dishes to wash and house to clean. As long as the work was done, it was taken for granted.

Not too long ago, a group of mixed-age women were talking about our experiences as homemakers. Helen, one of the older women who rarely spoke on any subject, told of the time she heard her husband and a neighbor discussing furnaces. The neighbor complained about how his coal furnace fumes dirtied the rooms of his house. Helen's husband however, was quite pleased with his furnace. He thought it was because he had a better brand. Helen told us with an odd expression on her face, "My husband didn't know I washed the walls while he was at work. He never noticed."

> Now Dearie, 'tis said God hath wrought
> The part that we play, so we're taught,
> To resignedly drone.
> But we say with a groan,
> Convince us it was not for naught.

Women were a constant target for jokes.

"Who was that lady I saw you with last night?"

"That was no lady. That was my wife."

In the days before turn signals, right or left hand turns had to be signaled by the driver with an arm out the window. The standard joke was that if a woman driver had her hand out the window, she was probably checking her nail polish.

A practice by some men was to stop after work for a drink with the boys. The man who had the courtesy to call his wife to let her know he would be late, was mocked by the other men with big "yuk yuks" or "poor guy has to report."

Casey, Frank's friend, often referred to his wife as the "War Department." This bothered me. After all, she was his wife and the mother of his two children. When I protested to Frank, he dismissed my concern by saying, "Don't be silly. Casey's only kidding. He doesn't mean anything by it."

There were gym classes for girls in schools, but by far, major funding went for sports for boys. Girls weren't encouraged to pursue sports. Parents hoped their "tomboy" daughters would "grow out of it" or "settle down." It was 1973 before Title IX of the Education Act ordered that equal funds (proportioned for the female population) should be set aside in schools for sports for girls. Of course there were dire predictions about this act leading to destroying men's sports in schools and colleges. Instead, women athletes have been encouraged and supported, and sports for both sexes have thrived.

There were different standards for sexual conduct for young men and women. "Nice girls didn't."

They were expected to remain virgins until they married, while "sowing wild oats," a euphemism for sex for young men, was accepted with a wink.

Pregnancy was usually a private matter until it became obvious. Then the husband might acknowledge this to friends with, "Yep, the little woman is expecting," as if it was all her doing. At that another man was likely to comment, "Keep'em barefoot and pregnant, I say. Ha Ha!" It was another "joke" followed with chuckles and a poke to the ribs.

For most couples, birth control information was uncommon. Diaphragms were available to women who could afford the costs of a doctor and diaphragm. For others abstinence was the alternative. It's hard to believe that owning even one condom was a crime in thirty states in the country.

Margaret Sanger, a nurse, was the driving force behind making birth control information available for everybody. She had a personal interest. Her own mother, a devout Catholic who had seventeen pregnancies that included seven miscarriages, died when she was fifty years old. Mrs. Sanger opened her first family planning center in Brooklyn in 1920. It was raided by the authorities. She and her staff were jailed, but her crusade continued. She was the founder of Planned Parenthood whose mission has been, and still is, providing family planning information to anyone who comes to them. Ms. Sanger's major legacy is promoting research and development for The Pill that was approved by the FDA (Food and Drug Administration) in 1960. It was five more years before a Supreme Court decided that birth control information should be available in all the states.

Especially incomprehensible is how rape was regarded in those days. Most cases of rape were not considered to be a crime. There was very little sympathy for any girl or woman who was raped. The social judgment was that she probably "asked for it," shouldn't have been where she was vulnerable, or that she must have done something to provoke or entice her attacker. Attempts to bring charges of force were almost impossible to prove. Very often, not the attacker's, but the victim's sexual history, was used as evidence against her.

Whether sex was consensual or forced, if an unwed pregnancy was the result, it became a major problem. Abortions in the United States (not in all countries) were illegal. However, money made a huge difference in how the situation was handled. With money, a girl could be sent out of the country for a "vacation." Or as happened with one of my friends, she was able to consult a psychiatrist who was willing to state that continuing the pregnancy would be harmful to her state of mind. His prescription made her abortion legal.

If money was limited, there were other options. The young man could do the "honorable" thing, and they could marry. Or the girl could carry the baby to term and give it up for adoption. Or the girl could take a chance on her life with an illegal abortion. It was done under the conditions that were not sterile, by some unqualified person, and still costly for too many. Yet thousands of desperate women died taking such chances.

Or she could choose to keep her child. The consequences for keeping her baby were not as obvious as Hester Prynne's punishment of wearing a "Scarlet Letter" in Nathaniel Hawthorne's novel, but the stigma for unwed motherhood was there. The disgrace was felt so strongly by some unwed girls, that with or without money, suicide might be considered as another option.

"Blossoms in the Dust" is an excellent movie about the life of Edna Gladney, who spent a good part of her life in Texas trying to persuade the state's legislature to remove the word "illegitimate" from the birth certificate of such children. This became Edna's cause when her adopted sister discovered this label about herself just before she was to be married. The sister felt so disgraced that she did commit suicide.

During the earlier years of our marriage, it was assumed by everyone, including me, that I would support and help my husband during his studies. I did so willingly. Most of the time I had a full time job as well as all the usual household duties. Although I admit my house cleaning standards weren't the highest, I did those duties as well as helping Frank with research, proofing, and typing papers.

When it was my turn to go to school full time, a person could assume there might be some help offered with my duties. There was not. I continued all my household work as usual. Frank's help to me was to build a radio from a kit to occupy himself so that he wouldn't interfere with my studies. Honest! Back then I accepted this arrangement without question and was even happy that he "allowed" me to complete my degree. What's more, the college sent my grades to Frank. His grades had never been sent to me.

I did get my degree and taught sixth grade for six years. We also took steps to correct problems in our marriage and adopted two children. There was no doubt but that I would stay home with the children. After all, I was a product of the times. I loved the children. It was a joy to see the almost daily changes in their development. There were also homemaking projects. It was all new, exciting, and fun.

At first being a stay-at-home mom was challenging and satisfying. Without me being aware of what was happening, gradually my life narrowed to the children and me. Of course I could take them places and arrange for play dates and other diversions. I did that, but whatever we did was usually child centered. If I visited women friends, they had children, too. Whether it was adult conversation in person or on the phone, trying to read anything at all, watching a favorite talk show (not a soap), or trying my hand at writing, there were constant interruptions. Sometimes I thought if I heard "Mom!" one more time, I would run out the door.

Once when I was talking to a very nice woman who had eight children, I told her I admired her and asked how she managed with her brood when I knew how hard it was with just two. She answered, "Nobody knows how many times I went into the closet to cry."

I knew exactly how she felt. I loved my children and being a mother, but there were times when my image of me as a mother was spoiled by my own actions. I wasn't always patient, kind, and understanding. Yet, that's what I expected of myself and what I felt others expected of me. When I didn't live up to those standards, there was guilt. There were two men who helped to perpetuate the guilt by their influence.

Sigmund Freud, an Austrian psychiatrist, wrote articles and books about patients of his who were mostly neurotic women. These cases became the basis of his theories about mental illness that were widely accepted in the field of psychology.

The other man was Philip Wylie who wrote *Generation of Vipers.* The book was an uncomplimentary description of American women as compared to women in other cultures. The "viper" in his title was his special target, American moms. According to Wylie, they were so demanding of their children that a cult of "Momism" developed to maintain Mom in the exalted status that she required. His book was a best seller.

Both men had theories and opinions that women caused many mental problems for themselves as well as for their children, especially the sons. The message from both authors was that if a woman was just more compliant and accepting of the role assigned to her, she and her husband and children would be ever so much happier, and the world would be an altogether better place. All the woman had to do was conform. Never mind her own inclinations or talents or ambitions.

Women's magazines, that should have been examining the plight of homemakers, were instead filled with articles that laid all the responsibility of family happiness and success on the shoulders of women. One woman author suggested an occasional surprise to keep a husband interested. A wife might appear at the door wrapped in clear cellophane to welcome him home from his hard day at work. Apparently after her day of work, a woman didn't need attention. After all, very little of what a woman did routinely was recognized as important or worthy of respect.

There was a young wife who expected
That her daily chores were respected.
She cleaned toilet bowl
With pride in her role.
The reward was her face there reflected.

Throughout my life, books and reading were important to me. At times I became so engrossed in a good author's words on the page, that I didn't see or hear anything actually happening around me. My kids learned early on that sometimes the only way they could get my attention was for one of them to lean over whatever I was reading. As a Mom, very soon I relegated my reading or my writing attempts to their naps, or after they were in bed for the night.

I'm not sure whether it was through a friend, or because of a review, or because of plain curiosity, but I did have a copy of *The Feminine Mystique.* The book had gotten much attention because it had some controversial ideas about the part that women played in our society. It sat on the coffee table for a while until one evening when Frank was gone, the kids were in bed, and the house was peaceful. I picked up the book and started reading. The first chapter was titled "The Problem without a Name."

From the first few pages, I couldn't believe what I was reading. Betty Friedan, the author, was describing everything I was doing, feeling, and thinking: the house in the suburbs; the drudgery of housework; the feeling of isolation; constant chauffeuring; and the countless demands on me that were taken for granted with no thanks or appreciation.

I stopped reading and let the book fall to my lap. There were other women who felt as I did. Ms. Friedan had studied and documented them. They were here on these pages. These women who worked conscientiously at being good wives and mothers were asking, "Is this all there is?" Those words hit me in the gut. On these pages they were saying what I couldn't allow myself to think.

There were many other important contributors to the surge toward allowing women more options in what and how they wanted to live their lives. Betty Friedan's book was the breakthrough for me. There were changes in my thinking and in my actions, but they were gradual and many remained private. Maybe Ms. Friedan's book wouldn't have had as much impact if my marriage had been more stable, but I doubt it. The "problem that had no name" was one component. The isolation I felt was real. Too many times it was just me and the children.

The limericks included were some of the writing I tried to do. I probably have twenty or more verses. They were a way of letting off steam. Well then, sez I to myself, "I have them. Why not use them? After all, it's my memoir." A few of my therapy limericks are on the next page.

LIBERATION LIMERICKS

There she stands, the big bust you adore,
On a pedestal gracing your door.
Demeanor so stoic,
An act quite heroic.
As a bust, she's a bust, and a bore.

There was a young single named Bill.
As a host he was proud of his skill.
Invited his steady
To make everything ready,
While Bill did the steaks on the grille.

Both he and she worked every day.
Shared chores seemed the fair way.
But when work was done,
Her chores had begun,
And he chided, "You're too pooped to play."

What joy to be free to explore
All the options that life has in store.
Take the mole in his hole
With his circumscribed role,
To the world, still bores more than one door.

Consider the cost for ignoring
Flyers confined to the flooring:
The clippers who clip
Wings could well trip
On the bird who's prevented from soaring.

Just what are these radical views then,
That threaten men's egos and bruise them?
A terrible thought:
That each of us ought
To choose our own Muses, then use them.

Which is what all this is about:
Until we can find a way out
Of the horrible hex
Of worth based on sex,
Each sex will suffer, no doubt.

CHAPTER 32
THE DARK SIDE

Frank and I were married for twenty-two years, and then divorced. Some experiences that we shared during those years were almost idyllic. I wouldn't trade many of them for anything. But there was another, darker side to the marriage. In writing these pages, one of the hardest parts has been whether or not to include this unpleasant side. After a prolonged inner debate, I have decided to include it. The main reason for this decision is that what happened in our marriage was so insidious that it took me twelve years to recognize that we had a problem. After useless arguments about drinking; after several separations; after countless promises made and not kept; after marriage counseling that I thought was successful, it took another five years to realize that even though we thought we took the right steps to correct them, the problems were getting worse. That's because my husband was an alcoholic. Alcoholism is not a matter of will power. It is an illness. Like other illnesses that go unrecognized and untreated, it gets progressively worse.

The very word "alcoholic" was part of the problem. It conjures up pictures of the derelicts of society like the Skid Row bums. It never even occurred to me to consider alcoholism in relation to my husband. There was nothing, absolutely nothing that could pin such a label on Frank even during the later years of our marriage. He was ambitious. He studied and worked hard. He got and kept responsible jobs. He was reliable and well regarded at work and by friends. Much of the time he was a good husband. These were qualities that helped to disguise the other side. Oh sure, he did drink too much at times, but then so did some of our friends. Drinking was a part of our social life. (Looking back, it probably was not a coincidence that most of our friends were drinkers.)

At first the drinking bouts were so sporadic that each time one happened, it was a surprise all over again. Besides, there was usually an excuse that both of us accepted: a buddy and he stopped for "a drink," somebody's birthday, bad day at work, etc. etc. Except that after a few years, the incidents were more frequent, the reasons less excusable, and my resentments accumulating. There were embarrassments and disruptions. Plans and dinners were ruined. The man who was so responsible in other parts of his behavior seemed to be deliberately inconsiderate toward me. According to him, everything would be fine if only I wasn't the heavy who was making unnecessary waves. And so there were arguments that resolved nothing.

There were other factors that made it harder to identify problem drinkers. During the '50s and '60s, there was a much greater acceptance of drinking and drunkenness. These were the days before MADD (Mothers Against Drunk Driving) who still fight for enforcement of drunk driving laws. Back then it was the rare drinker who would concede to turning over car keys to another driver. If a drunk driver was stopped by police, they were often sympathetic enough to give warnings or repeated tickets.

Wives were expected to be understanding and supportive. If she treated her husband right, there would be no reason for him to drink (or stray, or gamble). If he did any of these, she probably drove him to it. At least that was the common assumption. Of course, I wanted to be the understanding, supportive wife. That helped to create my own doubts. Was I being the nagging wife making unreasonable demands on her husband, or were Frank's drinking habits really as excessive as I thought they were?

After one of these arguments that resulted in a short separation, a condition of reconciliation was that we would get marriage counseling. There followed every Monday evening for three years, a group marriage counseling session with three other couples, under the guidance of a psychiatrist. During that time, every troublesome topic that could be a problem in a marriage was discussed. I did bring up Frank's drinking, but the group's response was to analyze why his drinking bothered me. *No one, including the therapist, ever tried to pin Frank down as to how much and how frequently he did drink, and how he behaved under the influence.*

There were other positive results from the counseling. Issues that had developed in our marriage were resolved. The most important one was that we had stopped talking altogether about having children. By the end of our sessions, we made the decision to adopt. That was the most wonderful result. We adopted an infant son, Christopher, and a year and a half later, an infant daughter, Melissa. As was common then, I quit my teaching job to be a stay-at-home mom. A whole new world opened to us. Both of us loved the children and loved being parents. Our marriage was not only saved, it seemed to be much more stable. We had the two most beautiful and the smartest children ever. We were a family.

During this time, my Mother was diagnosed with cancer. She had a series of three surgeries over two years. She died in May of the year we got Chris. I think of her always and wish so very much that my children could have known this wonderful woman. Except for that great loss, the four years after counseling were absolutely the happiest period of my life.

It was a stable, happy time. Frank didn't stop drinking, but the drinking did seem to lessen and to be much more under control. Another positive development, was that Frank was accepted into the doctoral program at the University of Buffalo. Not long after that however, the same old habits began to reappear. At UB, as in thousands of schools across the country, there were student protests against the Vietnam War and for Civil Rights. Without doubt, there were also added pressures on Frank with his studies and with work. Instead of trying to keep a clear head, for him these were excuses for drinking.

For me it was fear and more questions. We had taken the right steps. I thought our problems were solved. Why was he turning to drink again? Was there anything I could do? Who could I turn to now for guidance or advice? Certainly not to family or friends. There was also my pride. How could I admit that counseling was unsuccessful? Somehow, somewhere, I had to get an objective answer as to why this was all happening again.

I don't remember how I learned about the Alcohol Information Center in Buffalo, but I made an appointment and went. In the office,

I was given a half sheet of paper with 23 typed alcohol related "yes" or "no" questions. I quickly answered 17 of them "yes" and hesitated on six others where I put question marks. The counselor informed me that only three "yes" answers indicated a problem with alcoholism. I sat stunned, trying to absorb what I had been afraid to admit to myself. I had an answer at last, but it was not welcome. My husband was an alcoholic. I was numb. There wasn't much else I could absorb that day. The counselor gave me some pamphlets and advised me to learn all I could.

One of the pamphlets had dates and locations of Alcoholics Anonymous meetings. I went to several open A. A. meetings and was surprised to see ordinary looking people, mostly men. Rarely did any of them look like bums. There was usually a speaker who told his story. One of them was the handsomest man that I had ever seen (including Hollywood). He told that as a boy, he was always fascinated even looking at whiskey. He came to A.A. in his thirties after he woke up in the rain in a gutter beside the road. He was dressed in a sweater and slacks, but what made his story especially compelling, was that he was still a practicing priest.

I also went to several Al-Anon meetings for family members of alcoholics. These were discussion groups where the problems of living with drinkers were discussed. Almost everything I heard from other women at these meetings were what I also had experienced. I wasn't the only one with these problems. I wasn't alone any more. A heavy burden was eased. I couldn't wait for the next meeting.

There was always helpful literature available. One pamphlet was titled "Alcoholism, the Merry-Go-Round Named Denial." It described very clearly what I could recognize as the merry-go-round Frank and I had been, and still were, on. There was also a sad, disturbing picture of the long-suffering wife who was one of the contributors to this pattern of denial. She continually tried her best, and yet it was never enough. I was getting an entirely new perspective on the role I was playing in this drama. The description was sympathetic, but not at all complimentary. Nothing would change until someone had the courage to get off that destructive ride.

For about three or so months, I went to these meetings secretly. I learned enough to give me some hope. If Frank would go to the Information Center, maybe he would recognize that he did have a drinking problem. One day when I thought conditions were right, I told him what I had been doing and challenged him. If he thought my accusations were so very wrong, go to the Information Center and prove me wrong once and for all.

He made the appointment, went, and came home furious. He was given the same 23 question sheet that I got, except he refused to answer any of the questions. His argument to me was that as usual, I was making a mountain out of a molehill. How could he be an alcoholic and do what he was doing? I was the one who had the problems and needed help.

When I got accusations like that in the past, I argued and tried to prove him wrong. These days I was trying not to get defensive. It was true. I did need help. I wanted to continue going to Al-Anon meetings. The result was that for two years after, usually on Monday night, Frank stayed with the children while I tried to learn more and to gain strength for whatever was in the future.

I attended two separate Al-Anon groups and found them to be quite different from each other. I went less often to the one in Lackawanna because it was farther away. The general consensus there was to be far less tolerant of the drinker and his put-downs. It was not at all uncommon to hear, "Why are you paying attention to what he says whether he's drunk or sober?" Because the other group in Hamburg was closer, I went there more often. Overall, this group was much more "Stand by your man." At first, that's what I tried to do.

Frank had reached the last step in his doctoral work, the dissertation stage. He was doing the writing, and I was doing the editing and typing. I had resolved that I would avoid doing anything that could be blamed for interfering with getting his degree. In this one area we were cooperating. Otherwise our marriage was pretty much a facade.

In my two years of Al-Anon meetings, I saw the merry-go-round repeated over and over with other wives. One of them, an otherwise capable woman with a responsible job, would appear every three months or so. The sad part was that she was repeating the same complaints each time, and nothing was changing. Once I got annoyed with her for this pattern. In time I was able to understand her because I was gripped by the same thing. By now I had learned and was practicing one very simple, very obvious rule: "You can't reason with a drunk." That alone changed the dynamics between Frank and me. Unfortunately it was not for the better. Our situation was deteriorating. It was then I realized, that woman and I were both facing the unknown, and whatever the future held, it was frightening.

Through the years, one of the patterns of our marriage was I made threats, in hopes they would bring changes. It took me a long time to learn threats mean nothing if they're not carried out. A lesson from Al-Anon was not to make threats unless you mean them. I was reaching that crisis point. Should I stay on the Merry-Go-Round or get off and take my chances?

I made lists. On the one side were all the problems I would be facing after the divorce: There was still the stigma of divorce. I would be raising two children as a single parent. There would be lifestyle changes, more limited finances, as well as reentering the job market. These were some I could think of. There were probably others lurking. There were two other considerations. I could now see for myself that alcoholism was progressive. Whatever improvements I thought we had made were gone, and matters were steadily getting worse. The most important concern though was the children. Whether I stuck it out or divorced, neither option seemed to be good for the children. And so I stewed and fretted, made more lists, and see-sawed.

One evening at the Hamburg group, a woman introduced herself as Jean. She had attended our group regularly before my time. Jean didn't say much at first, but our discussion that evening must have had something to do with leaving the drinker, when she spoke the words I never forgot, "It's not so bad to be alone."

From her mouth to my ears! No one that I heard had said anything like this at our meetings before. Afterwards I cornered Jean outside on the church steps. It was a warm September evening. She was kind enough to talk to me for an hour or more. We exchanged phone numbers, and she has been my friend ever since.

Jean understood what I was going through. She had survived a similar experience. She was wonderful not only as a sympathetic ear, but also in providing therapeutic escapes. Jean, Missy and I spent a weekend at her parents' home. (Chris was with Frank.) The visit with those kind people was good for my soul, and Missy, who was six years old then, remembers it to this day. Jean was also an admirer of Eda LeShan, a rare woman psychologist who was coming to speak at Chatauqua Institute, about an hour from Hamburg. We went. This is the gist of the story the audience and I heard from Eda LeShan that afternoon:

At a dinner I was seated next to a marine biologist and wondered what we could possibly talk about. After a few small-talk exchanges, he started telling me about lobsters. I was fascinated. Apparently at a certain point in their life cycle, lobsters have to shed their shells. For some time, shedding makes the lobsters very vulnerable, but without shedding the old shell, they cannot grow. I believe that most humans come to a time in their lives that they have to become vulnerable by shedding their old shells so they too can grow.

I was sure that Eda was speaking directly to me. At a time when I was feeling such anxiety and fear, no words could have been more welcome or more inspiring.

Frank did get his Doctor of Education degree. I could not be accused of being responsible for any failure there. But the drinking episodes were an ugliness between us that he chose to ignore, and that I couldn't forget. Somebody had to get off the merry-go-round. I finally made the decision to file for divorce. What should have been a simple process took three years, since he contested the divorce.

The divorce was granted in December of 1974. Chris and Missy were ten and eight years old, and I was 45. I thought I had analyzed pretty well what to expect after the divorce. What I didn't anticipate was that the changes would be as drastic as they were, or that other misfortunes would happen. They did. It was one thing after another, big and small, from my car being totaled by another car with no brakes, to getting a ticket in the middle of a snowstorm because I didn't come to a full stop at a stop sign. It was as if I were under a heavy black cloud that every so often just opened up to pile on another problem.

The first year after the divorce was the hardest. I couldn't have picked a worse time. The country was in a recession. Finding a job was the first priority. The old standby "You can always teach" didn't apply. All jobs were scarce including teaching. I called several school systems and was given discouraging figures like "400 applications and no openings."

Eventually I did find a job in Buffalo. Under the best non-snow conditions, it was a forty minute one way commute so that I didn't get home till 6:00 p.m. or later in bad weather. That was how I learned the I.R.S. was not sympathetic to working mothers. At that time it never occurred to me that something as essential as sitter charges for the kids would not be a deductible expense. The I.R.S. disagreed. In June I got a dunning letter complete with compound interest charges if I didn't pay my government debt promptly. In this case I brought it on myself, but I surely could have done without the government as part of that black cloud.

The house was sold after a year. I thought it would be less disruptive for the kids if they didn't have to change schools, too. I found an apartment close to their school, but it was small and a huge change from the only home they had known with its land and woods.

In one way Frank's irregular comings and goings were less aggravating, but in another way they were worse especially for the kids. His visits with them were more sporadic than ever. Sometimes he would make arrangements to pick them up and not show up at all. Or he would show up an hour or two late while the kids waited and released their frustration and disappointment by crankiness and bickering toward each other and toward me.

I tried my best to plan activities and distractions for the kids with their friends or for the three of us. It was much different for me. The life I thought I had built through the years was gone. There were slights and hurts until I realized that I was no longer a part of the couples' world.

I came to believe that every person could benefit from A.A. and Al-Anon principles. The Serenity Prayer that we recited at every meeting is a bit of profound philosophy:

God, grant me the serenity to accept the things I cannot change;
the courage to change the things I can;
and the wisdom to know the difference.

There were also simple concepts that I repeated to myself often, and in times of stress, constantly. Saying them was like taking a deep breath. *"Easy does it, "Let go and let God," "One day at a time," "Keep it simple."* They seemed to comfort, guide, and soothe. I could stop and think! Nothing had to be done this minute.

Words like those, Al-Anon meetings, family, a few loyal friends, and putting one foot in front of the other even when it was an effort to lift the foot, helped to get me through the gut-wrenching anxieties of those four dark years.

One of the books that was popular in the 1950s that Frank and I both read was *Knock On Any Door.* There was a line from the book that Frank often quoted, "Live fast, die young, and leave a good-looking corpse."

Frank died unexpectedly in 1994. He was 65 years old. My children told me that he did begin going to A.A. meetings a few weeks before he died.

CHAPTER 33

RECONSTRUCTION

Buffalo was in a serious recession in the early 1970s. Steel plants that had been the major industry were closing. As a result the unemployment rate in the area was above 10%. These were bleak times. I was job hunting and took whatever job I could get. One of them, trying to sell office equipment, was a mistake that lasted about two months. The three work experiences that followed were interesting and challenging enough to describe a little.

The manager of a Buffalo nursing home was a nepotism appointee. In spite of constant poor citations from New York state overseers, he was just becoming aware that the State Nursing Home Codes were actual laws that were meant to be followed. I was hired as administrative assistant to bring the constantly changing Code Book up to date and to bring the manager's attention to the changes. His attention span however, was limited.

The professional staff helped to make the situation tolerable. They were all in their thirties, mostly unmarried, and fun. Since I was older, they set out to re-introduce me to the singles scene that had changed considerably during my married years. I am still friends with Virginia Kelley who was then Recreational Director. She is an artist who did the illustrations for my book, *Prisoner Prince*.

Within a year, I interviewed at the Gow School in South Wales, New York that allowed me to cut my commute time in half. It was a boarding school for boys with learning disabilities like dyslexia. The school was founded in 1926, had an impressive success rate, but had done almost nothing with promotion and expansion. The Trustees decided it was time and hired a Development Manager, Jay Longacre, who hired me as the first Alumni Secretary. David Gow was the son of the founder, and my other boss.

Looking back, this was my favorite job, partly for the variety of my duties and partly because of David and Jay. Both men were considerate, told me what they wanted done, and left me to do it.

Jay was gone much of the time, but I worked closely with David. Among other things, we started an alumni newsletter. I researched, located, and interviewed former students, many who were successful in various fields, and wrote the articles. David was the editor-in-chief. The year at Gow School was challenging and satisfying, and two men that I admired and respected made the work a pleasure. In the years since, Gow School has expanded considerably and is thriving.

Just like Eda LeShan's lobster, I was feeling very vulnerable. The life that I thought I had in Buffalo was gone. More than once I had thought about moving back to Akron, but I had my doubts. Could I go home again, or was I idealizing something that might no longer be there? Also, would it be fair to the children to take them farther away from their father? Then several things happened that helped me to decide.

First, in July of 1976, my father died unexpectedly from a heart attack at 72. So many friends, relatives, and neighbors that I had known all my life came to pay their respects that it was like being enfolded with their warmth and sympathy into the comfort of a clan.

Regarding my doubts about the move for the kids, Frank helped me to decide. He saw them on the last day of school in June, but I couldn't reach him to tell him about Pop's death, and he did not call or see the kids again until late August.

Not long after Mary Anne was married, her husband was diagnosed with multiple sclerosis. MS varies from person to person, but it is a progressive disease. Forty years ago, there were fewer medications to retard MS. Besides, Terry's was particularly virulent. Within ten years he was in a nursing home. Mary Anne and I had always been close, but now more than ever, since we were pretty much in the same predicament. We talked about different possibilities, did some investigating, and thought that getting a house together might work the best both for her as well as for me and the kids. We found a house we both liked one door away from Garfield High.

In spite of all the arrangements that had to be made, the move to Akron was completed in about a month. It wasn't too long before I realized the decision had some unexpected benefits. Now it was no longer just me and the kids. Now it was Aunt Marn, Aunt Vicky and Uncle Dick and their three boys. (Uncle Russ lived farther away.) As well there were other cousins around the same ages as my kids, and various relatives and friends. The four of us began attending St. Nicholas Church regularly. We became a part of an extended family and community.

Melissa entered sixth grade at Firestone Park School (where incidentally, one of my classmates from Voris was teaching. She was Mary Lengyel Becker, Jack Lengyel's sister.) Missy's nature is sociable and she adapted very easily to new surroundings. She always did very well with her studies in Hamburg and in Akron and was valedictorian when she graduated from Garfield.

The move was much harder for Chris whose nature was more reserved. He was never fond of school and entered Roswell-Kent Junior High on the brink of the teen years with all those uncertainties, at a time when he could have benefitted from a strong male influence that he didn't have.

The arrangement Mary Anne and I made with the house was not intended to be permanent, but it did serve our purposes very well for six years until Mary Anne took an interesting job as a resource librarian for small rural towns in Iowa. For me the house has been a refuge, a great satisfaction, and is still my home.

As far as employment in general went, Akron wasn't much better off than the Buffalo area. Specifically for teaching, I would have to be re-certified in Ohio by taking additional courses, and there weren't many teacher openings here either. Instead of the usual frustrating, time consuming, disappointing, and sometimes demeaning experiences of job hunting, I lucked out because of old connections. Charlie Anthe, the former chef at the Garden Grille, and his wife, Pauly, and their two grown sons now had one of the outstanding restaurants in northeast Ohio. They were adding a new banquet facility for 500 and hired me as banquet manager. Charlie and Pauly were pretty much retired. I worked mostly with their two sons, John and Jimmy, that I remembered from when they were boys of eight and ten. I worked at Anthe's Restaurant for 18 months. My job was meeting with possible banquet customers, interviewing them for needs, and then relaying those needs to the kitchen and servers wherever the orders needed to go. For the most part, I enjoyed the work and got lots of satisfaction from setting up the procedures, many of which were continued after I left. The worst part of that job was that there was no way to cover my mistakes. I was the only one getting the information from the customers, and it better be right.

These work experiences in Buffalo and in Akron, mostly paid less than what teacher's earn. They forced me to re-think my options yet again. Should I re-train or re-certify, or continue work experiences like the ones I had taken that offered few chances for improvement?

But there was another idea that kept interfering repeatedly. Although I had no particular qualifications for any of the jobs, the work was done to my employer's satisfaction, responsibly, and usually with a minimum of supervision. It occurred to me that if I could set up systems and be responsible working for others, why not try to do the same and work for myself?

CHAPTER 34
INCUBATING OK FAST PRINT

The thought of going into business was a bold idea. In the 1970s, very few women owned businesses. They may have worked behind the scenes with their men, but it was understood that the man was in charge. I had no business experience – didn't even know anyone who had a business. It was nervy of me to consider such a thing, but the thought wouldn't go away.

I had loads of questions. Most important, what kind of business? Where do I start? I did know enough to realize that it took money. I did have some. Was it enough? I surely didn't want to lose what I had. I'd better find out first what I was getting myself into. That's what started me on a year of serious research.

The first two positive steps were: to call SCORE, the Service Corps of Retired Executives (more about them later); and to take a class in Continuing Education at Akron University on "How to Start and Manage Your Own Business." The $45 for the eight week class turned out to be the best investment I ever made. That class became my bible. The instructor (cannot find a record of his name) was a small business owner who repeatedly said, "Talk to people who know. Learn anywhere you can. Research!" Sometimes I didn't understand why I had to do what he suggested, but I did it anyhow, and a good thing I did. I had about six ideas for businesses. As I did the research, one by one they were eliminated. Some needed more experience than I had; others needed too much capital; and one wouldn't have earned enough to support the children and me.

At the time I had not heard the term "business plan," but our instructor taught us all the essentials that went into one. These days if you're planning to borrow money, you must have a BP. My advice would be that even if you don't need to borrow money, do a BP anyhow. It should be what it says it is: a plan for how you will run your business.

In finding answers to all the things that he recommended we know, for me it all seemed to come together for an instant print shop, something that hadn't been one of my original ideas. What decided me was that it didn't take too much capital, didn't require too much training, and most important, there was a need in south Akron where I lived. I developed from a hesitant know-nothing to someone who was making decisions about a possible business based on solid information. I was getting there.

During this year of research, my sister Mary Anne, had been my sounding board. The fun part was picking names for my various business ideas. The one that stuck for the print shop was Mary Anne's suggestion of OK FAST PRINT. The OK was for Olga Kurtz.

One of the many pitfalls when starting a business, is not having enough money to tide you over the months your business is growing. The business term is *undercapitalization.* If you're leasing space, paying utilities, insurance, and other expenses, whether money is coming in from your business or not, the monthly bills have to be met. The way to avoid running into not having enough money to pay those bills, is to estimate monthly projections of what your business might bring in. For me this was the hardest part of all. I considered my figures to be guess work and didn't trust them. In time I learned although the figures were guesses, they were realistic, educated guesses that turned out to be quite accurate. They were used to help me determine how much money I needed to borrow.

I got much satisfaction from different experiences with two bankers I approached for loans. I knew I was bucking the system. First, for a woman to borrow money on her own for anything in those days, was rare. For a woman to try to borrow money for starting a business, especially with no business experience, was almost laughable. The first banker that I approached was at my bank where he knew me by name. I told him what I wanted to do and handed him my papers. He flipped through the papers, started sputtering and asked, "What makes you think you could run a business?"

That got to me. He had every right to ask pertinent questions. Instead, his attitude was at least a put-down if not downright insulting.

He didn't even do me the courtesy of pretending interest. He did question one of my conclusions, but he was wrong, and I knew it. That was sweet!

Without hesitation that same day I approached another banker whose attitude was entirely different. He was receptive and respectful. He led me to his office, looked at my plans seriously, asked question for which I had answers, and then told me he thought I would get the loan. I can tell you, I floated out of his office and out of the bank. When I got the actual check two weeks later, it was without doubt, a high point in my life.

The next three months were very busy. Since a small garage on Wilbeth Road close to Arlington was being remodeled for me, printing equipment was delivered to the dining room of my house. The basic printing press was the A.B.Dick 360 and a service contract from the same company. Their guarantee was that the company would train anyone to use their equipment. The plan was that while waiting to move into the shop, I would learn to print. With manual in one hand, I did learn to operate the machines, but producing printing good enough for actual orders took more doing orders over than I anticipated. I do believe that in my case, the A.B.Dick Co. probably came to regret its commitment. I called on the service department so often that I got to know all the servicemen by name. None of the men at any time were rude or even impatient, although my SOS calls must have been irritating. In later years I described to one of the men whose name was Bill, how my calls were probably received. "The supervisor said, 'Hey fellas, it's Olga again. Who wants to take it?' Nobody answered."

Bill chuckled, nodded, and said, "That's about the way it was." Still, of all the contacts I had early on when times were toughest, The A.B. Dick servicemen were the most encouraging. I appreciated it then and have not forgotten.

My marketing plan had three main parts to reach potential customers. Flyers were sent out to other businesses to let them know about my print shop. Cold calls were to be made to introduce me to the same people. Most important was the Yellow Page ad in the phone book. Also on a length of white butcher's paper in magic marker, I made a huge sign for the large front window of the garage:

OK FAST PRINT

GRAND OPENING OCT. 16

That day I got all gussied up in preparation for customers. I waited. And waited. And waited. Nobody came.

I made cold calls the following days while Mary Anne came with her knitting to shop sit. The flyers and my calls did bring in a very few customers, but total money that came in the first six weeks was under $200.00, and my first loan payment was due. Not at all a good spot to be in. However, my research indicated that for printing, the most productive advertising was the Yellow Page ad. The new phone book with my ad in it was due to come out the first of December. I kept telling myself I wouldn't panic till then.

My information was right. The Yellow Page ad did it. During December, customers came trickling in on their own. Within four months, I had enough business to hire a woman and train her to print while I did everything else. I kept a graph by month of my gross sales. It was a steady upward climb every month for the next three years. Later the pattern was more erratic, but each year showed an increase during the thirteen years I had the business.

Even though women managed and worked behind the scenes in print shops, for the most part the public saw printing as a man's job. When a man came in as a customer the first time, very often his manner tended to be condescending or skeptical of information from me. Although I was never very good at it, by learning to print, I knew the pitfalls. After I explained some more technical printing process in terms he could understand, he knew that I knew my business. When these same men became regular customers and even asked for my advice, it was a private reward. I developed a personal relationship with most of my customers and knew them by name. That was the part I thoroughly enjoyed and missed when I retired.

There were things I had to do that I disliked, like collecting money owed, or firing employees which I had to do more than I ever dreamed I would. I did not work 60 or 80 hours a week like some business owners. I tried to keep a 9 to 5 Monday through Friday schedule but in truth, the business was always on my mind. Also, during the print shop years, a three day weekend or Christmas holiday was my only vacation. I couldn't seem to get a system where a longer vacation was possible. I made up for those no-vacation years later with travel to Russia, China, Thailand, Turkey, Spain, Morocco, Portugal, Italy, and Norway and loved every bit of it.

I did not get rich, but I did make a living and then some for me and my children. If you look around you, that is what most small businesses that survive at all, do achieve. That in itself is an accomplishment, if I do say so. In 1991, I sold the business to a young woman who talked the talk, but had done no research and was not inclined to ask or take advice. She probably thought buying the business and giving orders would be enough. Within five years, the business went bankrupt.

She could have benefitted from SCORE (mentioned earlier), a part of the Small Business Administration. It is an organization of retired volunteers from every area of business who try to help establish and maintain businesses with advice or guidance that is provided at no cost. I went to them for help twice. Also, there was so very much that I learned through the process of starting and managing my print shop, that after retirement, I volunteered at SCORE and have been a counselor for twenty years. I can empathize with some of our clients who come in with an idea for a business and have no idea where to begin.

Been there. Done that.

CHAPTER 35
OUT OF THE BOX

The hardest years were the five years before the divorce, but the five years after it weren't much easier. My life had changed completely, and I was trying to find my way. The trouble with memoirs is that you spend a lot of time in examining your life and coming to some conclusions. But then when I was younger, I had so many more pat answers than I have now. Maybe a part of wising up is to accept that there are very few pat answers and to recognize that conclusions you've made may not always be correct.

It seems to me that for a large part of my life I was playing roles that I thought were expected of me: the good daughter, the older sister, the loyal friend, the reliable employee, the supportive wife, and the understanding mother. Whatever decisions I made in those relationships weren't so much based on what I wanted or even on what was necessary. Mostly I did what was expected. I thought that if I followed the rules, everything would turn out all right. That's why I think the divorce was especially hard. I thought I had followed the rules, and surprise, surprise, things didn't turn out the way they were supposed to. I was in a muddle without guides I could trust.

Not so much in recent times, but for a good part of my life, being part of a married couple was the most desirable and acceptable status. Of course there were men and women who had never married. They were included in the social world of couples, but sort of on the edges, somehow "incomplete." Most marrieds, even those in a poor marriage, didn't consider that remaining single could be a matter of choice. Rather being unmarried was a poor reflection on both men and women, but more so on women. He might not have found the right girl, but there must be something wrong with her that she couldn't hold on to a man. As for divorcees, there was a lingering stigma.

Now I hasten to add, I was not looking to find another life mate. What I wanted to find was an acceptable place for me. I turned to self-help articles and books and followed some of those suggestions: joined a bowling team, went to PWP (Parents Without Partners) meetings, went to singles' dances, and even tried the bar scene as well as a few dates arranged through friends. What I learned through these experiences was that single, middle-aged women, but especially divorcees with or without children, were a glut on the market. And it was a market. At one of the dances, I felt like I was in seventh grade again. The boys were on one side and the girls on the other. Some of the girls were resorting to attention-getting ploys that were sad to see. At the church coffee hour, a recently widowed man was constantly surrounded by women. It took a while until I decided most of that was not for me.

Little incidents along the way helped to reinforce my thinking.

One evening I went alone for dinner to a restaurant. (That in itself is a test of character.) In the booth next to me was a woman with a man, his arm around her shoulder, very attentively talking close to her ear. I have to admit I felt a twinge of envy. The next time I glanced at them, they had a drink, but he was still talking. Inadvertently, my glances continued. In the hour or so during dinner, she may have nodded, but I never saw her say a word. The man never stopped talking. My twinge of envy disappeared forthwith into a bit of insight. Conversation should be taking turns, sometimes shorter and sometimes longer, but give and take; talk and listen. That poor woman was stuck!

I'm not sure of the time sequence of these little lessons, but right about the same time, one of my customers who had a business across the street, asked me to go out. He seemed pleasant enough and was decent looking, so I agreed. No big deal. While we went out for pizza, he told me all about his first marriage. It did occur to me that as far as getting acquainted, he surely wasn't very curious about me, but then I scolded myself, "Don't be making snap decisions. He might turn out to be a gem." When He asked me out the second time, I went, to my regret. It was the same monologue about his marriage, this time embellished with how good he was to her, and how she done him wrong. I could hardly get through dinner. I was reminded of that woman in the booth. Maybe she was willing to tolerate her bore, but

I could not. I would not. Furthermore, why should I even consider doing such a thing?

No question about it, dating is a winnowing process. It's time consuming and takes work to separate out the chaff. I had been through the process once before. I was much less willing to do so again. However I will add that if by some weird happenstance, someone came along who thought I was the best thing that ever came his way, I might reconsider, but he better be willing to listen as well as talk.

The print shop wasn't making a fortune, but the business was steadily improving. My children had acquired some friends. We were attending church, and there were also family social events. It seemed we had settled into our new life. Still Saturday nights were difficult. After all, that was when most people, married or single, had plans. By now Mary Anne had moved to Iowa. Here was another Saturday night. The kids were out and around, and I was alone: no invitations, nowhere to go, nothing to do. Poor me.

Then something clicked. It was as if I heard a voice say, "You know, you can do anything you want. Nothing is here to stop you. Go to a movie. Go for a drive. Visit a friend. Anything." Then the critical question came: ***What would you really like to do?***

Aha! What did I want to do? I looked around. There were records and TV. I had just been to the library, so there were books waiting. The house was quiet. Did I want to go out anywhere? Not a chance. It didn't take me long to realize that what I'd really like to do is start one of those books. And that's what I did.

Somehow that simple question and simple answer settled my thinking. My Al-Anon friend, Jean, was right. It's not so bad to be alone. I've grown to appreciate it more and more.

I was busy with home, parenting, and business, but I had acquired some friends. Besides family, there were a few men and a few married women, but mostly it was single women like me. On a whim one Wednesday, I made some calls to invite whoever could come for Saturday evening. The excuse was to play Trivial Pursuit that was a fairly new game at the time. Eight women did come. We decided we would play as two teams. That decision was a happy accident. As a team tried to come up with answers, the ladies often got side-tracked way off the question. That led to silliness, clever remarks, stupid associations, lots of laughs, and just plain fun.

We had such a good time, that we became a nucleus that developed into monthly Trivial games. These usually included food that could be cover dish, ordering in, or cooking together. We also met for dinners out about once a week, and there were summer day trips. We took in whatever suggestion anyone came up with. Whoever could go, went. Everything was Dutch treat, and we chipped in for gas. Once in a while we got into a serious discussion, but mostly it was companionship and good times. Most important, we were support for one another. Others joined us off and on, but the original group continued meeting for some twenty years. There are fewer of us now, and we are not as active, but we are still friends.

It's easy to mouth platitudes or to fall in with group think. That Saturday night that I asked myself what I really wanted to do was a turning point, and what I've tried to practice since: What do I truly believe? Is that really what I want to do or say?

Wise Shakespeare said it best, "To thine own self be true...."

CHAPTER 36
NOT AS I DID

I must say with pride that Christopher and Melissa, my two children, are now thoughtful, considerate, gracious, sociable, ambitious, productive, and a few other complimentary and honest adjectives I could use, but I don't want to overdo it. Besides, I lucked out. Chris married Sara, and Missy married Hank. It's a pleasure to be around all of them. That is, now that they're adults. For what seemed much longer than a few years, it was not so pleasant with my two children.

Frank's sister Mary and her husband Ted had three children who were eight, six, and two when Frank and I married. During the thirteen years we had no children, I became a teacher and Frank a psychologist. Between the two of us we acquired many modern theories of raising children. I'm sorry to say, we did not always keep our opinions to ourselves. Years later I said to Mary, "Before we had kids, Frank and I had all the answers about how to raise kids. How could you stand us?" Mary gave a little laugh and then honestly said, "It sure was hard sometimes!" I'm sure it was. Nothing cured me of having all the answers about child rearing as much as becoming a parent. This of course will not stop me from continuing to offer opinions. In my own defense though, what I'm offering is the result of experiences after many mistakes big and small.

Chris was six weeks old, and seventeen months later, Missy was ten weeks old, when we got them. (Neither child was officially adopted until nine months later.) At first, it was the wonderful happy glow of having these two marvelous, beautiful babies. I used to say that we couldn't have done any better if we had picked them out from a catalog. Every day it gave me so very much pleasure to watch my babies grow, learn new skills, and develop personalities. Little by little, that's when the problems began to appear. As my beautiful babies became more capable, they also began to assert themselves.

Here was my little darling learning to say the cutest things and struggling to walk. And my, he (I'm saying he because Chris was the first, but most of this applies to both children.) was so adorable when he discovered the toilet paper and unrolled it all over the bathroom and into the living room. What didn't sink in at the time was that a child's development is a continuum. The child will grow. There was very little to indicate that the same wonderful child, before very long, will be defying me in almost everything, and too many times, shockingly topping off a tantrum with, "I hate you!"

That's where I went wrong. What I didn't know was that during those testing years, even had I been Saint Olga, my chances of being beloved were, at the very best, slim. That being the case, I should have been setting very firm guidelines. The hard-earned conclusion that I hold now is that since I was going to be hated anyhow, better to be hated for what was important to me rather than some silly, childish outburst.

Most of us learn to be parents by osmosis, without knowing what we absorbed from our parents. Some of us consciously might reject what we absorbed, but we shouldn't kid ourselves. The model is probably there lurking in our DNA. My parents were authoritative, so of course, I was going to be different. Supporting my modern views was my reference authority, Dr. Benjamin Spock and his book, ***Baby and Child Care.*** It was my underlined, starred, stained, dog-eared, highlighted bible that I referred to more than once daily for whatever uncertainty came up.

Dr. Spock has been accused of encouraging the permissiveness that led to the rebellion of the "flower children" of the 1960s. Child rearing theories and practices before his time discouraged any coddling: no kissing, strict schedules, letting babies cry, etc., etc. I think the accusations against Spock are too harsh. What he did encourage was that parents should consider even infants as individuals with needs at different stages of development and needs that vary from child to child. That made sense to me. Without realizing it, I (and I was not alone by a long shot) carried the advice a tad further by being the modern democratic parent. My practice then was not to give orders, but to make suggestions, give reasons, and explanations. This in turn produced more questions from my darling children and more explanations from me that resulted in frustration for both of us and quite often (oh horrors!) conflict. Furthermore, there were occasions when in spite of my zeal to meet the individual needs of my darling children, my modern, reasonable approach frustrated their immediate needs. What then? Did I assert my wiser adulthood? Sometimes. But when I did, the price was analyzing self doubt. Is it possible that by denying their wishes, what I was doing might leave a permanent scar on my darling children's future psyche? Oh, my heavenly days, and it would be my fault! (No thanks to either Freud or Wylie.)

One night after the kid's were in bed, I was reading a historical novel about a pioneer family. I remember very few details, but the mother was alone with her two small children when something life threatening (prairie fire? tornado?) was approaching. She took the children to a safe place, but had to leave to take care of something vitally important. She sternly ordered the children to stay there, while she left. The children obeyed without question. I stopped reading. The children obeyed!

I knew it was fiction, but that last short sentence did it. I think that's when the parental DNA kicked in. I imagined myself in the same situation, giving the same order. If there really were danger, would my children obey me? The truth hit me. I would have gotten a series of questions with no time for answers, and worse, my kids certainly wouldn't have stayed put. Fiction though it was, that incident made me aware that something was out of kilter. Right about that time I started resorting to answering with, "Because I said so!" That helped a little, but I didn't start soon enough, nor was I consistent.

Michelle and Greg who live next door are caring but strict parents. They have two boys, twelve and five years old. Michelle surprised me one day by saying in fun, but with no apology whatsoever, "My job as a mother is to provide material for my sons' therapists."

Good for her! I wish I had had the gumption to think like that instead of worrying that what I did would scar my children. Cruel, weirdo parents scar their children. Most of the rest of us stumble along and try to do our best. I didn't stop to think that if a parent makes a mistake or commits some injustice (and which of us doesn't?) there is time enough to correct the error many times over and in many different ways. Or maybe being the mean ogre isn't all bad. The teen years come way too fast. The mean ogre might be a means for self preservation.

Under any circumstances it's difficult to be a parent in our culture. The problems multiply when there is remarriage either by death or divorce. Whatever the new arrangements might be, they're surely easier when there is cooperation. When there is continued conflict or disagreement in parenting styles, it aggravates everything. The teenage years are no doubt difficult for any parents. For me, a single mom with recurring conflict, those years were certainly not easy. I remember thinking at times, "How could this be happening between me and the children I love?"

One of my customers at the shop was an older woman who was doing office work for her son's landscaping business. I had learned enough from various customers to know that family relationships in business took extra care. She and I had talked often. I knew she had five children and seemed to get along well with her son and her other grown children. One day she came in after I had a run-in with one of my kids. I must have needed to vent because I blurted out, "Mary, how did you manage to get through the teen years with five kids?" With no hem-hawing whatsoever, she bluntly said, "Oh, you can't count the teen years at all. You have to wait and hope the kids get human again. I'm lucky. Mine did. Now we get along, but it took years." Her words came when I needed to hear it wasn't just me.

"Speak softly and carry a big stick!" Oh, how I wish I had talked less and threatened less as well, and acted on the threats I did make. Talk and threats are useless if no action is taken.

My sister Vicky and her husband Dick had three boys. (Niece Julie wasn't born yet.) I noticed when Dick spoke the first time, without raising his voice I must add, the boys obeyed immediately. I asked Vicky one time how Dick managed to accomplish that. Did he punish the boys, or what? She said the most Dick ever did now was to repeat the boy's name sharper, or to rattle his belt buckle. He never actually used his belt. She did add that earlier Dick would take a boy by the ear if he didn't respond fast enough.

I, on the other hand, repeated myself over and over. Not smart at all. It wasn't until much later when I heard other parents doing the same that I comprehended how futile repetition was. Why should kids listen the first time when they're going to hear the same thing over again? How much better it is to take immediate action no matter how small. It was probably Dick's DNA influencing him, but he sure had the right idea. Get the kid's attention immediately! You can always ease up if you've been strict. It's much harder to get strict if you started too easy. Or, as a wise counselor once told me, "You can't squeeze the toothpaste back into the tube." So true! Vicky also told me that she and Dick did not contradict each other where the children were concerned.

Before I had children, I heard a father say, "Children have to be civilized!"At the time I didn't want to accept such a thought. I've come around to agree with him, at least partly. There are some kids who are downright mean and badly need civilizing. They're the ones whose behavior is destructive; the ones you don't like being around because you have to be on guard. They steal and have very little respect for the property or the privacy of others. They can be cruel to other children or to animals. If it comes to assuming any responsibility for their own behavior, they will blatantly look you in the eyes and lie. These are not childish pranks that can be minimized or excused. These are serious offenses that should have immediate consequences that make a serious impact on the child.

As much as I used to rely on Dr. Spock during the early parenting years, as time went on I started to have a different view of his ideas. My DNA inclination was to assert myself as the parent and adult. Dr. Spock's theories emphasized the psychology of parenting. It could have been my interpretation of his ideas, but the result was that I often doubted my own decisions.

Our local newspaper, "The Akron Beacon Journal," used to carry a column by Dr. John Rosemond, a psychologist and family counselor, who answered behavior and health questions from parents about their children. I wish he had been around when I needed him. There weren't many recommendations of his that I disagreed with. His approach to child discipline was so practical and down to earth.

Not so very long ago, I was invited to a baby shower where the women were of mixed ages. The talk turned to (surprise!) children and their behavior. Kate, one of those present, said she liked Dr. Rosemond's theories. I agreed with her, and the others wanted to know why. Kate said, "Let me tell you what's been going on with my wonderful son, Jimmy, that Bob and I waited for and adore."

Someone asked how old Jimmy was, and Kate answered, "He's thirteen now, but this started about two years ago. At that time Jimmy was giving us problems in lots of different ways, but what finally did it was when our smart, straight A student announced that he didn't like school and wasn't doing any more homework."

Obviously Kate and Bob considered Jimmy's announcement to be a serious offense. The other women responded with: "He didn't!" "Oh boy, I know what that's like!" "What did you and Bob do?"

"For a while we tried the usual stuff like taking away privileges, grounding him, etc., etc. Bob and I were always big on preaching about how each of us in the family has a responsibility. The parent's job is to work and to provide, and the kid's job is to go to school and learn. This time Jimmy wasn't buying it. Our punishments for him worked before, but in this case, nothing was working."

Kate had our attention. You could hear sympathetic sounds as she continued.

"Now you know, Bob isn't one to take this kind of guff from anybody, much less a bratty kid. He was ready to try anything. That's when I remembered Dr. Rosemond. What Rosemond says is that our responsibility as parents is to provide basic needs like food, clothing, shelter. Everything else we do for our children are privileges. So many of our kids live in kind of a paradise of privileges. That's the part I like best. When you think about it, look around at all the things our kids have: the clothes, shoes, toys, electronics, sports equipment, and on and on. What are we, the parents getting in return? Bob says we get too much smart-mouthing and disobedience. I agreed with him. It was time for drastic action."

"So what else could you do?" "Are you going to take a belt and beat the kid?"

Kate sort of giggled, "If we had a woodshed, we would probably have used it, but there was something else. We could take Rosemond's advice and banish Jimmy from his paradise."

"You did what?!" "You didn't throw him out of the house, did you?"

"No, of course not." She giggled again, "We were tempted, but that would be illegal, and we would be negligent. Instead, we decided to remove his paradise. Not only did he get all extra privileges taken away, I took Jimmy to his bedroom with garbage bags. HE was the one who had to put EVERYTHING, except his clothes, in the bags. I certainly wasn't going to do it. His paradise was disappearing, and the whole time I was telling him HE caused this because he wasn't assuming his responsibilities. What's more, if he didn't shape up, his stuff would really end up in the trash. If he showed improvement, his things would be returned a little at a time. It was up to him."

"You must have felt awful!"

"Tell you the truth, it felt kind of good. Don't forget, Jimmy had given Bob and me headaches and worries for quite a while."

Someone asked, "Do you think it's done any good?"

"Well, he is getting his homework done without a fight, at least most of the time, and we're not hearing as much griping about school. That's something."

"How long do you expect to keep this up?"

"When Jimmy slips up, it's still going on. Sometimes I do complain to Bob about how much effort all of this takes. He says, 'You know, I think the harder it is, the more worthwhile the results will be.'"

That last remark that came from Bob just might be the whole parent thing in a nutshell, but it sure is painful for parents to learn.

CHAPTER 37
SEDUCTION

Twice in my life I have been seduced. Not, I am sorry to say, by anything as exciting as a suave, handsome, romantic man. Instead, both times I was seriously seduced by my own words. It didn't start as a passionate romance, but more as a slow flirtation. What you're going to get here, is the slow, sometimes painful development of that romance.

In the days when letters to family and friends were an important means of communication, and more than e-mail shorthand abbreviations, I wrote three and four pages (or more, though my family says not often enough) as well as composing silly verses for family festivities. I also worked on different newsletters and as a newspaper stringer. Those two experiences were probably the first steps down the slippery slope. No matter how limited the circulation of the newsletter, or how small the article, seeing my words in print was alluring. My words took on an aura. I read and re-read them lovingly, which eventually led me to conclude (with no bias, of course) that they deserved to be developed and nurtured. That's what I set out to do.

I enrolled in a night school course, "How to Write and Publish Your Work," at the University of Buffalo. It was taught by a free lance author who had many articles published in various magazines. The class was worthwhile for several reasons. Among them, we were introduced to **The Writers Market**, an invaluable reference whose title says what it is, a listing of most available markets where writers can send their work for possible acceptance. Our instructor made becoming published seem do-able. She also encouraged us to start a writers group to critique each other's work. Of the nine or so in the class, six of us agreed to meet once a month which gave me an incentive to produce work. I wrote short stories for adults and children, opinion pieces, satire, verses, and brought select pieces to the group, whose members offered constructive criticisms as well as favorable comments.

For a stay-at-home-mom, writing seemed to be the ideal solution. I could write at my convenience and still continue my household duties as well as commitments to husband and kids. I had by now file folders full of material. Why not begin to send some of it off to publishers? Each of my entries had to be sent off with an SASE (with appropriate return postage). Then there was the interminable wait for a response, often weeks and sometimes months. It developed that the arrival of the mail was the high point of my day. If there did happen to be my easily identifiable SASE, I sat down before I opened it. Whatever the response was, standing could be tricky. But the aspiring author has to be optimistic. The envelope was opened, only to find yet another rejection. After months of disappointments, it began to sink in that perhaps other work might be a more reliable source of income.

Much of this was going on during the last of the Dark Side years and some during the variety of jobs after the divorce. As alumni secretary of The Gow School, I was able to continue enjoying my words in print through its newsletter. There was even some writing during the OK Fast Print years. Often customers would come in with a need for flyers or something else that needed guidance or editing. To have a part in producing a better product was also satisfying. However, it was not until the print shop was sold and I retired, that I got the second major writing spurt. This time I knew more of the pitfalls, but it didn't keep me from being seduced all over again.

How I got involved with writing books rather than the usual shorter pieces is a long story that I'll try to summarize briefly. Many years ago I heard of a prince that was raised by Indians. For some odd reason that insignificant bit of information stuck with me. Very recently something gave me a hint that that prince might be Marie Antoinette's son. I knew almost nothing about her, and certainly not that she had children, but a little research took me to Marie's youngest son. He did become King Louis XVII of France for a few months, but died when he was nine years old. I was intrigued enough to ask for more material that brought me a two volume, authoritative history of the boy's sad life. It was more information than I wanted, but I skimmed some pages and couldn't stop reading. It was a captivating story. The boy was protected and cared for while his parents were alive. After they were guillotined during the French Revolution, this child of pampered privilege, was ordered by the revolutionary forces to be placed in the care of an ignorant, brutish, cobbler for several months. Later his situation got much worse. He was imprisoned in an isolated cell with no human contact. When he was discovered some months later, he was in rags, filthy, covered with sores and lice, seriously ill, and traumatized. I was appalled at the cruelty to this child. That should not happen to any human or beast.

On C-Span 2 one Sunday, I was watching an "In Depth" interview with Stephen Ambrose, a noted historian who has died recently. "In Depth" is a three hour program where calls are taken from listeners who can ask any questions of outstanding authors. A high school history teacher called and asked Mr. Ambrose how she could make history more interesting to her students. His answer was, "Don't forget the *story* in history."

My feelings exactly. Too many times history is taught through dates and battles rather than through the people and the circumstances in which they lived. I was lucky. My history teachers were able to convey the drama of particular periods as well as to humanize our heroes and the villains. For me, that was the spark. Favorite reading for most of my life has been historical fiction which is a painless way of absorbing history. That's how I learned that Henry VIII of England defied the all-powerful Pope in Rome so that he could divorce his first wife who had provided him with fourteen children. (Only one daughter, "Bloody Mary, survived to adulthood.") Henry wanted the divorce so that he could marry again to produce a male heir for his kingdom. He married five more times by beheading two wives. Sometimes life itself takes revenge. Rather than the son he had wanted so desperately, Henry was succeeded by a daughter, Elizabeth I. That whole story isn't easy to forget.

That's the way I felt about my boy, Louis XVII, the innocent who was caught in the violence of the French Revolution. I felt like I had discovered Charles, as the boy was called, and that everyone should know about his short, sad life. I felt almost obligated to attempt to tell his story and started writing.

The Akron Manuscript Club is the oldest writing group in Ohio. It has been in existence since 1929. The members meet primarily to help improve their writing by critiquing each other's work and by offering suggestions. They also share what they have learned about the publishing business. I had been attending the monthly meetings for about a year and bringing in my usual assortment of short pieces. When I brought in my first writing about Charles, the group was encouraging enough that I continued writing.

At first it was the pleasure of discovering the story and the decisions about how to write it. Who would I be writing for? How much history should be included? What characters to include? I had played around with the idea of having different narrators to present opposing views about the events. Research had introduced me to a few real people that I wanted to include. Several references had identified Turgy, a palace cook who had followed King Louis XVI, Marie Antoinette and their children from the glory of the palace at Versailles to their Tower prison and execution. It occurred to me that Turgy was probably knowledgeable about palace personalities and events, and could be a narrator. . However the only thing I could learn about him was his name and that he was a cook. But I also wondered why a cook would feel such loyalty to a king.

On one of those C-Span2 "In Depth" interviews, one author said he didn't believe in writer's block, and that he often spent hours at his desk gazing out the window. He also said those quiet sessions were productive. What a relief to hear this! I write on the kitchen table. Not only am I a slow writer, but I spend a lot of time just sitting and staring, time that I thought was totally wasted. Now I agree with the gazing author I heard on TV. Mostly that time is not wasted. It seems to me that there is much problem solving during the writing process. The germ of an idea comes to mind. While driving, or doing chores, or yes, sitting and contemplating, options are being considered. Then a decision is made. But there is often a doubt as to whether or not one of the other choices might not have been better. Not that the decision can't be changed, but I tend to get fond of my solutions.

That's how the idea came to me to have King Louis, who really loved to tinker with mechanical things, come to solve a pilfering problem in Turgy's kitchen at Versailles, and why Turgy began to respect the King as well as to identify with him for his craftsmanship.

That's where historical fiction can be misleading. The incident in the kitchen with the King never happened, but I used it to show the King's love of mechanics as well as my own purpose of Turgy's loyalty. Maybe that's how George Washington got stuck with the cherry tree story. (I, however, have been conscientious about including End Notes in my books to explain if the incident never happened, or if I embellished a bit.)

So there I was, nine months later plodding along with a story that I called "Prisoner Prince" when it dawned on me that this might be a book. But adult books are sometimes 80,000 words or more. I had somewhere around 40,000 words and yet I felt I had told the important parts of what I wanted to tell. There was even one chapter on the impersonators of young Charles that included the prince raised by Indians as well as, believe it or not, John James Audubon, the famous botanist, as one of the impersonators. It did occur to me after some time that this shorter book might work for the Young Adult market.

Creeping seduction was whispering, "The book is finished. It's not doing you any good stuck away in a drawer. Why not try some Query letters to publishers to see if there is any interest?"

To create a Query letter that might inspire a busy, often overwhelmed editor to request a manuscript by an unknown author is an art form in itself. After umpteen variations, I must have put together a Query that worked, but again, it was waiting weeks or months for a reply. I did get manuscript requests. The pages were sent off this time not with high hopes, but with the remote possibility of 'maybe,' and again the interminable wait for a response.

Meanwhile as I'm sending off Queries and going through that process, I missed writing. I needed another project and remembered Alexei, the hemophiliac little son of Tsar Nicholas II and Alexandra of Russia. When I started, it really wasn't research. It was sort of a lazy curiosity. I knew movies had been made on the subject, called the library to get one of them, and got hooked by accident.

I wouldn't say that research is my favorite part of writing historical novels, but so many times surprising gems turn up that make it all worthwhile and even fun. It happened several times during *Crazy Spider,* the first time with the movie from the library.

The three Barrymores, Lionel, Ethel, and John were Hollywood movie actors in the '30s and '40s, but they only made one movie together, "Rasputin, the Mad Monk." In this version, Hollywood suggested that the Tsar's niece, Irina, was raped by Rasputin. Those of the Russian royal family who were still alive after the Communists took over, were incensed. That was not true. Irina had never met Rasputin. The family sued MGM Studio, took the case to the Supreme Court of the U.S. and, with a woman lawyer no less, won the case. To me it was one of those interesting historical sidebars that I had to use somehow.

There again was a problem. How can I incorporate that little sidebar into the story without making it sound like a footnote? More mulling and staring, until I came up with the idea of re-telling my own experience with the movie into a character. A high school computer whiz got interested in Russian history through that same library movie. That student's story became the first chapter, and the student's nickname, *Crazy Spider* because of his skill on the Web, gave me the title for my second book. Till then the working title was *Caught in a Revolution.* It didn't appeal much to me either, never mind attracting a Young Adult reader.

Then Jim Hercules appeared in two references. He was an African-American who worked in the palaces of two Tsars. How in heaven's name did he, a young black man from America get to Russia, and why would he go there? At the time I was writing, all I could find about him was his name and the description of the outfit he wore as a door opener in the palaces. Still, I thought he could be an excellent narrator for the Young Adult reader. Since I wanted to describe a little about life in Russia at that time, my solution was to create a biography for Jim and let him tell his neighbors in Peach Creek, Mississippi, his parents' home that he visited, what he saw as he crossed the great Siberian expanse from Vladivostok in the east to St. Petersburg where he found work in the palace. After the book was published, one of my friends gave me a small article that told that Hercules actually was a boxer from New Jersey, but with no indication of how or why he went to Russia. Fine with me. It was not enough information to effect what I had written. By now I had grown attached to my version of Jim Hercules. They were my words.

Another part to putting together an historical novel was deciding about possible art. It seemed to me that pictures, especially portraits were essential. Many pictures are covered by copyright and stored in archives. It could cost $40.00 or more per picture to retrieve any and to get permission to use it. Instead, I decided to ask my niece, Michele Montgomery, an artist in San Francisco, to do the portraits for *Spider.* I was delighted when she agreed and then did such excellent work. Michele had other commitments and could not also do the art for *Prince.* Luckily I knew Virginia Kelley, an artist friend from our days together in the nursing home in Buffalo. She also agreed, and the book benefitted.

Now I was juggling several projects: completing *Spider*, reviewing art for it, revising *Prince* and continuing queries for him, when I heard the seductive voice again, "Might as well start query letters for *Spider,* too." Oh no! My reaction was almost a shudder.

I heard somehow that Stephen King (or maybe it was some other well known author) had a room in his house papered with rejections of his work. I could probably match that, except in my case, I wouldn't want the décor to be a depressing reminder. I have though, kept a record of every publisher large and small that I queried and also kept the results. One day just to reassure myself that all of this effort wasn't a total loss, I tallied the rejections and gave them a rank.

The worst rejection was a form note on a postcard.

The next up was a form letter with an editor's name, but no signature.

A little better was still a form letter, but personalized to me and with a real editor's signature. From these three groups, I have a plentiful supply, enough to redo at least one wall.

The best were those that not only were personalized to me, but also included a sentence or two complimentary to the manuscript and with a signature as well. I have nine of these letters from important publishers. They were still rejections, but to the editors who took the time to write a few kind words, I am grateful. Those letters, along with the members of my writer's group, gave the encouragement that kept me going.

As I'm writing this, it sounds so futile, but there were satisfactions. There must have been. Otherwise, why would I have continued? I may have been an optimist, but not a loony, at least I don't think so. Yet, rather than giving up on what seemed unattainable, a third book about Pancho Villa in the Mexican revolution, was well on its way. Go figure. But I was retired. In the four years or so of writing and trying to get published, I was completely occupied, absorbed, productive, and enjoying the work. Another year and there were three completed manuscripts. Again the seductive voice reminded me, "Time is fleeting! Do not forsake us!" Truthfully, I couldn't. I didn't expend all that effort and time to give up now.

The technology of publishing had changed drastically since the days of OK Fast Print. The digital age allows small quantities of books to be printed by independent publishers. This produced a whole new area of 'print-on-demand" or POD publishing. Most PODs are 'vanity' publishers. That is, authors pay to have their work printed. There are also a few POD publishers who require no payment from authors. In both groups, some are reputable and some are not.

Those POD publishers who are not reputable, have tainted the entire process. An established publisher makes use of many controls to ensure a quality product. Many POD publishers use none. They take the author's money and print whatever they get with no regard for quality. I have seen POD books that are downright shameful: poor punctuation and grammar, repetition of sentences and whole paragraphs, misspelling, and poor or no organization. Obviously, there was no editing whatsoever.

I was not about to invest more money in what might prove to be a dry well. From the 'no pay' publishers, I chose Publish America. Since I didn't know what to expect from them, I kept very close controls on the printing process. For the most part, I am pleased with the finished quality of both *Spider* and *Prince,* and now *The Way It Was.*

When retail sellers order books from an established publisher, they can be assured of quality. With too many PODs, retailers have no indication of what they might get. Rather than taking chances, most of them have refused to look at any POD products. Therefore, some authors like me don't reap the advantages of the new technology. They have a hard time getting their work on store shelves.

At last my works were in print. *Crazy Spider* was published in 2006 and *Prisoner Prince* in 2008. My two babies were also listed on line with Amazon and Barnes & Noble. Our local paper, "The Akron Beacon Journal," was kind enough to review both books, and I'm happy to say, favorably. The Akron library that has been such an important part of my life, bought a number of books that could be available to book clubs as well as a few for branch libraries. Through contacts with thoughtful and helpful friends and my own efforts, I was invited to speak to a number of groups. And, I was receiving small (very small) royalty checks. I thought I was on my way. Not so. It was then that I met the final hurdle.

As wonderful as it would be to have the sales that "Harry Potter" had, I never aspired to be a best seller. I would be perfectly happy with small, but steady sales. What I did learn should have been obvious: any kind of sales at all, depend on books being available on store shelves. I discovered before long that being published is half the battle. The other half is MARKETING. Making the book available to retailers who will be selling them is just as important and also takes know how. There is a good reason why students work toward a four year degree in the subject. Marketing is a complex field with all kinds of connections, techniques, and specialties. I didn't know, for example, that publishers pay stores to prominently display their authors. Also it is true that independent and chain book sellers welcome authors to speak in their stores. The connection is easier to make with independents. As for the chains, it's often difficult to get through to the person who makes the decision and does the scheduling. Whatever marketing methods are attempted or used, all of them require much diligence and have their costs.

About twice a year I try to attend writer's workshops where authors and publishing people speak about their experiences. I always pick up some worthwhile information. The most recent was an author who gave us statistics on number of books sold by the average author. What we hear about mostly are the best sellers who get large advances and then sell millions of books. (Like J.K. Rowling or Bill Clinton.) Our speaker gave us some figures I had not heard before. I wish they hadn't been quite so negative. He told us the average book in print sells about 200 copies, hardly any books at all, a mere **200!** Sales of 10,000 books would be considered excellent. Advice from him and from others as well was, "Keep your day job." For most of us, writing is not the path to wealth and glory.

Writing for me really was a seduction. At each progression, I got in deeper and deeper. It started with the attraction of reading and being transported by words on a page. Then there developed an interest in and affection for vocabulary. There was the attraction of seeing my own writing in print; discovering the drama of history; trying to re-create that drama; and finally, the fulfillment of being published. The trouble is that as in any seduction, the victim is lured into further commitment. My supportive daughter reminds me quite often, "Mom, you have two books published. That's an accomplishment!"

Logically, I know this to be true, but as in any romance, logic has nothing to do with it.

An aside:
Most times after dinner, my husband would dutifully compliment a meal with, "That was good." I suppose 'good' is better than a negative or no comment at all, but as appreciation for my efforts, it was not at all satisfying. Once in frustration, I consulted my dictionary, a worn, outdated Funk and Wagnall that sister Mary Anne the librarian, gave me years ago. It is my favorite dictionary because it's almost as good as a thesaurus. Right where you need them, synonyms are listed for certain words. I turned to 'good' and counted 73 synonyms for the word. Choosing the right word is one of the valid reasons why I'm such a slow writer. English is descriptive, diverse, and versatile. My F&W synonyms even differentiate the nuances of a word. It leaves me with numerous ways to say the same thing. The challenge becomes how to express precisely what you want to say, so I ponder.

I wondered if the same variations are possible in other languages. That information was not so easy to find. It's hard to get accurate language word counts because of verb forms, technical and scientific terms, etc. However, Harvard University in a 2010 study, credited English with over 1,000,000 words and constantly adding new ones, more than any other language.

One of my pet peeves is to be forced to listen to other languages in automated phone messages, or to wade through manuals to find written English directions. Why, I ask in frustration? True, I am aware of globalization, and that we are a nation of immigrants. I have no objection to immigrants. I and my parents are among them. But I feel very strongly that other languages should not be imposed on the American culture. Preserve your own language, honor your heritage, but learn the language of your new country and respect it. English deserves respect. We should be doing everything possible to encourage its use and to improve the way we use it.~

CHAPTER 38
EXOTIC PLACES

Probably if we had had our druthers, we would have taken a safari in Africa or gone to some remote Pacific island. It didn't happen because of time limitations and also because of costs. But when Mary Anne, Vicky, and I first started talking about traveling together, the word that came up quite often was 'exotic.' Vicky and her first husband, Dick, had gone to Germany. Mary Anne and her husband, Terry, had visited Hawaii. My international travel as an adult was limited to camping in eastern Canada. All of us had enjoyed the traveling we had done, but now we were eager for more.

Vicky and Mary Anne were both working, but I was retired. Casually we started talking about taking a trip, but to where and how? I got two brochures from travel agents just to see what was possible. Every variety of trip was available, costs seemed reasonable, and were determined by the number of days and distances. After charting the advantages and costs of several trips that appealed, in 1993 we agreed on a Portugal, Spain, and Morocco twelve-day tour. Morocco in AFRICA was the lure. It included Casablanca and Tangier, both cities glamorized by movies and certainly exotic to us.

In the following pages I'm going to describe a few highlights from each of our tours, but you should know that the experiences I tell about do not include everything we saw or did.

Portugal, Spain, and Morocco - 1993

Our plane landed in Lisbon, Portugal. Our first lunch was outdoors at a café overlooking the Atlantic Ocean. Portugal is beautiful. We'd love to go back and spend more time there. That night we had dinner at a restaurant where we heard *fado* music for the first time. A woman with a deep voice sang this gutsy, peasant, blues-like music that reverberated in the soul. That entire day was an auspicious beginning.

We crossed the border into Spain by bus and visited Seville and Barcelona. Spain also is beautiful with history that includes a

Moorish influence present in much of the architecture. Of course each city had experiences and sights to offer, but should you ever have an opportunity, Toledo, that till then I knew only by its name, is a must see. It is outstanding in its history, its art, and the beauty of its setting. It is a walled, fortress city on an island in the Tagus River that divides and flows around the city. It is accessible only by bridges with gates to the city that are themselves works of art. Most of the city developed during the 13th century, but it had its beginnings even before the 5th century. I bought two books about Toledo. When I look through it, it's hard to believe so much beauty is present in one city. Later we crossed the Strait of Gibralter by ferry into Africa, right past the Rock that looks exactly like the Prudential Insurance logo. It doesn't seem right to describe the natural wonder of the Rock to a commercial logo, but that's how it looks.

From the little we saw of Casablanca and Tangier, their glamour was well hidden. They seemed not much different from other large cities. Marrakech, however, made up for them. Most of the buildings are of a bright orange/rust colored material that looks very much like adobe. Homes are surrounded by the same color walls. Contrasting over the walls are feathery, green leaves of jacaranda trees with brilliant purple flowers. Beautiful!

Morocco is a third world country. Phone service is very expensive and unreliable. The Town Square in Marrakech is where contacts are made just as they were long ago. Everywhere we walked and looked were sights and sounds and smells. There was a man with an ordinary chair looking for customers who needed a tooth pulled. On a tray beside the chair were all the teeth he had pulled. Jugglers and wrestlers were performing. A snake charmer was tootling his flute; wonderful smells were wafting our way from a three-stool counter offering grilled meat. For us it was a culture shock all the more fascinating because it was all so different.

Not far from our hotel in an open field were two young men with a camel. We bargained with them for a camel ride. Normally there would be a stool or platform to step on to mount the camel. This camel obligingly knelt on all fours so we could get on it. I was the first, got on, and sat. What I didn't know was that when a camel rises, it does so hind end first. There I was hanging on for dear life, face down, trying not to slide down over the camel's head that was just inches off the ground. I managed to stay on when the camel stood up on all fours,, but then the animal started moving. I learned why camels are known as "the ship of the desert." My ride gave me motion sickness.

In nearby Fes, we were taken to the Kasbah, the fortress part of ancient cities. It is a maze of narrow streets and alleys with apartments and shops. A donkey bumped my rear as we walked, while a motor scooter with a young couple on it, whipped by; modern and old side by side in constant contrast.

That first tour hooked us. About thirty people made up this group. We traveled by bus between destinations, and got acquainted quickly. Since single travelers pay more, most people traveled in pairs of every mixture. All of them were pleasant and sociable. In less than two days, we were our own cohesive group with lots of travel stories, good natured kidding, and laughs. We had an assigned tour guide with us the entire trip and an added guide for the five days in Morocco. The guides were always helpful. Our luggage was transferred for us. Money exchanges were explained. Must-see sights were arranged. The food was always good and quite often excellent, introducing us to local cuisines.

There is an ongoing difference of opinion between those who prefer independent travel and those who take tours. Independents maintain that they see far more out-of-the-way places and have much more contact with local people. I'm sure that's true, but if I had to make all the language arrangements myself to make this happen, it probably wouldn't. Tours are the answer for me. I'm perfectly happy to go along with the plans of the tour that's chosen. Besides, most tours have optional side trips that are an additional cost. We tended to sign up for almost all of them. We sure didn't want to take a chance on missing something.

Over ten years, we went on six tours. To other travelers that we met, our travels would be insignificant. Some of them went on two and three tours a year. To us, each of ours were unique and memorable experiences that I'm happy to tell about at any opportunity. One of the questions that comes up is "What country did you like best. The answer is "None," because each of them had special, wonderful things to offer.

* * *

China - 1995

Two years later in 1995, Vicky and I decided on a fifteen day tour to China. Overseas to Europe takes about seven hours. Across the Pacific to Japan en route to Shanghai, took over twenty hours. I'm not sure how long because we crossed the International Date Line that tested my comprehension. For the length of those flights, Japan Air Lines was the way to go. Later in our travels, in contrast to other airline crossings to Asia, we could compare JAL very well in comfort and service.

I'm happy to say we've had very few unpleasant experiences in our travels. This one was the first. Our tour guide was to meet our group in Shanghai airport. Vicky and I were in the back of this huge, full plane and were among the last to get off. It was late at night. Hardly anyone was around, we didn't speak the language, and there was no guide to meet us. Near panic, scary! But we calmed down, realized we had our tour information. We found a polite young Chinese man who made sense of our predicament and told us in halting English that we could take a hotel bus that would be here soon. What a relief to find our guide and group at the hotel. Our guide had waited for us, but apparently, not long enough. This time there were sixteen in the group. Five of them were an interesting, friendly, Chinese family from Brooklyn that was going back to a small village to visit their roots and relatives.

We visited five cities in China, and Hong Kong as well, and flew between cities with Chinese pilots whose takeoffs and landings were near perfect. Shanghai is the largest city, our first in China, totally interesting from the moment we landed. In the European part, there was a raised wall promenade where every activity was carried on including speeches, musicians, children's performances, and line dancing to American music. Also, everywhere were street vendors, but the shock was from our room window. When we looked out at night, there were only a very few lights, not at all what you would see in other major cities of the world. We later learned that China has far less electric power than it needs so that sometimes there are blackouts.

The Shanghai station where we waited to board for a three hour train ride through the countryside to Suzhow, was itself an experience. It had curtains at the windows and overstuffed sofas and chairs much like a 1930 living room in America. Where Shanghai was a city of skyscrapers, Suzhow was picturesque, old China with sampans, laundry fluttering from homes, and traditional architecture with carvings and curved rooftops. Here was China. We did a lot of gawking here and all through China.

Our next city was Beijing, the capital. Our hotel was quite modern with a full orchestra playing western classical music every afternoon. One of our first scenes was the sheer magnitude of Tiananmen Square. The pictures on TV, where not so long ago the government used tanks and weapons to subdue anti-government demonstrations, gave no indication of its size. The Square is immense with the entrance to the Forbidden City on one side, and the gigantic rectangle of the People's Republic government building on the other. Photographs of people in front of the building look like insects.

A few miles outside the city was the most visually powerful sight all of us agreed that we had ever seen. It is the Great Wall of China snaking over the mountains as far as the eye can see. It is a humbling, overwhelming sight, unforgettable and truly awesome. Vicky and I took a walk on it. It is wide enough for a truck, and about every fifty yards is a guard tower. We looked over the wall on both sides. On the outer, enemy side, the drop to the ground is maybe two or three stories below the wall. On the other side, the drop is not nearly so deep. A Chinese mother, father, and son near us were also taking pictures. With smiles and lots of hand motions, we traded posing for each other. It's one of the very few pictures from this trip that Vicky and I have together.

China is a Communist country, but it is undergoing profound changes. Mae Li was our guide throughout the tour. She was a government trained young woman in her late twenties. She was pleasant, knowledgeable, always helpful, and spoke excellent English. Everywhere, in front of large buildings or small alleys, we saw carts, tables, bikes or even blankets with displays of everything (including a mesh bag of snakes) on display for sale. To us this was non-communist free market. In answer to our questions, Mae Li explained that some years ago, the communist government realized the collective farms were not the panacea they had expected. These huge farms were divided among the farmers in 99 year leases. The deal was that 40% of whatever was grown was given to the government as rent payment. The farmers could keep or sell the rest. This drastic change-over to individual ownership was and is a huge success. Unproductive collectives became thriving small farms. The result was what we were seeing: free market entrepreneurs selling anything that comes from a farm in any space they can find.

In spite of what we knew about human right issues in China, in no way did we feel restricted, that is, as long as we kept with the tour plan. Usually Mae Li was very accommodating, but twice I asked what I thought were simple, certainly non-threatening, requests. Once was on the train to Suzhow, where we were in a car with white tablecloths, fresh flowers, and served hot tea. There were empty seats, but no Chinese. I asked if I could go to the car with Chinese people. I had read this was a unique experience. The other time was when Mae Li pointed out the direction where Beijing University was. I asked if we could possibly drive through the campus. Both times the answer was a firm "No," with no reason offered, and a quick subject change.

Remarkable artistic and historical treasures are the terra cotta warriors discovered by a farmer in 1976 outside the city of Xian. This is a full army of thousands of sculptures complete with horses, carts, weapons, and soldiers with armor and facial features that make them individuals. An emperor may have ordered these to be created to protect him in the afterlife. They are displayed in a structure built right over the excavation site. Visitors can walk on a ramp surrounding the site for close-up views. All of the sculptures are life size and were buried for centuries, yet they are extremely well preserved with most being intact. This army is being excavated during the past twenty-five years. There could very well be thousands more still buried.

In Xian I got sick with a hacking cough and much fatigue that refused to get better. It gave Mae Li and Vicky an experience both could have done without. Mind you, there are no convenient drug stores for medicine. In a situation like this there are practical problems like medical translations as well as possible conflicts with other medications. Mae Li found an English/Chinese medical dictionary and a woman doctor. Somehow we agreed on some kind of a shot. I spent the next day in bed, but did improve enough to continue the trip. Poor Vicky had spent two scary days considering worst scenarios. At the beginning of the coughing, one of our tour members gave me some eucalyptus cough drops he had that did help. From him we learned that it was smart to come prepared by carrying a pharmacy.

At the city of Guilin, we boarded an open-sided boat for a three hour cruise on the Li River, probably one of the most scenic landscapes anywhere. The Li has eroded a meandering path through the mountains that have left huge rock formations of such a variety of shapes that all of them have been given names like "Elephant Trunk" and "Snail Hill." Some are cone peaks, but all shapes are blanketed with greenery so they look like green silhouettes. Along the river bank are narrow strips of farmland with water buffalo at the water's edge, and graceful fronds of bamboo tree branches swaying in the breeze like immense Hollywood fans. It is beautiful and serene. Some pictures show scenes when there is a mist that gives a fairy-like quality.

Hong Kong is a major world port and a free market business center. It has been a British colony since 1841. The big unknown when we were there was what would happen to the city when it reverted to Chinese control in 1997. The agreement was that it would not become Communist, but there were doubts. (As I write some fifteen years later, the fears were not justified.) We did take a cable car ride to Victoria Peak where we got a panoramic view of the harbor with huge liners, freighters, as well as sampans and junks, just like pictures.

It is true that in China there are human rights injustices and that the print press is controlled. Although we had no contact with slum areas or dissidents, the overall impression that we came away with after our visit was that for the general public (non-dissidents) this is not an oppressed society. Just the opposite. We saw an awful lot of Chinese people bustling about their daily business with good nature. The scene that comes to mind is the traffic. Bicycles are still very common transportation, but there are more and more cars and trucks and more pollution. In spite of all the congestion, it's hard to believe that there are very few stop signs and traffic lights even in the large cities. It seems that chaos would be the result, yet traffic moves steadily and with a minimum of hostility. A few main routes have bike lanes, but mostly cars and trucks make room for bikes, bikes move for bigger vehicles, and all vehicles take turns at crossroads. This was remarkable to me, and I commented about it to the group. One of the men said, "You didn't see the accident? Two men were going at it hot and heavy." I didn't see the accident, but for the hours we spent on the bus in heavy traffic, one angry incident is a pretty good record as far as I'm concerned.

Always breakfast and most lunches and dinners were provided as part of this tour. Breakfast was continental style at the hotel. Lunches and dinners were very efficient; all self serve at a table for eight with a large turntable in the center. Always there were two soups in tureens; always bottled water and tea and usually at dinner either wine or beer for those who wanted it; and always there were 6-8 entrees and rice. The entrees were well flavored with a variety of meats and one or two vegetable mixtures. There was ample food, but somewhat of a disappointment. Chinese is one of the great cuisines of the world. We made a large circle of travel in China which should have introduced us to different schools of Chinese cooking. Instead it was mostly Cantonese style that seemed to be geared toward tourists. We once got what was called Peking Duck. I've roasted duck. What we got was very much like mine, nothing Peking about it.

Once I heard a commentator say that where the U.S. makes short-sighted decisions usually for the profit, the Chinese make plans for the next century. I'm inclined to agree. In spite of profound, historical changes, China has maintained stability. Our next trip to Russia was a sharp contrast to China.

* * *

Russia - 1997

First I have to say up front that our Russia visit was wonderful in so many ways. There were sixteen people in this group including Vicky, Mary Anne, my dear daughter, and me. Also a part of our family group was our friend, a Vietnamese/American doctor, Thien Chu, that we met on the Morocco trip. This one was a ten day tour. We visited St. Petersburg and Moscow in September of 1997.

The beginnings of Russia date back to about 1000 A.D., but it has had a complicated and rich history. In spite of the damage done to churches and tsarist era treasures by the Communists, there is much history, art, music, architecture and beauty to see and hear. The five of us thoroughly enjoyed each other's company without the usual distractions of home, and the rest of the group were interesting and fun. But our first evening in St. Petersburg was as unpleasant as it could be. I'm going to tell about it not to bad mouth another country, but to show conditions as we experienced them.

The breakup of the Union of Soviet Socialist Republics (U.S.S.R.) into separate republics came in 1991. Russia is one of the republics. The security of free education and healthcare, pensions, and full employment (as basic and corrupt as it often was), was suddenly gone, and there was very little left of legitimate government functioning to ease the alarming downslide in conditions for the people.

We left New York City on a pleasant, fall evening. It was a long, crowded and cramped flight with a five hour layover in Helsinki, Finland. Our total travel time amounted to about twenty hours. We arrived in St. Petersburg hungry and badly needing rest.

St. Petersburg is the second largest city and considered to be the cultural center of Russia. Most international airports at such an entry try to reflect the best image for their countries. On our arrival in St.

Pete, there was nothing to indicate this importance. The place was dimly lit with an altogether drab and shabby appearance, no art, no ads, no busy hustle. We waited for our luggage by the rickety carousel with its torn rubber strips. We waited and waited. No luggage. To make matters worse, our tour guide, who would normally handle such inconveniences (that can happen any where) was not there to meet us.

Some of our group found an office while the rest of us waited. Vicky started snapping pictures: of the shabby office with one end of the carpet left uncut in a dusty roll; of the attractive woman clerk at the desk; of the young soldier in camouflage with a serious looking rifle in his arms. This uniformed young man moved toward Vicky with a frown, shaking his head 'no,' and with hand reaching out for the camera. It was a scary moment. Vicky's hands were trembling as she tried to open the camera case to take out the film to give him. That made just enough delay for a well-dressed, good looking, woman in a business suit, to interfere. She spoke a few words to the soldier who immediately turned away. The woman nodded at Vicky, and just that quickly, it was over. Later we wondered what civilian woman was important enough to have the authority to give orders to a soldier.

The woman at the desk, who spoke excellent English, requested that each of us fill out baggage claim forms. During that time, our guide did appear. She was an attractive young woman who introduced herself as Marta. She was very apologetic and explained that the delay was because someone wouldn't allow her to enter the passenger arrival area. Most of us agreed that this kind of a snafu at a major airport was unheard of. Marta spoke to the clerk who by now had learned our luggage was still in NYC. She also emphasized several times that this was an American error, not Russian.

It was now about 8:00 p.m. The temperature had dropped to a cold 45 degrees, and our warmer clothes were in NYC. At our hotel, there was a buffet waiting for us, but the servers had to stay two hours longer because of our delay. No one made us feel welcome, sympathized, or even smiled. The food was the worst: the cold cuts looked dry and greasy, and the hot foods were cold and greasy. Nothing was appetizing. We thought a bottle of wine would warm us up and maybe improve the mood. Too late we realized we probably should have ordered vodka. The wine was almost vinegary.

Tour brochures explained that hotels in Russia were either 'good' and $500 and up per day, or 'tourist class' and reasonable. Our hotel was selected for its central location and considered to be clean and adequate. Fine with us. It doesn't have to be fancy, but after a day of travel or sightseeing, it is a quiet refuge. Missy and I came into our room expecting that.

The one lamp provided dim lighting and that didn't help the somber colors. More important, the drape was blowing. Apparently the window was left open. Missy went to shut it and couldn't, because the window was so badly warped, it wouldn't close. She pulled it to as best she could, and we both hoped for the best.

The shower was a flexible, hand held tube over the tub (not unusual in hotels in other countries). Missy tested the hot water because we knew it could be erratic here. It was steaming hot. Good. A shower would be nice. She lathered her hair only to have the hot water stop altogether for no reason. Her anticipated, welcome, hot shower ended with a cold water rinse in a drafty room with warm robe back in the States. To top everything off nicely, the towels were not even a rough terry cloth. They were instead small, kitchen-size tea towels that some maid in her infinite wisdom had stiffened with starch and ironed.

Meanwhile in Vicky and Mary Anne's room, the toilet had to be flushed with the flexible shower hose. Towels were the same in both rooms except theirs were also threadbare. Our solution was bed, sleep, and hopes for a better start tomorrow.

A good night's rest helped. Breakfast was in the hotel dining room. There was plenty of good, hot coffee and tea, but nothing traditional like bacon or pancakes. Mostly it was bread, butter, cheese, and hard cooked eggs. At best during the tour, the meals were nothing to brag about, but adequate.

There was no word about our luggage, but most of us had some things in our carry-ons that we could layer for warmth. It was good that a bus tour of St. Petersburg was scheduled because the day was dismal and cold.

Tsar Peter the Great did much to try to make Russia more modern and more European. He needed a port in western Russia. He built St. Petersburg 300 years ago on 100 islands of marshland all connected by bridges. The city is beautiful. Because of the marshes, none of the buildings are taller than five stories. The variety of architecture comes through the pastel colors, the designs, and artistic details on the exteriors. It was a relief when our luggage arrived that evening.

In St. Pete there were three outstanding experiences. The best was a visit to The Hermitage, considered to be one of the great museums of the world, second only to the Louvre in Paris. Part of the Hermitage complex is the Tsar's Winter Palace. We toured both of them in one day. What we saw was overwhelming: original art by Rembrandt, Cezanne, Da Vinci, and so many others; a room all in white set for the Tsar and his family; and another room full of objects made from malachite, a semi-precious stone common to Russia. As in any great museum, repeat visits are the only way to do justice to what is there to appreciate.

Another sight was the Tsar's Summer Palace at Petrodvorets. Even though it was a gloomy, drizzly, cold day, the layout of the grounds and gardens was awesome in its symmetry and beauty.

The quality of ballet in Russia is considered to be top-knotch. We were privileged to see the Kirov Ballet Company perform "Swan Lake." The grace of the entire company was beautiful to see, but the leaps, twirls and pirouettes, most *en pointe* were breathtaking. From St. Pete, we took an all night train ride to Moscow that was an experience in itself.

At one time or another on a tour, there is usually something that happens that requires celebratory imbibing. Probably Thien prompted this one since he presented Vicky with a bottle of Cointreau liqueur. I had a plastic shot glass. It turned into a happening with everyone in our group collecting in our small compartment as the bottle and shot glass were passed around. I led the singing with the chorus of one of Pop's Polish Army songs (in Polish that the group learned). We sang Dark Eyes, *Ochki Chorniya,* in Russian that nobody knew, but we were strong on the la, la, las. Mary Anne led "On Top of Old Smokey" since she was the only one who knew all the verses to that one, and we all finished with "You Are My Sunshine." That scene was filed in my memory bank.

During the night when we were alone, Missy was startled by someone trying to break into the compartment. She must have said or done something that scared the intruder away, but in the morning, one of our group reported that some money and a camera were stolen.

The restroom on the train was not pleasant. By the time we reached our hotel, my first question at the registration desk was, *"Po Zhaluste, toilette."* Nothing subtle about it. It means, "Please, the toilet." Mind you, I asked a hotel employee. She directed me up the stairs to a dead end office and no toilet. I could not have misunderstood since she pointed the direction. I tried to excuse her directions as not being deliberately misleading, but it was hard to excuse.

Katya was our guide in Moscow. She was an older woman who lost her pension after the breakup. She was not sympathetic to the new conditions since she had to continue working. Katya looked and dressed much like pictures of Russian working women, no sense of style and on the stocky side. There seemed to be a generational difference in the appearance of most women. The younger ones were style conscious and used more makeup.

Our rooms in Moscow were better. A big plus was that the hotel was adjacent to Red Square where all important celebrations and military parades are held. At the edge of the Square on one side are the red brick, high walls of the Kremlin that is the seat of government. Inside the walls, we saw Vladimir Lenin's body on display. Every day it is visited by citizens who come to pay their respects.

St. Basil's Cathedral is on another side. Pictures don't exaggerate this structure. It is colorful, showy, and impressive, and in an unusual way, beautiful. In front of St. Basil's, Thien took a picture of the four of us together. Each of us have one or more of these pictures on display in our homes. Being together at St. Basil's was very meaningful.

St. Basil's is truly unique. That is exactly what Tsar Ivan "The Terrible" who had it designed and built, wanted. This Tsar deserves his name. To ensure that nothing like this cathedral would ever be replicated, besides many other cruelties to his subjects, Ivan ordered that the architect's eyes be removed. Not all tsars were such tyrants, but Russian rulers have always been absolute autocrats.

Susdal and Vladimir are two small towns about 60 miles outside of Moscow. They are tourist attractions because both are being restored. Leading to them is a two lane road with very little traffic. We went by bus so were able to see a little of the countryside. On either side of the road are small, individual houses very much like small houses in my neighborhood, but with a huge difference. Near me the lawns are cut, pretty with flowers and shrubs, and the houses well maintained. In Russia the houses were seedy looking, yards overgrown with weeds, broken or rusted fences, very few flowers, and very little to redeem the overall drab look.

Susdal is a restored 17th century all-wooden village. We were lucky to hear the church bells on the grounds of the monastery. As we passed the bell tower, we saw the bell ringer who had ropes tied to his ankles and hands to ring the bells. He looked like he was jiving to the rhythm as he tugged the ropes. It was a mini concert. Our dinner that evening was in the monastery. Afterwards, three Orthodox monks harmonized on *a capella* hymns. Lovely!

It was dark on our return to Moscow. Our driver stopped in the middle of nowhere with the lights left on. Before long a car stopped and four young men approached. The driver went out to them, and all of them went behind the bus. Of course, the questions and rumors started not knowing if it was a possible hi-jacking or what. Katya spoke to the driver and then told us it was a flat tire. She also explained to us that service garages and gas stations were few and far between. Drivers often stop to help one another just like these men stopped. For reasons like these, very few woman drive cars, especially not in unpopulated areas. The young men helped to fix the tire, got in their car and drove away, and our bus went on to Moscow. On the rest of the way back, there were no lights on the road. We did see lights from windows in homes, but not what looked like the bright lights of electricity; more like the dim glow of oil lamps.

The last day we spent at the Moscow Flea Market. It was a bit disturbing to see soldiers with Kalishnikov rifles at the entry, but our bus went in, and we thoroughly enjoyed as much as we could cover. The entire Market was huge. It covered a large paved area as well as a good-sized, grassy meadow. In stalls and booths and on tables, there was everything for sale: the ever present souvenirs like the nesting Matrushka dolls, wooden decorated eggs, and all kinds of trinkets; hand sewn and used clothing, knitted and fur hats; breads and pastries and produce from farms. A quartet of women in traditional costumes and tiaras were harmonizing very well on Russian folk songs. What was unexpected and what we enjoyed very much was the meadow where every genre of artist set up an easel, or his or her art displayed in any improvised manner. Some of the artists spoke English so that we were able to ask questions. The Flea Market was a great finish to a fascinating tour.

What I'm going to describe next may not be totally fair, since the observations are based not on the country as a whole, but on two cities. It would be like making conclusions about the U.S. by visiting only New York City and Chicago. But these were not just my observations, but our family group as well as most of the tour group. So many things about Russia were unexpected that they were often topics of conversation among us.

Our family has always been proud of our Russian/Ukrainian heritage. Most of the people we grew up with were sociable, caring, fun loving, hard working and with other favorable qualities. It was a real surprise to us that in Russia, among what we expected to be "our people," we saw hardly any of these qualities—certainly not friendliness or caring, and very little interest in providing any kind of service. Usually even on a tour, there are a few casual opportunities to make a connection with local people. Apart from our two guides, these connections did not happen in Russia at all. On the subway (and they really are showcases with sculptures and chandeliers) in both cities, there were no smiles or eye contact. In the Moscow subway right across from us, was a family with two children. None of them acknowledged our presence in any way. At best in too many situations it was as if we didn't exist; at worst there was rudeness, as when we tried to place an order and others barged ahead of us. At the hotel bar while we tried to get his attention, the waiter served everyone around us, but not us.

We tried to understand. Were Americans still considered to be the enemy? Is it possible this could be a national inferiority complex? After all, for seventy some years the people had been led to believe that the Communist system was the best. Then in a very few years the whole thing fell apart in a shambles. That kind of uncertainty was bound to have an effect. Did their living conditions make the people so distrustful? Had the Communist system conditioned the people to offer as little service as possible? In the ten days we were there, we saw ten minutes of sunshine on our very last day. Could this continual gloom affect the general mood?

We had interesting discussions, but came to no conclusions, except that we were sorry to see this great heritage of music, art, dance, literature, and history reflected in such inconsiderate, short-sighted behavior.

Another observation bothered me especially. It seemed that whatever was done in the USSR under Communism was fifth rate, like our hotel, the airport in St. Petersburg, and other examples too numerous to describe. Even to our untrained eyes, this shoddy work wasn't recent, but due to decades of government practice. It seems to me that something so obvious wouldn't take the CIA to deduce that the conditions in this country were anything but a thriving system. All the USA would have had to do was wait for the system to collapse from within. Instead, we spent billions of dollars in an arms race with the USSR. What a waste of resources that could have been better spent to benefit our own country and people and Russia as well.

Both China and Russia are in profound transition. The long history of both countries was by absolute rule from the top. However, where Communist China has maintained stability, the breakup of Communist USSR six years before our visit, brought lawlessness and hardship to the people in most of the republics. Our observations certainly weren't scholarly or deep, but we felt sorry that the people of the great culture of Russia have such a distance to go to improve their lives.

* * *

This chapter is the longest in the book, and there are three more tours to describe. I'm going over the limit of incidents I set for myself (surprise!). However I will continue to write, and give you permission to stop reading if you so choose. O.B.K.

Turkey - 1998

A fourteen day tour of Turkey was our choice a year later in 1998. Vicky and I and our friend, Linda Pence, traveled together and again, Thien Chu who lives in Los Angeles, joined us.

Turkey and Morocco are both Islamic countries, and both are friendly to Americans. That's a good start, but in addition, very soon we concluded that Turkey was for us a well kept secret.

Turkey is an ancient country. It has served as a trading crossroad between Europe and Asia for centuries. Its history is complex, but in the 1920s, Kemal Ataturk instituted reforms that helped to bring a medieval country into the modern world. Ataturk is revered as "The Father of Modern Turkey."

We made a wise tour choice. Many tours to Turkey cover only the Mediterranean coast. Our tour made a circle to Ankara, the capital. The farther east you travel in the country, the more fundamental the Islamic practices. Turkey's eastern border touches on Iraq, Iran, Syria, and Russia. The people are more nomadic and more backward.

We visited some of the oldest ruins in the Near East, and walked in areas that Alexander the Great conquered. We visited the city of Ephesus to whose people St. Paul wrote "A Letter to the Ephesians."

There we also visited the little house where St. John brought St. Mary to live after her Son, Jesus was crucified. In Istanbul we saw the Blue Mosque, St. Sophia's cathedral, and the Topkapi Palace, all of them spectacular in art and architecture. And then there was the overwhelming Istanbul Bazaar with its maze of shops and stalls that display and sell everything, not only made in Turkey, but made all over the world. Two sights among many others however, are unforgettable.

Near Ankara is Cappadocia, an area covering many square miles that has one of the truly unique landscapes of the world. It has volcanic shapes that have been sculpted by wind and weather into huge moonscape formations. Many of the shapes are cones, some several stories high, others with mushroom caps. What we saw had no vegetation at all so that they vary in color from beige to steel gray. What the forms did have were windows and doors. For centuries past, these formations were excavated to act as homes and towns that were hiding places from various conquerors. Early Christians hid in them to escape the Romans. Living areas, storage rooms for provisions, and ventilation systems were developed within the formations. Today some of these spaces are apartments and hotels. On Google, you can see pictures of modern interiors. But to look at the landscape is as if you were looking at an alien planet.

I had heard the term "whirling dervish," but had no idea what it meant. In Turkey, we had the privilege of seeing an authentic group of whirling dervish practitioners. This is a sect of Islamic ascetic monks who whirl to achieve a state of ecstasy for meditation and prayer.

We entered a very plain room with benches along the walls where we were directed to sit, and an open space in the center. There was steady background music of soft drums and flute and a somber atmosphere. One figure in a long, brown flowing robe (really a one piece dress) and tall head covering appeared to begin the ritual. The music changed. About twelve men entered the center space. They wore long robes like the leader had, only theirs were white. They also had tall white hats that looked like a top hat without the brim. Slowly they began to turn in place. Every posture of arms and head had a symbolic significance. Gradually the speed increased to a stately, steady twirl. The full robes expanded like an umbrella, and the arms took prescribed positions. The monks moved around on the floor, always twirling, but with intense concentration during the thirty minutes or so of the ritual.

When it was over, most of us came away speechless. I think we were trying to comprehend this extraordinary practice.

It seems almost disrespectful to follow what I just described with this next story, but I have to tell it. Vicky was the star. She and Metin, the young man who was our guide, had a kidding back and forth relationship. One of our planned visits was to a pottery factory. There were several other busloads of tourists present. We were all seated on benches in a very basic, dusty, factory setting. In front of us was a pottery wheel. The host asked for a volunteer, and Metin "volunteered" Vicky. She went up to the host, was provided with a covering to protect her clothes, and sat at a stool beside the wheel. All she had to do was work the treadle with her feet and work the wet clay with her hands as the pottery wheel turned.

She began pedaling, took the wet clay and began shaping it. It looked like she was trying to form something slender like a narrow vase, but the clay wasn't cooperating. Just as she worked the form to an appropriate height, the clay began to sag and lose its shape. There were a few chuckles from the audience (maybe in sympathy), and Vicky tried again. Her hands molded and manipulated the clay while her feet pedaled. She was obviously working to keep the shape erect. Not good enough. The form wilted again.

The audience began to catch on to what they were seeing. Chuckles became guffaws. And Vicky, in what seemed to be innocent bewilderment, continued pedaling and stroking. In spite of her best efforts, at just the right size, the shape would go limp and droop, and the audience roared.

About an hour later as people were leaving, there were comments like, "That's the best pottery demonstration that I'll ever see!" One woman said to another, barely loud enough to be heard, "I have something at home that acts just like that."

There is no record of Vicky's starring performance. Nobody in our tour (including Thien who videoed everything) taped her show. They were all watching and laughing too hard.

On one of our last days in Turkey, we were at a rest stop that also had Turkish souvenirs. I bought two bagsful and then went to use the facilities. Several Turkish women, not in the coverup burkas but with head scarves, were there. One of them with smiles and gestures, offered to hold my bags. I gave them to her with no hesitation. Immediately it occurred to me that this could be a stupid move on my part. However, a few minutes later, there was the woman, again all smiles toward me, and from me, too as she gave me my bags.

It was a small incident, but it was a connection. I'm glad I took the chance. Now years later, I can see the Turkish woman's smiling face clearly. She is a part of my warm memories of Turkey.

* * *

Thailand - 2002

Smart Tours was a company that other travelers told us about. We went with them to Turkey and liked the price and accommodations. Since we were on their mailing list, I read all the brochures if only to salivate. When I saw a fourteen day tour to Thailand for $1273 with air fare included, I started recruiting anyone to join me. It was a disappointment, but for some reason nothing worked out. When I saw the same tour for the same price offered the next year, I resolved to go even if I went alone. That's what I did. On Saturday, February 23, 2002, I left Akron for NYC and a flight to Seoul, Korea and then on to Bangkok, Thailand.

Probably the nicest thing I can say about Thailand, is to describe the people. Thai names are long. Our guide was a young woman whose name was unpronounceable to most of us. She asked that we call her Nok. Besides being knowledgeable, Nok was at all times, smiling, helpful, courteous, and friendly. She was a constant example of Thai people in general. The contacts we had were mostly like Nok. The dominant religion is Buddhism that may also account for a gentleness and good humor that I felt and experienced as well. One day I sat on a bench with two teenage girls who were peeling an odd fruit I had never seen. It looked like it had red spikes protruding from the skin. The girls saw that I noticed. With friendly giggles, they offered some to me. I couldn't help but compare this incident if it had been in America.

Restaurants everywhere often have themes in décor. We went to a restaurant in Bangkok that is probably one of a kind in the world. At the beginning of the AIDS crisis, Thailand had an alarming increase in the disease. A wealthy citizen took AIDs education to a very basic level. He opened a restaurant called "Cabbages and Condoms." The theme throughout was safe sexual practices all presented with humor: posters on the walls with cartoon condom characters; safe sex rules on each step leading to the upstairs; a gift shop with the usual key chains and T-shirts, but with comic safe sex subjects. The art everywhere kept us chuckling. No doubt we enjoyed ourselves. Besides, the food was excellent, here and throughout the tour. Thai cuisine has just the right mixture of sweet, sour, spicy, and hot (the hot can be milder for the uninitiated) that is a special treat for the taste buds.

Southeast Asia culture goes back to prehistoric times. Many temples that are still beautifully preserved date back to the 12th and 13th centuries. The architecture for all of them is very ornate with spires that are carved and decorated with mosaics, porcelain flowers and shapes in many colors, and gilded as well. Other temples have pagoda roofs and are also ornate.

One day we visited the Imperial Palace in a sixty acre complex that is beautifully maintained. Like the temples, every building was artistically decorated. The square in one courtyard had sculptures of spirits, dragons, and other mythical beasts. My eyes didn't know where to look. There was beauty everywhere.

In contrast we took a bus trip north to a tribe of hill country people. Thailand is a tropical country. On the way we saw poinsettia, rhododendron, and orchids growing wild along the road. When we got to the village, we saw extreme poverty; one and two room wooden huts with open spaces between the wall boards. There was one standing pipe with a spigot for running water for the whole village. The men were away working in the fields. We saw only small, skinny women and children with beautiful faces, but dirty with runny noses and bare feet. All were smiling and friendly. The women were eager to sell their small, handmade items.

Later on in the same trip we stopped at a one room school, every space filled with children. There was no electricity, only sunlight filtering into a dim room. Most of the children were barefoot. There was a blackboard. The teacher was a man, the children were reciting, and the atmosphere was informal and cheerful.

One of our stops was at an elephant camp. We arrived early enough in the morning to watch the elephant families frolicking in the water and spraying each other. There was also a performance by the animals and their *mahouts*. These are trainers who often start working with a particular elephant when they both are very young. The elephants did all kinds of work that brought "Oohs!" and "Look at that!" from the visitors. There were great comedy routines, too.

Almost everyone took a ride in the *howdah*, a two-seater like a roller coaster seat, on the elephant's back. Our *mahout* was a young man probably in his early twenties who sat with his feet behind the elephant's ears. In more commercialized tourist places, this probably would have been a ten minute ride. In Thailand it was a forty minute ride through woods, up and down hills, on a narrow path only wide enough for the elephant's feet, and a steep ravine on the outer edge. We called it an "Oh, my God!" ride. We heard the words often enough on the trail. None of us regretted taking the ride, though.

The Mekong River and the "Golden Triangle," where the borders of Thailand, Laos, and Myanmar (formerly Burma) abut, were familiar words to most of us from Vietnam days. A cruise on the river took us past interesting fishing villages and scenery along the way. The unforgettable sight though, was the border town with Myanmar. We could not cross the border, but we could see. At 6:00 p.m. while we were there, everything: cars, people, police, and traffic; everything stopped in place while the national anthem played all over the country, then and again at 8:00 a.m. No question but that we got a glimpse of a police state.

Early in our visit, we took a small rowboat tour through the canals of Bangkok. On the banks on either side, there were lovely residences with landscaped yards right next to very humble small houses. Not everywhere, but many of both kinds of homes had a small house, bigger than a bird house, on a pedestal on a corner of the property. Nok told us that these are "spirit houses." The spirit houses are built and maintained by the owners. The belief is that since these spirits have protected and cared for the land throughout time, the current owners want to encourage the spirits to remain, so they provide a place for them to stay. Sometimes the owners leave offerings of food or small gifts for the spirits. We also saw these spirit houses in front of banks, large stores, and all kinds of businesses throughout Thailand.

Spirit houses sort of encapsulate Thailand and its people for me.

Italy - 2004

I don't remember why, but for several years, nothing much was being discussed among us regarding major trips. It had been two years since Thailand for me, and six years since Turkey for Linda Pence. We were both restless and ready. After the usual elimination search, we decided on a ten day tour to Italy. Lois Hawk, a former neighbor and her daughter, Laura, joined us. We left from JFK Airport in NYC, on November 6, 2004 to Milan, Italy and then to Venice. St. Petersburg is sometimes called "The Venice of Russia" because of its rivers and bridges, but the city also has roads. In Venice, the canals *are* the roads. The city was built on hundreds of islands all joined by curved, picturesque bridges higher in the center to allow the standing gondoliers and other water traffic. Venice is the most expensive city in Italy because everything, all supplies have to be brought into the city. Still it is very cosmopolitan with high-end shops of leather, glass, lace, clothes and very smartly dressed citizens.

At the gondola stand, (a water taxi) each boat had a distinctive, elaborate décor that adds much to the local color. Our gondolier serenaded us in a not-so-good-bass voice, but since we were drinking champagne toasts between the gondolas, we weren't too critical. All along the route, we saw wonderful buildings, some of them hundreds of years old. We couldn't help but be impressed with the engineering accomplishments. Their foundations were on salt-treated wooden poles sunk into the water, but mind you, hundreds of years ago without modern construction equipment. Some of them are now being replaced with steel poles, but it is remarkable that the wooden poles lasted as long as they did.

Our bus took us from Venice through the countryside of farms, vineyards, rolling hills, and the tall, slender, tapered cypress trees that make it Tuscany. We traveled through Padua, Pisa, Florence, and Sienna. Each of these cities had beautiful and unique sights to see. Always there were cathedrals; In Padua however, was St. Anthony's Basilica. The difference is that a basilica also has some Christian relic. In Padua, it was St. Anthony's jawbone in a small chest set in an all gilt alcove. The interior of St. Anthony's was memorable because it had alternating perfect bands of black and white granite on the same column. How could this be done? Granite doesn't come that way.

Of course there was a stop at the Leaning Tower of Pisa, but it was a cold, drizzly day, so we were back on the bus after taking a few pictures.

The high point of the trip so far was Florence where we toured the Uffizi Art Gallery. Here were many original, old master artists that we had only seen in pictures before. There were too many feasts for the eyes. Repeat visits would be the only way to do justice to all that was on display. When we came out of the gallery, there was Michelangelo's fourteen foot tall Statue of David on a pedestal. The Master formed the ideal body of a beautiful young man. Details of hair, hands, veins, ribs, and muscles as well as his thoughtful face, all of it there chiseled in white marble.

Sienna is a charming town with, of course, a cathedral. Attached to it is a building with a display of the most exquisite illustrated medieval manuscripts with lots of gilt, beautiful colors, and infinite detail. It's hard to imagine how human hands and minds had the patience to create such artistry on such a small scale.

Florence and Sienna are not far from each other. From their earliest beginnings, there was a fierce rivalry (including wars) for territory. Rather than more bloodshed, the two city-states agreed to settle the boundary lines peacefully. Some genius suggested they use roosters and champions. Each city would choose a runner as champion. The runners would begin the race when the rooster in his city crowed. Wherever the runners met, would decide the boundary line.

The canny Florentines pulled a fast one. They kept their rooster totally in the dark for five days and then exposed him to artificial light. Of course, the rooster crowed early, and the runner from Florence gained the most territory. There is a purpose to my story, honest.

The whole area of Tuscany is chianti wine country. Some of the wine is excellent and some is not. The quality wine must pass approval. The symbol of the stamp of quality is the rooster on the label. If you like chianti, choose the one with the rooster. I told this story to a friend who kept a wine cellar. He checked his bottles of chianti and was pleased to have roosters among them.

Should you have an opportunity to visit Rome, do not go in the summer during tourist season. The day we went to the Vatican, our guide set bus time at 8:00 a.m., and a good thing he did. There were already groups of people lined up before we arrived. After us there came an endless stream. The farther back you were, the longer you had to stand and wait in the hot sun, and this was November. By 9:00 we were inside and on our way to the Sistine Chapel. We were entering a world of wonders.

There is a long passageway lined on one side with sculptures, some of them pre-Roman. On the other side are wall-size Gobelin tapestries of Biblical and mythical stories with minute details. To me it was incomprehensible that human hands could have woven such intricacies on a loom.

Then we entered the Sistine Chapel. Every surface is covered with something beautiful done by masters of art. Below the ceiling in other strata are portraits of popes. Below them are immense wall-size paintings of the life of Jesus on one side and Old Testament stories on the opposite wall.

And then there was the ceiling. Michelangelo spent four years of his life on his back with paint and water dripping into his eyes and on his body as he painted the frescoes. Not too long ago, the ceiling was meticulously restored. The colors are now bright and true, but small dark rectangles were left in places to show how candle smoked and dismal they had become through the centuries. All that glory that we were able to see was previously clouded. The Sistine Chapel itself was worth the trip to Italy. It seemed almost sacrilegious though, to pass by so many masterpieces in such a superficial way.

On every tour there are photographers and there are picture takers. The serious photographers keep a notebook, number their pictures, and then describe that picture in the notebook. When they get home, they can name what they saw. Picture takers on the other hand, keep clicking, and label nothing, so that at home, some structures are hard to identify. We picture takers make flippant comments like, "Seen one cathedral, seen them all." Or "Seen one ruin, seen them all." Not being students either of architecture or archeology, cathedrals and ruins, as awesome as they are to see, at home without labels tend to get muddled together.

Everywhere in Italy there is continual restoration to preserve these treasures for the future. Many countries and companies of the world are contributing in these preservation efforts, not only for altruistic reasons, but because it's also good business. Thank heaven for this farsighted outlook. The Coliseum is one of these efforts.

I thought the Coliseum would be only part of the outer wall like the common picture of it. When we drove up to it, it was fun to see entry gates numbered like modern arenas, except the numbers were XIII and XIV. Then we passed through the gate like a Roman spectator, and there was the whole arena before us with its three distinct tiers of seats. Paolo, our Roman guide, explained the lowest tiers of marble were the best seats for the elite; next were the tiers made of bricks for the middle class; the top tiers of wood were for the plebeians. The best part was what we could see now. Half the arena floor was being restored as it had been with a wood base and sand covering the wood (to absorb blood). The rest of the floor was not being replaced so we could see the labyrinth of cells for animals and gladiators under the wooden floor that Roman spectators never saw. The idea behind the restoration was not to redo the whole thing, but enough so that today we could see what it had been. It surely did that. The Coliseum now to me was much more than another ruin.

Rome was built on seven hills with the Forum on one of them. We walked on the road leading to the Forum on the original, large cobblestones where Julius Caesar walked. Smaller stones are being used where the road is being restored, but the large stones must have made a bumpy chariot ride. On the originals, we couldn't gawk and walk and talk, but that was a problem in many other places, too.

To sum up the Italian trip very briefly, I came away from Italy with a much greater respect for its contributions to the world. What a wonderful heritage Italians can claim.

Norway – 2009

My daughter Melissa and her husband Hank, lived in Oslo, Norway for three years. I visited them in September of 2009. Of course, I had a wonderful time with my children. That was the best part, but there were some experiences I would like to describe.

Missy took me on a two day trip, "Norway in a Nutshell," across southern Norway from Oslo in the east to Bergen on the west coast. The trip was mostly by train so that we could see the beauty and variety of the country. Part of the beauty was bridal-veil-like waterfalls that streamed down from mountain tops to the valleys below. Not only are they beautiful to see, but the falls supply hydroelectric power for the country so citizens don't get electric bills.

Part of this trip was a bus ride that was a knuckle gripper, but worth it. After each breath-taking hairpin turn on the mountain road, it was one lovely view after another.

There was also a boat ride on the Bergen fiord. What makes a bay a fiord, is that the mountain comes right down to the water's edge. There is a narrow ledge of land at the harbor for a few necessary businesses, but the rest of the city climbs up the mountainside. Bergen developed as a trading post during the 17th century. Historical parts have been preserved or restored. We took an open, small electric train ride that took us above the residences and gave us a marvelous view of the colorful buildings around the fiord. That scene is still vivid in my mind, although all of Bergen is picturesque.

Norway generally is very family oriented. On the train there was a compartment with toys, games, and interesting things for children to do. Parents could sit in seats near this compartment so that they could keep an eye on their kids. Many times on streets, I saw that even toddlers walked alone as they followed parents. There seemed to be a sense of security that no harm would come to the children. Of course that was before the bomb episode by the warped Norwegian man in the summer of 2011. What a shame if such a thing could change the atmosphere even in peaceful Norway.

In Oslo there is wonderful Vigeland Sculpture Park. There are some 200 life-size granite groups of figures that depict family members in different kinds of activities: children playing, families hugging or picnicking, grandparents with children, and one of a child crying alone. The park is beautifully landscaped, with large enough for spaces to walk or sit between the sculptures. It is a lovely, outdoor art museum honoring family.

I have often heard Norwegians being described as a "hardy people." I found this to be true on the first walk with Hank from the airport to public transportation to the apartment. There are many cars in Oslo, but it is an old city with narrow streets and limited parking spaces. Public transportation is excellent and driving is discouraged. People walk. That's all well and good, but there were also several sets of stairs on that first walk. I relied considerably on the handrails while people all around me were bounding along at a goodly pace. My first indication of "hardy" was when I was surprised by the palm of my hand. It was black. Oslo is a clean, orderly city. Apparently however, "hardy" Norwegians don't find the need to use handrails.

Missy and Hank had a very nice, homey apartment on the third floor. It had one drawback. No elevator, and 48 steps up to reach it. That first day, I took three rest stops on those 48 steps. I am pleased to report that by the end of the visit, I could usually (not always) do all 48 steps with no stops. All it takes is practice and the incentive of comfort to come. That was cocktail time while the three of us, under Hank's expert direction, prepared a yummy dinner. I thoroughly enjoyed my entire visit.

On Off Broadway - 2011

This was a short trip, but an unexpected Happening to four senior ladies and one tolerant younger one who shared a recent trip to New York City.

Mary Anne and I and a couple of friends in Akron, and Vicky and some friends in Florida for the last three years have been going to the HD live performances from the Metropolitan Opera that are being offered in select movie houses around the world. We got hooked from the very first opera not just by the music, but by all the extras that included interviews with the stars, conductor, engineers, and any other behind-the-scenes creators responsible for the production. Besides, there were the wonderful close-ups of the performances as well as impressive interior views of the opera house itself.

Mary Anne and our friend, Marie, started talking about how great it would be to actually be there. It got to be more than talk when Mary Anne did some research and much coordinating. She learned that tickets for any opera would not be for sale until August 1, 2011 at noon. At 12:15 that day she was on the phone and five of us had tickets for a performance of "Don Giovanni" for Tuesday, October 25.

On Monday the 24th, Mary Anne, I, our niece Julie, and Marie flew into La Guardia airport. Vicky flew from Boca Raton and met us there. The five of us took a van/taxi to our hotel that was on 77th Street at the corner of Broadway. (Remember the location. It's important). The Belle Claire is a very nice, small but picturesque hotel with pleasant rooms, attentive service, and close walking distance to essentials like food and shopping. Vicky made the arrangements, and they were what we had hoped for.

Mid-afternoon Monday there was time for super good hamburgers at the 5 Napkin (its name) and some quick stops to check out interesting shops. Then back to the hotel where for a short time we were at loose ends until we consulted the concierge who offered a suggestion for the evening that turned out to be a winner. But first so as not to minimize the purpose for our trip, I want to describe our Tuesday opera experience.

None of us knew that Lincoln Center was a complex of buildings with the Metropolitan Opera as one of them, Avery Fischer Hall as another, and Julliard School of Music across the street. Part of the Met building is the Gift Shoppe. Nothing was souvenir-like. Here was quality, as it should be.

The interior of the Met is grand with elegant, wide, curved, red carpeted staircases like parentheses on either side of the entrance to the restaurant where we also had dinner reservations. I tried not to gawk, but I'm not sure at all that I succeeded. Our dinner, the service, and the ambience altogether were wonderful.

One of the most impressive sights were the chandeliers. Pictures don't do them justice. They look like exploding stars. There were several huge starbursts and smaller satellites randomly surrounding them everywhere we looked and inside the auditorium, too. The interior was just as we had seen it on film; the main floor with its stage, and five tiers of balconies in a semi-circle around it, and all filled with people. Our seats were on the second tier to the right of center.

The orchestra and the singing voices were absolutely beautiful, but also amazing in another way. There is no sound amplification for the voices. Somehow, either because of skill or acoustics, the smallest pianissimo tone can still be heard in the highest balcony. In contrast, when the chorus, or a solo, or the orchestra cuts loose at full strength, the sounds reverberate in your body. Either way, it's goose-pimply to hear. We thoroughly enjoyed Mozart's "Don Giovanni."

After the performance, we took some pictures in front of the large bubbling fountain in the center of the plaza. Behind us was the front entrance to the Met that at night was lit with multi-colored lights so that it looked like giant stained glass windows. There was beauty everywhere. We told each other how fortunate and grateful we were to be there. Our Tuesday opera experience alone was unforgettable. However, Monday evening the night before, was an unexpected bonus.

We had considered either an Off or On Broadway show, but many were closed on Monday, and trying to get tickets for anything at five o'clock was nearly impossible unless we took a chance and just went to the theater. That was too iffy for us. That's when we talked to the concierge. He suggested the Stand Up/NY comedy club right around the corner from our hotel and offered free tickets to boot. Great. We accepted the tickets with thanks, and went.

It was a small theater, nothing fancy, with probably 75 or so people. There was an alcove toward the back that was just right for five. That's where we sat, four "older" women and Julie. The usual program at these clubs is an Emcee who warms up the audience by interacting with them and also introduces the four or five comedians scheduled to perform. The Emcee sized up his audience and must have figured we were among those that looked like good patsy material. Within minutes he directed questions at others and then at us. His question was bait, and I fell for it. I answered him. To my surprise, people laughed at my response. He directed another comment at us and again, I answered, and again people laughed. The Emcee continued leading me on, and the audience continued laughing at whatever I was answering, not just polite chuckles, but hearty, genuine laughter. Oh my! I have to admit, it wasn't at all hard to take.

I don't remember much of anything that was said, but I was aware that my group wasn't ducking in embarrassment. They were laughing, too. What's more, it went on for some time. As other comedians performed, some of their comments were also directed at us, so that Julie, who is a nurse, got into a clinical discussion about anatomy with one of them. More laughs. And so it went.

I can honestly say that this was one of the most fun evenings ever. What made it especially memorable was that this was New York City, the mecca for best performers in the country, and to really build this up, probably the best in the world. For one wonderful evening, Julie and I joined that illustrious company of performers. Now we can both claim that we entertained Off Broadway. And, as you can see, I for one, am not the least bit reluctant to do so.

* * *

I've loved the traveling experiences I've had. Even instances that were unpleasant at the time (and there were very few), make interesting stories now. If you have any inclination to travel at all, I would urge you to get started sooner rather than later. There is so much to see in our country and in the rest of the world. Besides the wonder of history, architecture, art, and scenery, there is also the diversity of cultures. Travel does broaden a person's outlook. Furthermore, anything can happen, and the best part is that sometimes it does.

* * *

CHAPTER 39
GROUP THINK

Black Joe

A part of the Ohio Canal passes about a half mile or **so** from where we lived. The neighborhood kids used to go swimming there in the summer. Some of us walked and some rode bikes along a dirt road with farmland on both sides of the road. On the right side as you went toward the Canal was a cornfield. Nestled among the cornstalks was a short path leading to a shed made up of tin, metal and tarpaper. That's where the only Negro (the acceptable term in those days) in our neighborhood lived. Everyone knew of him as Old Black Joe.

Sometimes while doing this writing, my mind would take twists and turns on its own. Now after all these years, I finally got curious. What was Joe's real name? Where did he come from? How did he happen to live in that cornfield? How did he manage to eke out a living? Old Black Joe lived among us for many years, and yet he was an unknown. Was it just my ignorance or others as well? I asked a few of us still around who had also known of Joe.

Across the road from Joe's cornfield was Kalman's farm where Russ earned money planting in the Spring and weeding in Summer. Russ remembered that occasionally Joe was hired to plow for Mr. Kalman. Mary Anne didn't like passing Joe's place because a barking dog, even though he was tied, scared her. A neighbor remembered Joe in his bib farmer overalls and boots walking across fields. She assumed he was going to Louie's, our local, all-purpose store/bar, but wasn't sure if he stopped there or not.

As far as I could find out, there was never an incident of vandalism, mischief, or disrespect for Joe. On the other hand, he may as well have been on a deserted island. He lived in isolation right in our midst.

* * *

A Man's Job

Rainy taught fifth grade and I taught sixth at Ebenezer School. Of the twenty some teachers in our building, all of them were women except the gym teacher. Of course, the authority figure was the principal. The principal was always a man not just in our school, but also in the eight or so other schools in the West Seneca District.

Rainy had one of the best understandings of human nature, both in adults and children, that I've ever come across. She was also an instigator. Where she was there was less "small talk" and usually some kind of pertinent discussion, and all of it with a sense of humor. She was my friend, and I admired her.

Rainy was finishing the work for her Masters of Education degree when she asked me what I would think if she applied for the next opening for principal in our system.

I did not say, "Why not? Go for it." Or, "Good idea. It's about time!" I did not even pause to analyze the qualities that my friend had that would have made an excellent principal. I did not encourage or support her in any way. Instead, my answer to her was, "Oh Rainy, being principal is really a man's job."

I cringe now at those words.

* * *

CHAPTER 40
PUZZLES

Home Grown Napoleon

I have known short men who were soft spoken and kind. They do exist. However, a good many are the other kind; the ones who try to compensate for their height by bluster and bravado. I'm inclined to think that if either Napoleon or Hitler had been six inches taller, the world would have been spared much anguish. These two had to prove to everyone (and I suspect to themselves) that short men can be as powerful as tall men. That would describe Mr. Berman, manager of Federman's Department Store on Main Street in Akron. I didn't have any personal contact with him until he fired me.

Federman's was my first full time job after high school. When I graduated, I had no marketable skills and no money to go to college. I applied at Federman's, got the job, and figured I could take classes at night school. I was assigned to selling purses on the main floor close to the entrance doors. It was a nine to five job, six days a week, with an unpaid half hour off for lunch. I think I may have earned about $25.00 a week plus commission which came to a grand total of $30.00 on a good week.

Federman's was like an early version of Big Lots. The store carried all kinds of discontinued and irregular items: towels, sheets, housewares, furniture, and clothes for the whole family. There was an employee discount. I needed a wardrobe, and the whole family needed so many things that probably half my pay went right back to the store.

I did as I was told, kept the purses stocked and neat, was pleasant to customers, and tried to keep busy even when I wasn't. For the most part, I enjoyed the work, made some friends, and worked there almost a year.

The store had five or six floors. There was an elevator with an operator. Mr. Berman seldom used the elevator. He used the stairs going down, so that from about the fourth floor, we could hear his approach until all five foot four inches of him (including his elevator shoes) came into view on the landing at the top of the first flight of stairs.

I would say a good 90% of store employees were women. None of them were working just to occupy their spare time. They worked because for whatever reason, they needed the money. They wanted to keep their jobs. You would never guess that from the way Mr. Berman talked. On his way down the stairs from his office, he spoke to all his employees as if they were slackers of the worst kind. You could hear him across two floors.

I was new to the work force. It didn't occur to me that there could be another or better way for bosses to act. But some of the older and more senior women complained and wanted to improve working conditions. They were trying to get signatures from other employees to sign up for a union. One of the women approached me, explained what they were trying to do and why. What she told me made sense. I signed.

I'm not at all sure of the time lapse between when I signed and when I was called to Mr. B.'s office and fired. I do know he talked to me, but I can remember nothing specific about reasons he gave for letting me go; maybe because he was good at doublespeak or maybe because to me it was such a total surprise and hurt, that I couldn't concentrate. I was rejected by Federmans. That in itself was a kick in the self esteem, but the worst part was coming home and telling Mom that I had lost that important first job. I was sobbing while I tried to explain that I thought my work was good, and I didn't break rules. Mom came through. She comforted me, told me not to worry, and that I would find another and better job. She eased me through what I thought at the time to be a monumental failure.

It could very well have been a coincidence that I signed the union proposal at the same time that I did something unacceptable. If I did, I have no idea what that error was. Losing that job has remained a mystery. But if the store had been unionized, could it have done anything to change that little tyrant?

* * *

Suspicions

Senator Joseph McCarthy was a headline hound who got much notoriety by accusing American citizens of being Communists. This was during the Cold War in the 1950s when the U.S. was very concerned about the spread, and even the domination, of Communism. Our country, and others as well, saw Communism as a threat to the Free Market, Capitalism, and basic freedoms that Americans enjoy. McCarthy helped to create an atmosphere of suspicion that permeated the whole country. In a very small way, I was caught in that suspicion.

No doubt about it, Communism was a very repressive system of government that was actively and secretly working to convert other governments. Just to give an idea of the mood at the time, Nikita Kruschev was Prime Minister of the U.S.S.R. (Union of Soviet Socialist Republics that was made up of Ukraine, Belorus, Georgia, and others. Russia was the dominant republic with Moscow as its capital. The terms Russia and USSR were used interchangeably, though they were not the same.) In a speech at the United Nations in New York City, Kruschev was said to have taken off his shoe and pounded the table with it for emphasis while he proclaimed, "We will bury you!" This was specifically referring to the U.S.

There were for sure many reasons for our country to be cautious and guarded. The U.S.S.R. and U.S. spent billions competing and trying to undermine each other. For thirty years or more there was fear, suspicion, and skullduggery between them. It may not have been an out and out war, but the animosity was there. It was rightly called the Cold War.

Senator McCarthy developed his own formula for capitalizing on those fears. He was chairman of the Senate Committee on Governmental Operations. In both houses of Congress, committees like his have performed useful funding and investigative functions. Usually (not always) the committees try to follow rules that are fair and orderly. Not McCarthy. His methods were calling people to testify before his Committee, and then accusing them of being Communists, not with evidence, but with innuendo and association. His targets included members of the State Department, Hollywood personalities, union members, and just about anybody who had ever been to a gathering where opinions were spoken. Artists were black-listed and barred from working, and careers were ruined.

Television was a new media, and McCarthy's rants were telegenic. There were people who began to believe that there really were Commies lurking everywhere.

I was teaching sixth grade in the West Seneca Central School in New York State. Usually the only contact teachers had with one another during the school day was in the lunchroom. At that time, women who worked were also expected to do all of the "women's work" in the home as well as the paid full time job. Our lunchtime conversation too often was concerned with which one of us conscientiously carried on with our home duties by ironing pillowcases or hand drying dishes with a dishtowel or, as an alternative, heaven forbid, just air drying the dishes on the counter, or folding the pillowcases.

As I've mentioned, my friend Rainy, quite often would throw into the mix, some current topic that invariably lead to at least a little pertinent discussion, and sometimes, to out and out debate.

The Russians had just put Sputnik into Space. It was simply a 22 inch aluminum ball, but it was a terrible shock to our national ego that the Russians had gotten ahead of us in Space technology. Our educational system was under attack. How could the country have allowed this to happen? How had we failed? It was a time of much discussion and dissection.

I've never been shy about my background and, as I have been known to do, I'm sure I did express an opinion or two. Whatever the discussion was that particular day or what my comment was, one of the teachers picked up her tray and flounced out of the cafeteria muttering just loud enough to be heard, "Why doesn't she go back where she came from!" I remembered her indignation later.

Part of the sixth grade social studies was the study of the U.S.S.R. and "Iron Curtain Countries" (forced satellites of the U.S.S.R.). The textbook was arranged so that the Iron Curtain Countries came first, before the kids were introduced to anything about Russia or Communism. It occurred to me that the Russian unit should come first. Everything concerning subject matter had to be cleared with Connie, the Curriculum Coordinator. I went to her with my suggestion, confidently assuming there couldn't possibly be an objection. Connie's answer was a "no", but it was the way she gave her verdict that troubled me about her decision.

We were sitting at a small table across from each other. My hand was on the table with some papers. Connie put her hand over mine, looked me directly in the eyes, and in a soft, very sincere tone said, "Olga, I just don't think it would be a good idea at this time."

I couldn't believe what I was hearing. To me, it seemed to be a logical request. Could there possibly be another reason?

I happened to be standing next to my principal in the cafeteria line. The incident with Connie hadn't left my mind. I briefly explained what happened with Connie and asked him if he had any ideas why she would have refused me. He too, looked me in the eyes. Then he said, "If I were you, I'd just let it drop."

That shook me up. "What are you trying to say, Art?"

He looked directly at me again and then very seriously added, "Don't say I was the one who told you, but someone reported you to the F.B.I. The Superintendent had to answer questions about you."

I stood there in that cafeteria line holding my tray, completely stunned.

One of the things I have always maintained is that immigrants are the most loyal citizens of this country. I know there are always exceptions, especially these days when a few have committed acts that are beyond understanding. But for the most part, who would know better than immigrants what this country has permitted us to achieve or how it has allowed us to live? I was appalled that anyone would question my loyalty.

It's been over fifty years and yet, not obsessively, but every now and then, that incident will surface in my mind. It still bothers me. I try to analyze what I could have said or done that anyone would report me to the F.B.I. The best I can come up with is the reaction of that teacher in the school lunchroom, but I don't know. Could stating opinions be considered dangerous?

Several months before the planes flew into the Twin Towers on 9-11, I decided to try to find the answer through the Freedom of Information Act. I wrote to the Cleveland F.B.I. office assuming that F.B.I offices shared information. After several months, I was informed there was no record of any inquiry about me in that office.

There was an investigation after 9-11 to try to determine how such a catastrophe could have been allowed to happen. The country learned much through that inquiry including that all the agencies concerned with national security, were separate "stovepipes." (The old stovepipes on roofs were placed parallel to each other. It was a good analogy for no way to share information.) From that I concluded that I probably should have written to the Buffalo, New York F.B.I. office. I haven't done so as yet. I'm inclined to think the F.B.I. may have more important things to do. So my small trauma remains a puzzle.

Question: Is a "small trauma" an oxymoron?

To me it was a trauma even though in the great scheme of things it was a small event.

* * *

Is it Ukrainian?

I was three-and-a-half years old when Mom and I came to America. I spoke mostly *"po nashimo"* among the family. The words mean "in our way." Mom, as well as most of Serednica, could also understand and speak enough Polish to get by. Among ourselves, no other name was given to our language. However, through the years, when Americans asked what we spoke, we always said it was Russian. For me, that was a problem. We went to the Russian Orthodox church where until some years ago, the entire service was conducted in Russian. Very few of the words I heard in church were words that I understood or spoke at home with my parents. Also, when I was about twelve, I had Russian lessons with a priest, Father Migdal. The basic textbook we were given had very few words that I recognized. It was almost a whole new vocabulary. I got discouraged and stopped going to lessons.

Most of the congregation came from the same part of eastern Europe that my family came from. Except for a very few words that may have differed, they spoke as we did. From time to time I asked others at church why we said we spoke Russian. I got answers that were rationalizations too lengthy to try to explain here.

Ukrainian is a separate, legitimate language. It is the main language of the Ukraine, the area that most of us from the church membership came from. Yet I do not remember that anyone ever named what we spoke as Ukrainian. Why would there be such a united denial?

I've come up with some theories, but that's all they are. I'd welcome information that might be more accurate.

As with many parts of Europe, Poland's borders were flexible, sometimes being a part of Ukraine, Russia, Austria and others. These separate incursions must have left an influence on where they had been. One of these influences may have been the church. Today, most of Poland and the Ukraine are Catholic. Yet the Orthodox church was brought to all of Russia by Prince Vladimir of Kiev in about 1000 A.D. Kiev is one of the oldest cities in the Ukraine. It's possible that during the centuries when the Ukraine became more Catholic, pockets of Orthodoxy remained. However, Orthodoxy became identified with

Russia, and Orthodox believers in the Ukraine, may have preferred being called Russian because of their loyalty to the church.

There is another possible reason that is more political. Throughout its history, Russia often claimed the Ukraine as part of its Russian Empire as it did during the Communist era. But the Ukrainians are a proud people who have no affection for the Russians. There was always a strong drive for an independent Ukraine, as there is now after the breakup of the Soviet Union. Our family and our church never identified with the independent Ukraine movement. The opposite question is why would we have identified so strongly with Russia? I know so little about the politics of our family who came to America. Could they have supported the monarchy during the Russian revolution? If so, in heaven's name, what for them would have been the advantage of such loyalty?

Just very recently I've resolved the question about what it was we spoke at least to my own satisfaction. It was the direct result of an argument I had with my cousin, Sandy (Alexandra) Molohoskey, Elias's youngest daughter. She only knew a very few words of *po nashimo,* but she studied Russian in college and maintained that what we spoke was a sort of hill-billy version of Russian. I objected and disagreed, but couldn't prove any reasons.

Coincidentally about the same time, I saw a Kent State University catalogue that offered a course by an instructor who was from the Ukraine. Of course her vocabulary was far more extensive than the words I remembered, but I could understand her much better than I understood Russian. The best result of that class was the Ukrainian/American dictionary I got at the bookstore. Now whenever I recall a *po nashimo* word, I look it up in the dictionary. There it is. I can finally say that what we spoke was Ukrainian. What continues to remain a mystery, at least to me, is why we always said it was Russian.

Chapter 41
A VERY BRIEF HISTORY OF EASTERN ORTHODOXY

After the death of Christ, Christianity continued to spread across the known world. Many decisions about Christian doctrines and practices had to be resolved. Most of these decisions were made by a council of bishops from important cities like Antioch, Byzantium, and Rome. Of course there was strife in the process of decision making, but the decisions of the bishops were generally accepted. Christianity remained unified and developed into a prominent force in the Mediterranean world and beyond.

When Barbarians invaded Rome, Constantine, who was the Bishop of Rome, was concerned about the paganism. He moved his headquarters to the city of Byzantium that was renamed Constantinople in his honor. It is now named Istanbul.

It was the beginning of the Dark Ages. Latin was the unifying language, and the Christian Church preserved the works of philosophers, mathematicians, and its own history. Since there was no opposition from civil governments, the Church continued to gain power. There was a Bishop of Rome, who till now had been co-equal with other bishops, but who began to assert his authority over other bishops, and kings and princes as well.

The first major division in Christianity came in 1054. It was brewing for many reasons, but finally came about when the Bishop of Constantinople refused to accept the authority of the Bishop of Rome. This led to a permanent breach and is named in history as The Great Schism. The Bishop of Rome was called The Pope and remains the authority for the Latin Church that we now know as the Catholic Church.

Constantinople became the seat of authority for the Church that became known as Eastern Orthodox. Its language was Greek, which was a more flexible language than Latin. As Orthodoxy spread across eastern Europe, the Bible was translated into Serbian, Greek, Russian, and others all under the Orthodox umbrella.

The Orthodox Church of today has no connection or allegiance to the Catholic Pope in Rome. Rather, Orthodoxy is governed by a conclave of co-equal Patriarchs from major Orthodox centers.

Both Eastern Orthodox and Catholics believe in Baptism and Transubstantiation.

The Credos for each are almost identical except for one phrase known as *the Filolique*. It came about because the Toledo Council in 569 A.D. added that the Holy Spirit descended from Father and Son. Orthodoxy rejects this and maintains the Holy Spirit descends only from the Father.

Catholic and Orthodox churches are fundamentalist in doctrine and heavy with rituals and pageantry.

Orthodoxy does not encourage missionaries, nor does it strive for conversions from other beliefs.

Orthodox priests can and do marry, but they must marry before they are ordained as it would be unseemly for a priest to go courting.

An aside:

All of us liked Father John Mason who was the priest at St. Nicholas for twenty-some years. He and his wife had four children. He was easy to talk to and encouraged questions, especially from the younger ones. One day my son Chris, who was about twelve at the time, asked Father Mason if he always wore the same white clerical collar that other priests wear. Father Mason answered with a chuckle, "Well, I didn't when I went out in public with my pregnant wife. I didn't want to be mistaken for a Catholic priest."

I had to explain to Chris that Catholic priests take vows of celibacy.

* * *

CHAPTER 42
ELLIS ISLAND

The Statue of Liberty had been a gift from France to the United States after the Civil War in 1865. Through blistering sun and raging storms, it had been standing in the New York City harbor for almost one hundred years. Thanks to President Ronald Reagan, experts were called in to evaluate the condition of the Statue that had become an icon of democracy to the world. As a result of the study, a commission was formed with Lee Iacocca, chairman of the Chrysler Corporation, appointed as the head of the commission. He, himself, was the son of immigrants from Italy. Mr. Iacocca was charged with raising funds from private sources for the restoration and preservation of the Statue of Liberty.

Ellis Island had been the entry point for millions of immigrants to America. There was already a group of citizens who were involved in restoring the administrative buildings on the island. The Statue of Liberty and Ellis Island Foundation, Inc. was combined into one of the most successful fund-raising efforts ever. The Foundation raised $295 million for both projects, all from private sources.

One of the ideas for raising money was what became known as the Immigrant Wall of Honor. Immigrants who came through Ellis Island could be registered by family members for $100. The donor received a certificate of registration, and the immigrant's name was entered into computer records as well as inscribed on the Wall of Honor. So many names have been inscribed on the Wall of Honor that the Wall now goes around a good part of the Island.

My sister, Mary Anne Bechkowiak Smith, had the foresight to enter our mother, Julia Molohoskey Bechkowiak for the Wall of Honor.

Elias Molohoskey, and his mother, Anastasia, (Julia's mother and our grandmother) were also entered by his daughter, Alexandra Molohoskey.

* * *

Would you like to see your manuscript become a book?

If you are interested in becoming a PublishAmerica author, please submit your manuscript for possible publication to us at:

acquisitions@publishamerica.com

You may also mail in your manuscript to:

**PublishAmerica
PO Box 151
Frederick, MD 21705**

We also offer free graphics for Children's Picture Books!

---

www.publishamerica.com

CPSIA information can be obtained at www.ICGtesting.com
Printed in the USA
BVOW031337281012

303984BV00004B/2/P

9 781462 665785